HER HOUR COME ROUND AT LAST

The History of Psychoanalysis Series
Professor Brett Kahr and Professor Peter L. Rudnytsky (Series Editors)
Published and distributed by Karnac

Other titles in the Series

Rescuing Psychoanalyis from Freud and Other Essays in Re-Vision
  By Peter L. Rudnytsky

HER HOUR COME ROUND AT LAST

A Garland for Nina Coltart

edited by
Peter L. Rudnytsky
and Gillian Preston

KARNAC

First published in 2011 by
Karnac Books Ltd
118 Finchley Road, London NW3 5HT

Copyright © 2011 to Peter L. Rudnytsky and Gillian Preston for the edited collection, and to the individual authors for their contributions.

The rights of the contributors to be identified as the authors of this work have been asserted in accordance with §§ 77 and 78 of the Copyright Design and Patents Act 1988.

All rights reserved. No part of this publication may be reproduced, stored in a retrieval system, or transmitted, in any form or by any means, electronic, mechanical, photocopying, recording, or otherwise, without the prior written permission of the publisher.

British Library Cataloguing in Publication Data

A C.I.P. for this book is available from the British Library

ISBN: 978 1 85575 878 0

Edited, designed and produced by The Studio Publishing Services Ltd
www.publishingservicesuk.co.uk
e-mail: studio@publishingservicesuk.co.uk

Printed in Great Britain

www.karnacbooks.com

CONTENTS

LIST OF ILLUSTRATIONS	xi
ACKNOWLEDGEMENTS	xiii
ABOUT THE EDITORS AND CONTRIBUTORS	xv
FOREWORD Brett Kahr	xxv
INTRODUCTION Peter L. Rudnytsky	xxix
PART I: TRIBUTES (A) PATIENTS	1
CHAPTER ONE Nina-isms *Susan Budd*	3
CHAPTER TWO Ways of knowing *Muriel Mitcheson Brown*	11

v

CHAPTER THREE
Nina and the parcel　　27
Alex Douglas-Morris

CHAPTER FOUR
A Buddhist way of seeing　　31
Barbara Hopkinson

CHAPTER FIVE
A one-off visit　　35
Kathleen Murphy

(B) SUPERVISEES　　37

CHAPTER SIX
A whole attitude to life and work　　39
Michael Brearley

CHAPTER SEVEN
Charisma　　41
Mary Twyman

CHAPTER EIGHT
Nina Coltart the consultant: hospitality conditional
and unconditional　　43
Pina Antinucci

CHAPTER NINE
My Nina　　59
Maggie Schaedel

CHAPTER TEN
An "internal supervisor"　　67
Elizabeth Wilde McCormick

CHAPTER ELEVEN
Baby Peter　　71
Mary Leatt

(C) FRIENDS　　75

CHAPTER TWELVE
Homage to a valued friend　　77
A. H. Brafman

CHAPTER THIRTEEN
A recollection of friendship   83
Nina Farhi

CHAPTER FOURTEEN
My pen pal   89
Gill Davies

CHAPTER FIFTEEN
The silent listener   95
Mona Serenius

CHAPTER SIXTEEN
Nina Coltart: a person of paradox   113
Stuart A. Pizer

CHAPTER SEVENTEEN
Cometh the hour   117
Brendan MacCarthy

(D) SCHOOLMATES   121

CHAPTER EIGHTEEN
School friends   123
Janet Mothersill

CHAPTER NINETEEN
That sense of awe   125
Jane Reid

CHAPTER TWENTY
A knock on my door   127
Antonia Gransden

CHAPTER TWENTY-ONE
A very special time   129
Anne E. Knight

(E) FAMILY   131

CHAPTER TWENTY-TWO
Little Christmas   133
Mary Nottidge

CHAPTER TWENTY-THREE
A chink of craziness   137
Penelope Twine

CHAPTER TWENTY-FOUR
Memories of Neen   139
Martin Preston

CHAPTER TWENTY-FIVE
Word games   143
David Preston

CHAPTER TWENTY-SIX
A five-minute introduction   145
Gillian Preston

(F) READERS   149

CHAPTER TWENTY-SEVEN
Bare attention: the love that is enough?   151
Gherardo Amadei and Sara Boffito

CHAPTER TWENTY-EIGHT
In praise of Nina Coltart   163
Peter L. Rudnytsky

CHAPTER TWENTY-NINE
For Nina Coltart: in memoriam, or calling the thing by its name   187
Anthony Molino

PART II: UNCOLLECTED WRITINGS   195
(A) TRAVELS

CHAPTER THIRTY
The Grand Tour of New England   197

CHAPTER THIRTY-ONE
The Trans-Siberian Railway   223

CHAPTER THIRTY-TWO
A Tuscan holiday   231

CHAPTER THIRTY-THREE
Hotel drama in New York   239

(B) ESSAYS   247

CHAPTER THIRTY-FOUR
Diagnosis and assessment of suitability for   249
psychoanalytic psychotherapy

CHAPTER THIRTY-FIVE
The assessment of psychological-mindedness in the   261
psychiatric interview

CHAPTER THIRTY-SIX
To go or not to go   267

CHAPTER THIRTY-SEVEN
Psychoanalysis and Buddhism: does the ego exist?   271

CHAPTER THIRTY-EIGHT
Self-regarding   279

CHAPTER THIRTY-NINE
Ingredient X   283

(C) REVIEWS   297

CHAPTER FORTY
Reason and Violence, by R. D. Laing and D. G. Cooper   299

CHAPTER FORTY-ONE
The Technique at Issue: Controversies in Psychoanalysis   301
from Freud and Ferenczi to Michael Balint,
by André Haynal

CHAPTER FORTY-TWO
Mother, Madonna, Whore: The Idealization and Denigration   303
of Motherhood, by Estela V. Welldon

CHAPTER FORTY-THREE
Forces of Destiny: Psychoanalysis and Human Idiom,   307
by Christopher Bollas

CHAPTER FORTY-FOUR
Ignatius of Loyola: The Psychology of a Saint,   311
by W. W. Meissner

CHAPTER FORTY-FIVE
Body, Blood and Sexuality: A Psychoanalytic Study of   317
St. Francis's Stigmata and Their Historical Context,
by Nitza Yarom

CHAPTER FORTY-SIX
The Electrified Tightrope, by Michael Eigen   321

CHAPTER FORTY-SEVEN
Cultivating Intuition: An Introduction to Psychotherapy,   327
by Peter Lomas

CHAPTER FORTY-EIGHT
Some comments on "The silent cry", by Mona Serenius   333

(D) OBITUARIES   337

CHAPTER FORTY-NINE
Dr Maurice Friedman   339

CHAPTER FIFTY
Jafar Kareem   343

(E) CURRICULUM VITAE   349

CHAPTER FIFTY-ONE
Nina Elizabeth Cameron Coltart   351

Afterword   357
   Gillian Preston

INDEX   359

LIST OF ILLUSTRATIONS

Nina Coltart at High Leigh, Buddhist   xxxiv
Society Summer School, 1982.

Alex Douglas-Morris's "Lighthouse letter",   29
read by Gillian Preston at the Memorial Gathering
and Tree Planting Ceremony at the Amaravati
Buddhist Monastery, Great Gaddesden,
Hertfordshire (UK), 4 October 1997, 100 days
after NECC's death.

Lithograph by Matthew Wright of New End   144
leading to Well Road, mid-1980s, with NECC's
house at 1A Well Road indicated by an arrow.

"A Human Being", calligraphy by NECC, a practice 278
piece with arrows, lines, and spacings, etc., showing
how she worked.

"And the sprawling Bear", calligraphy by NECC.   355

ACKNOWLEDGEMENTS

My greatest debts are signaled in the introduction: those to Gillian and David Preston, for making this book possible and for the bountifulness of their hospitality in Sway; to Cheryl for accompanying me on journeys physical and metaphysical; and to Neville Symington for serving as a transitional object. To all the contributors, both those whom I have had the pleasure of meeting in person—Muriel Mitcheson Brown, Alex Douglas-Morris, A. H. Brafman, Nina Farhi, Gill Davies, Stuart Pizer, Gherardo Amadei, and Sara Boffito—and all the others who, sight unseen, entrusted me with their portraits of Nina Coltart: this book, like Nina herself, belongs to each of you. It is a source of acute sorrow to both Gill Preston and me that the "other" Nina—Nina Farhi—did not live to see her "Recollection of friendship" in print.

I would be remiss if I did not also voice my gratitude to Brett Kahr—scholar, clinician, and kindred spirit. I am honoured to have been invited to join him in serving as general editor of the History of Psychoanalysis Series at Karnac, and could not be more pleased to be launching our new venture with this book. He and Kim Criswell have provided me with a secure base in London. Special thanks go to Oliver Rathbone, publisher extraordinaire, for his statesmanlike blend of idealism and practicality.

Finally, Gillian Preston and I have done our best to secure the requisite permissions to reprint the previously published work of Nina Coltart, as well as the obituaries by A. H. Brafman and Brendan MacCarthy. With apologies for any oversights, we are grateful to Ivan Ward, editor of the collection *Is Psychoanalysis Another Religion?*, as well as to the editors of the *Scientific Bulletin* of the British Psychoanalytical Society, *Contemporary Psychoanalysis*, the *British Journal of Psychiatry*, *Raft*, *Interbeing*, *The Sunday Times*, the *International Journal of Psychoanalysis*, the *British Journal of Psychotherapy*, *Free Associations*, *Winnicott Studies*, and the *International Forum of Psychoanalysis* for their kind co-operation. The original provenance of any portion of this book that has appeared elsewhere is specified at the foot of the first page of the given chapter.

ABOUT THE EDITORS AND CONTRIBUTORS

Gherardo Amadei is a psychiatrist and a member of the Italian Psychoanalytic Society. He is an associate professor in the Department of Psychology at the University of Milan–Bicocca, where he works on psychopathology and psychoanalytic studies, focusing particularly on developments in interpersonal, relational, and intersubjective psychoanalysis. Among his recent publications are *Come si ammala la mente* (How the mind makes itself ill; 2005) and, with Ilaria Bianchi, *Living Systems, Evolving Consciousness, and the Emerging Person: A Selection of Papers from the Life Work of Louis Sander* (2008).

Pina Antinucci is a Full Member of the British Psychoanalytical Society and of the Milan Centre of the Italian Psychoanalytic Society (SPI). She is also a training analyst for the Italian Association for Child Analytic Psychotherapy (AIPPI), the Italian branch of the Tavistock training in child psychotherapy, and teaches in the Child Training Course of the SPI. While training in London, she worked both in private practice and in institutions for severely ill adult patients. She also worked at the Anna Freud Centre, where she was a toddler group leader in the Family Service for children under three. Moreover, she lectured in the MA programme in Psychoanalytic Theories of Child Development, which the Anna Freud Centre runs in collaboration with University College. In 1998, she joined the team of diagnosticians who served as consultants for the London Clinic. She moved back to Italy in 2003, and at present lives in Milan, where she maintains a private practice with adults, adolescents, and children. She has a special interest in the constitution of the bilingual/polyglot subject and in the vicissitudes of migration, topics on which she has published articles in professional journals. She is on the European Editorial Board of the *International Journal of Psychoanalysis* and on the Editorial Board of the Italian Annual of the *Journal*.

Sara Boffito is a psychologist working in Milan. She is the author of a thesis, *La più indipendente degli indipendenti: La psicoanalisi e vita di Nina Coltart* (The most independent of the independents: the psychoanalysis and life of Nina Coltart).

A. H. Brafman is a child and adult analyst in the British Psychoanalytical Society and worked in the National Health Service as a Consultant Child and Adolescent Psychiatrist. He and Nina Coltart trained together at the British Society, and they together founded "Group 64", which brought together several of that year's trainees for regular discussions of their work in progress. In addition to his scientific papers, he is the author of *Untying the Knot: Working with Children and Parents* (2001), and *Can You Help Me? A Guide for Parents* (2004). He is the editor of the You and Your Child series for Karnac, in which his most recent title, *You and Your Five to Ten-Year-Old* is published.

Michael Brearley is a Fellow of the Institute of Psychoanalysis in London, and currently its President. He works in private practice and does some teaching, writing, and lecturing. In earlier life he was a Lecturer in Philosophy at the University of Newcastle-upon-Tyne as well as a professional cricketer, captaining the England cricket team between 1977 and 1981.

Muriel Mitcheson Brown studied history and social science at University College London, the London School of Economics, and the University of Manchester, and for many years taught social policy and researched various aspects of social deprivation at the Universities of Manchester and Bristol as well as the LSE. She trained as a psychoanalytic psychotherapist with the Guild of Psychotherapy and is currently a member of the Severnside Institute for Psychotherapy and the Forum for Independent Psychotherapists.

Susan Budd was an analysand of Nina Coltart's. She was until recently a Member of the British Psychoanalytical Society, but is now retired from clinical work. She was for many years involved with teaching and supervising psychoanalytic psychotherapists in training in London, Oxford, and Birmingham, and was Editor of Books for the British Society. Together with Richard Rusbridger, she edited *Introducing Psychoanalysis—Essential Themes and Topics* (2005), and she has published papers on the history of psychoanalysis and its relations with other disciplines. Previously, she wrote several books on sociology, intellectual history, and alternative medicine. She lives in London and in Devon.

Gill Davies was for twenty-six years a publisher, and during that time she worked on and developed some of the UK's leading lists in psychotherapy and psychoanalysis, first at Tavistock Publications, then Routledge, and finally at Free Association Books, from which she retired as a publisher in 1988. Not long after leaving publishing she was persuaded to become a publishing educator and is now director of the MA in book publishing at the University of the Arts in London, where she recently became its first Professor of Publishing.

Alex Douglas-Morris lives in Richmond on the outskirts of London with her husband, David. They have two daughters, Freya, a painter and writer in London, and Tamara, a film composer living in New York. After a three-year textile course at Bournemouth School of Art, followed by a Montessori Teacher Training course, Alex taught art in various schools around London. She now works on commission from her studio in Richmond. Alex saw Nina Coltart over a period of twenty-eight years, in both Hampstead and Leighton Buzzard.

The late **Nina Farhi** was for many years a training therapist and training supervisor at the Guild of Psychotherapists. As an analytic psychotherapist who has also taught, lectured, and written over the past thirty-five years, she was for more than twenty years first assistant and then the Director of The Squiggle Foundation, a "place" where analysts, teachers, nursery nurses, doctors, writers, artists, et al. weekly studied and cultivated the tradition of D. W. Winnicott. Formerly a literary and political editor, she was married to the writer, Moris Farhi, with whom she had a daughter and a precious granddaughter.

Antonia Gransden attended Somerville College, Oxford, as a Coombs Scholar from 1947 to 1951, graduating with a First Class degree in Modern History. She received a PhD from the University of London in 1957 and a DLitt from Oxford in 1984. She was from 1952 to 1962 Assistant Keeper, Department of Manuscripts, in the British Museum. After being a Tutor at University Hall, Buckland, Berkshire, from 1963 to 1965, she subsequently taught medieval history at the University of Nottingham, retiring as Reader in 1989. She has published four books, three editions of texts and many articles and reviews, mainly on medieval historical writing and on the history of the abbey of Bury St Edmunds.

Barbara Hopkinson won a scholarship to grammar school, but her formal education ended when the school was evacuated in 1939. She learned shorthand and typing, and had her first job in a large insurance company. She then worked at Elizabeth Arden, the top beauty salon in London, before joining the Navy from 1943 to 1945. In 1947, she married for the first time and set up a mink and poultry farm in the country. Her daughter, Susan, was born in 1950. After living briefly in Canada, she returned to England and, in 1956, she became Secretary to the Assistant to the Superintendent at Claybury Mental Hospital. Remarried in 1963, she took over a lovely country house hotel in Suffolk. In 1968, she made contact with Nina Coltart. After the death of her second husband in 1970, she took over management of a bookshop, and in 1974 left to open her own shop. She sold the business after a few years and took up publishing, dedicating her first book, *Suffolk in Colour* (1982), to Nina Coltart. Reprinted in 1987, it has sold more than 22,000 copies.

Anne E. Knight grew up as an "army brat" in places including the Philippines, and graduated from Radcliffe College in 1946. After working in Occupied Japan, she attended Somerville College, Oxford, from 1948 to 1950, where Nina Coltart became her best friend. Their voyage on the *Queen Elizabeth II* in 1950 brought Nina Coltart to America for the first time. Anne Knight worked as a stockbroker in New York, New Haven, and San Antonio, where she lives with her husband, Graham, a chemical process engineer and rancher. They have a daughter, Ellenore.

Mary Leatt, born Mary Macklin Webb in Dartford, Kent, worked during the Second World War in Wartime Nurseries as a nursery assistant and then as a warden responsible for arranging meaningful activities for children aged three to five years. After the war, she taught for eight years as an infant teacher and nursery teacher at Dudden Hill Lane Infant's School in London. In 1955, she married John Leatt, a secondary school teacher, with whom she had three children, Pamela (b. 1958), Peter (b. 1961), and Jeffrey (b. 1963). The Leatts met Nina Coltart when she needed to study a baby, their son Peter, on weekly visits for a year as part of her psychoanalytic training. In 1966, the family left London and moved to Broadstairs, Kent. Although Mrs Leatt did not see Nina Coltart again after leaving London, they exchanged letters, every year, at Christmas.

Born in 1927, the late **Brendan MacCarthy** trained as a physician at University College Dublin, qualifying in 1951, then proceeded to become a psychiatrist, receiving his Diploma in Psychological Medicine in 1956. After training at the Institute of Psycho-Analysis, he rose to prominence as both an adult psychoanalyst and as a child psychoanalyst in the British Psychoanalytical Society. As a Consultant Psychiatrist at the Cassel Hospital, in Ham, Richmond, Surrey, and then at the Child Guidance Training Centre, attached to the Tavistock Clinic in North London, and as a psychoanalyst in private practice on Harley Street, in Central London, he became increasingly interested in the treatment of trauma, especially incest. He eventually became Chairman of the Child Guidance Training Centre from 1977 to 1981, and soon thereafter became the Director of the London Clinic of Psycho-Analysis from 1985 to 1993, as well as a Training Analyst at the Institute of Psycho-Analysis. From 1993 to 1996, MacCarthy served as President of the British Psychoanalytical Society. He died in 2005, and is survived by his wife Doreen MacCarthy, a former psychiatric nurse, and by their three sons and two grandchildren.

Elizabeth Wilde McCormick has been a writer and psychotherapist, in London and Suffolk, for thirty years. With a background in social psychiatry, humanistic and transpersonal psychology, and cognitive analytic therapy, she is a founding member of the Association for Cognitive Analytic Therapy. From 1996 to 2001, with Nigel Wellings, she was Director of Training at the Centre for Transpersonal Psychology in London. She currently writes and practises as a contemplative psychotherapist in Suffolk. Her books include *Change for the Better* (1990), *Surviving Breakdown* (1997), *Living on the Edge* (1997), *Transpersonal Psychotherapy: Theory and Practice* (2000, with Nigel Wellings), *Your Heart and You* (2001, with Leisa Freeman), and *Nothing to Lose: Psychotherapy, Buddhism and Living Life* (2002).

Anthony Molino is a practising psychoanalyst affiliated with the National Association for the Advancement of Psychoanalysis, an anthropologist, and a literary translator. Based in Pescara, Italy, he is best known for the award-winning *The Couch and the Tree: Dialogues in Psychoanalysis and Buddhism* (2001), as well as for *Freely Associated: Encounters in Psychoanalysis with Christopher Bollas, Joyce McDougall, Michael Eigen, Adam Phillips, and Nina Coltart* (1997). Other works include *Where Id Was: Challenging Normalization in Psychoanalysis* (2001) and *Culture, Subject, Psyche: Dialogues in Psychoanalysis and Anthropology* (2004). He has also compiled the two-volume *Squiggles & Spaces: Revisiting the Work of D. W. Winnicott* (2001). His most recent book, co-edited with Sergio Benvenuto, is *In Freud's Tracks: Conversations from the Journal of European Psychoanalysis* (2009).

Janet Mothersill was a school friend of Nina Coltart's. After graduating from Cambridge with a degree in classics, she taught for a year, then married and devoted her time to raising a family. When her children were in their late teens, she worked from home as part of a team under the leadership of Professor John Morris of London

University preparing for the first time an edition of the *Domesday Book* with a translation alongside the original text. After that, she worked part-time for fifteen years as paid adviser and tutor to her local Citizens Advice Bureau. She was also governor of a girls' day and boarding school in the 1970s and 1980s.

Kathleen Murphy was a very ordinary, down to earth basic bank clerk—in the days when all bank clerks were hardworking and honest, and not involved in the financial world as the banking industry is today.

Mary Nottidge was born in 1967 and grew up in Essex. At the age of eighteen she spent a year in Zimbabwe teaching English, history, and RE at a rural mission school. She studied modern history at Jesus College, Oxford, and has lived in the Hebridean Isle of Coll, in the former East Germany, in Frankfurt, and in London, working variously for a gap-year charity, as an English teacher, in sales and marketing, and as a head-hunter. She is married with four children and lives in London, where she is writing her first novel.

Stuart A. Pizer is a Founding Member, Supervising Analyst, and former President of the Massachusetts Institute for Psychoanalysis; Assistant Clinical Professor of Psychology, Department of Psychiatry, Harvard Medical School; and Past President of the International Association for Relational Psychoanalysis and Psychotherapy. He holds honorary and visiting appointments at the Psychoanalytic Institute of Northern California, the Toronto Institute for Contemporary Psychoanalysis, and the Institute for Contemporary Psychoanalysis in Los Angeles. He is Associate Editor of *Psychoanalytic Dialogues*, Corresponding Editor of *Contemporary Psychoanalysis*, and an editorial reader for *The Psychoanalytic Quarterly*. He is the author of *Building Bridges: The Negotiation of Paradox in Psychoanalysis* (1998).

David Preston, who celebrated his ninetieth birthday in 2008, was educated at Rugby School and Oriel College, Oxford, where he read Politics, Philosophy and Economics, taking his degree in 1939. In March 1940, he was commissioned as Second Lieutenant in the Green Howards, and was a platoon commander in the Battle of

Arras. From 1940 to 1945 he was a prisoner of war in Germany and Poland. He qualified as a solicitor in 1948, and from 1949 until his retirement in 1981 he was a partner in a family firm of solicitors in Bournemouth. He married Gill Coltart on 3 April 1956 in Hampstead Parish Church, North London, and at present lives in the New Forest, Hampshire.

Gillian Preston, née Coltart, was born in Kent on 30 April 1932. When her family home was bombed in May 1940, she was moved to a "holiday home" in Cornwall that had recently been purchased for such an eventuality. She was educated at Sherborne School for Girls in Dorset from 1942 to 1950. She trained as a primary school teacher at the Roehampton Educational Institute, West London, from 1950 to 1953. Until her marriage to David Preston in 1956, she taught Reception Class in Middlesex and Northwest London. After the birth of her four children, she established a branch of the Preschool Play Group Movement in Bournemouth. In the early 1980s she joined the newly formed Adult Literacy Scheme, aimed at helping adults—chiefly immigrants—with reading and language difficulties. From 1983 to 1997 she worked as a Welfare Officer for the Donkey Sanctuary, in Sidmouth, Devon, covering West Hampshire and the New Forest. She is currently involved with local groups of Friends of the Earth and Amnesty International.

Martin Preston is the youngest of David and Gillian Preston's four children. After taking his first degree in Biochemistry and Genetics, he went into public relations and marketing. He returned to university to become an osteopath and founded his own clinic, building it up to become a leading regional centre for natural healthcare. He has recently qualified as a Personal Trainer and a Life Coach and works part-time as a Clinical Studies and Technique tutor at Oxford Brookes University. In 2002 he was appointed Team Osteopath to the Red Devils Freefall Team, the display team for the Parachute Regiment and also for the British Army as a whole. The team trained him in skydiving, and he was one of the jumpers on the First Everest Skydive. In addition to enjoying other sports including skiing, motorcycling and martial arts, and to being a registered Tai Chi Chaun instructor, he plays mainly baroque and early classical music on a wooden treble recorder and tenor saxophone with a slightly mad local jazz band. He lives and practises in Wiltshire, on the north edge of the Salisbury Plain, near Stonehenge, and is the father of two teenage sons.

Jane Reid was a school friend of Nina Coltart's. She received her MA in English from Oxford in 1954, and an MA with Distinction from Cape Town in 1982. Owing to her husband's work as a diplomat, her career has been varied, and included journalism, teaching at school and university levels, research, and trust administration. Since 2000 she has served as Administrator of the Incorporated Edwin Austen Abbey Memorial Scholarships.

Peter L. Rudnytsky is Professor of English at the University of Florida and the editor of *American Imago*. He is an Honorary Member of the American Psychoanalytic Association and a Corresponding Member of the Institute of Contemporary Psychoanalysis in Los Angeles. He recently became a Licensed Clinical Social Worker and has opened a part-time private practice in Gainesville. A Fulbright Freud Scholar of Psychoanalysis in Vienna in 2004, he received the Gradiva Award for *Reading Psychoanalysis: Freud, Rank, Ferenczi, Groddeck* (2002). His numerous edited books include *Transitional Objects and Potential Spaces: Literary Uses of D. W. Winnicott* (1993), *Ferenczi's Turn in Psychoanalysis* (1996), and *Psychoanalysis and Narrative Medicine* (2008). In addition to *Rescuing Psychoanalysis from Freud and Other Essays in Re-Vision*, published concurrently by Karnac with the present volume in the History of Psychoanalysis Series, he is the author of *Freud and Oedipus* (1987), *The Psychoanalytic Vocation: Rank, Winnicott, and the Legacy of Freud* (1991), and *Psychoanalytic Conversations: Interviews with Clinicians, Commentators, and Critics* (2000).

Maggie Schaedel is Consultant Lead Adult Psychotherapist for Oxleas NHS Foundation Trust, where she has developed a specialist psychotherapy service for survivors of abuse and trauma. She holds an Honorary Lectureship at the University of Kent and has a private psychotherapy practice in Kent.

Mona Serenius was born in Finland and in her early childhood twice evacuated to Sweden for periods of 1½ years each during the Second World War. She studied German and French at the

Universities of Helsinki and Stockholm, earning an MA, and spent several years in Nashville, Tennessee, and Riyadh, Saudi Arabia. She married and moved to live in Sweden in 1963, and is the mother of three grown children. She is the former production editor and managing editor of several scientific journals, including *International Forum of Psychoanalysis*.

Penelope Twine (née Preston) is the niece of Nina Coltart. Happily married to Dave with two children, Sam and Tara, she enjoys the wilds of Dartmoor and the seas of beloved Cornwall. She holds a BSc (Hons) in Social Psychology and a Diploma in Psychiatric Social Work. She has served in various posts within Social Services, and is currently working in Devon.

Mary Twyman is a psychoanalyst in private practice in London. She was for thirteen years Principal Social Worker in the Adult Department at the Tavistock Clinic. She has been an Honorary Lecturer in the Masters course on psychoanalytic theory at University College, London. In recent years, she has chaired the Ethics Committee of the British Psychoanalytic Council and been the lead in drafting its Code of Ethics, Guidelines, and Complaint Procedures for the profession. She has contributed chapters to several books, mainly in the area of Independent theory and practice. With Hester Solomon, she co-edited *The Ethical Attitude in Analytic Practice* (2003).

FOREWORD

I recently attended a clinical discussion group during which a senior colleague presented the case of a troubled borderline patient who, after attending regular psychoanalytical sessions on the couch, would then, afterwards, visit a Buddhist retreat. The patient also displayed marked suicidal tendencies and had once taken an overdose of barbiturates. After listening to this highly abbreviated report of the patient's long and intricate life, an even more senior colleague in the seminar arched his eyebrows and muttered, in a sneering tone, "Oh, dear, that could be Nina Coltart."

As we know, Dr Nina Coltart practised psychoanalysis for many decades. She also subscribed to the tenets of Buddhism. And in the end, she made the decision to terminate her own life, having developed progressive osteoporosis. Yet, one would have to be a very small-minded, limited, and ill-informed person to remember Coltart as nothing more than a devotee of some mystical Eastern philosophy who died from an overdose.

Psychoanalytical clinicians endeavour to keep a very open mind about our patients, striving to suspend judgement and final diagnostic conclusions until we have accumulated all the evidence. If only we applied that quality of care and thought to our assessments of colleagues.

One need read no further than the opening tributes in Peter Rudnytsky's and Gillian Preston's moving *festschrift* to Coltart in order to appreciate the remarkable way in which this seasoned psychoanalyst transformed so many lives and moved so many others. As Muriel Mitcheson Brown, Coltart's one-time analysand, has observed, "From the start, analysis with Nina was a totally different experience: she made it seem natural, desirable, and above all, full of potential for change. She gave me a new experience, a wonderful sense of optimism." Brown then elaborates that,

> Analysis with Nina was a fascinating mix of a very correct, classical approach to technique and an intensely real personal relationship. The sessions were often hard, timing was impeccably accurate, the transference was interpreted over and over again, but there was a flexibility that allowed for the interplay of humour, shared experience, practical advice, and a good dose of common sense. I felt both held and contained and, at the same time, that I had the space to move around.

In truth, I cannot recall such a touching and thoughtful assessment of a psychoanalytical experience.

Another former patient, Alex Douglas-Morris, has described Coltart as a "lighthouse", poeticizing that, "she stood at the mouth of all our harbours—her lights constantly flashing the message—"I am here". And still another sometime patient, Barbara Hopkinson, has reflected that, "Her wise and benign influence has not ended with her death."

Her Hour Come Round at Last: A Garland for Nina Coltart brims with similarly loving, reflective personal testimony from other former patients, as well as from supervisees, colleagues, friends, schoolmates, and relatives. Some had only brief contact with Coltart, but nevertheless found themselves very touched and enhanced by their acquaintance. At least one contributor, Mona Serenius, a resident of Sweden, knew Coltart only through correspondence: "I never actually met Nina Coltart in person. Nevertheless, I came to regard her as one of my most intimate friends." Others testify to Coltart's capacity for enduring attachments. Mary Leatt first met Dr Coltart in 1961 when Coltart came to observe Mrs Leatt's baby son Peter for an infant observation as part of the psychoanalytical training. Many infant observers lose contact with the families whom they study after the completion of the formal course requirements, but Coltart remained in contact with the Leatt family for more than thirty years, and even contributed £500 towards the cost of Peter's college tuition (a princely sum in those days).

Others have noted Coltart's erudition, her lifelong love of learning, her gargantuan capacity for work, her deep devotion to psychoanalytical causes and committees, her practical and financial generosity to those in need, and her healthy suspicion of authority. As publisher Gill Davies has recalled,

> Nina's views were such a relief to a publisher in daily receipt of too many self-important, yet inhibited, letters from those who had appointed themselves to the High and Mighty and the Precious. They made me grind my teeth. She told me I had reason to.

This array of beautifully written, heartfelt tributes provides abundant evidence of Coltart's sanity, zestiness, wisdom, good humour, spontaneity, rigour, reliability, and professionalism, as well as her deep capacity to love. These reminiscences challenge and scotch for all time the stereotypes and the gossip that have threatened to surround Dr Coltart in the years since her death.

But Rudnytsky's and Preston's "garland" offers us much more. The editors have treated us to no fewer than twenty-one of Coltart's previously unpublished or uncollected essays, diaries, and reviews, encompassing her travel writings, as well as her considered psychoanalytical observations on a range of topics from Buddhism, to "Self-Regarding", to "Ingredient X", as well as her two classic papers on assessment and psychological-mindedness, arguably her most famous and evergreen clinical contributions based on her extensive experience of conducting consultations at the London Clinic of Psycho Analysis and in her busy Hampstead private practice. These writings bring Coltart back to life with a touching immediacy, and one can enjoy her *joie de vivre*, her intelligence, and her quest for truth as though listening to a living, breathing person.

Rudnytsky and Preston deserve our thanks for having assembled the contributions, testimonials, and reminiscences of no fewer than thirty people, itself a proof of the love and respect that so many have for Nina Coltart. Peter Rudnytsky, an experienced historian, clinician, author, and editor, has deployed his characteristically meticulous scholarly skills to shape a durable and inspiring *festschrift*, and Gillian Preston, Nina Coltart's beloved sister, has collaborated closely with Rudnytsky, providing unparalleled access to unpublished materials and contacts. Above all, Gillian Preston deserves our inestimable thanks for her tremendous generosity of spirit in sharing her precious sister with the wider psychoanalytical and historical communities in such a selfless manner. No doubt she possesses many of her sister's fine qualities, and no doubt she helped to foster and facilitate some of these qualities in Nina Coltart as well.

Although deeply appreciative and respectful, this "garland" never becomes hagiographical, and it treats all the aspects of Nina Coltart's life in a refreshing, transparent manner. When I received the first draft of the manuscript for this book, I read it straight through in one or two sittings; and then, some months later, when I received the revised version, I read it again with a complete sense of wonder, as though encountering the chapters for the first time—a rare experience indeed. This book possesses all the best qualities of a riveting biography that one cannot put down.

Sadly, I had only brief contact with Nina Coltart while researching my own biography of Donald Winnicott. After reading Rudnytsky's and Preston's garland, I deeply regret that I did not have a fuller association with Coltart. But reading these tributes allows one to enjoy a rich engagement with Coltart, offering a deeply satisfying experience, as well as a master class in the clinical arts, and a benchmark against which to measure one's own professional and private life.

Professor Brett Kahr,
Series Co-Editor

Introduction

Peter L. Rudnytsky

"*Si monumentum requiris, circumspice*". This epitaph on the tomb of Sir Christopher Wren, enjoining those who wish to see the monument of the architect of St Paul's Cathedral to look around them, which is quoted by Nina Coltart in both her published obituaries of others, stands fittingly also at the head of the present volume. For Coltart, who was singularly unconcerned with any form of personal immortality, is here remembered in the two ways that would undoubtedly have pleased her best: first, by an outpouring of tributes from people whose lives she touched; and second, through her own writings.

The inspiration that has eventuated in this book befell me when I read in the interview Coltart gave to Anthony Molino shortly before her death that "a lot of my papers aren't anywhere to be found . . . an awful lot of them haven't been published" (Molino, 1997, p. 184). Since, unlike almost all the other contributors, I never had the good fortune of encountering Nina Coltart during her lifetime, and hence had come to "know" her solely through her writings, the prospect that there might be unpublished manuscripts of hers still extant riveted my attention.

To find out more, I realized I would have to make contact with Coltart's sister, Gillian Preston. But how to do this? Although I had not met Neville Symington, I noted he was one of the contemporary analysts most often cited by Coltart, and I hoped he might be willing to help me. I obtained Symington's co-ordinates in Sydney, Australia, from an article in the *International Journal of Psychoanalysis*; we arranged to speak on the telephone, and in due course he graciously provided me with Mrs Preston's address. She and I entered into a correspondence, which culminated in my making two trips to the south of England to visit Gillian and David Preston, in Sway, Hampshire—the first in November 2007, and the second, together with my wife Cheryl, almost exactly one year later.

This book would not have been possible without the steadfast support and unstinting co-operation of Gillian Preston. In addition to making available to me all her meticulously preserved files of Nina's manuscripts—Nina having destroyed all her records of patients prior to her death in 1997—as well as of her own voluminous correspondence with the people whom she had notified of this sad event, Gillian was indefatigable in reaching out to everyone in Nina's vast circle to invite them to contribute to what was now our joint project. For it immediately became apparent during our first meeting that, in order to do justice to Nina's memory, this volume needed to contain not only her own trove of unpublished or uncollected writings but also essays in her honour by those who, through having known and loved her, were best equipped to celebrate the greatness of her spirit.

In weaving our garland, we have been guided by a principle of inclusiveness. This means that we have welcomed each and every person who came forward and offered to write about Nina. We likewise made diligent efforts to recruit all those whom we knew to have been close to Nina, including the members of the British Psychoanalytical Society who were her colleagues or her analysands in the Independent group. The reader may, therefore, conclude, if one or another name that one might have expected to find among our contributors happens to be missing, the explanation is that that individual, for whatever reason, chose not to join us in paying homage to Nina Coltart—a decision we naturally respected, however much we might have regretted it.

The same principle of inclusiveness steered us in compiling Coltart's own writings. To the best of my knowledge, this volume now makes available all the texts by Coltart that cannot be found in the three books she published during her lifetime: the two collections of her papers, *Slouching towards Bethlehem* and *The Baby and the Bathwater*, as well as *How to Survive as a Psychotherapist*. The only exception to this statement is that we have not included any of Coltart's letters. As many of our authors testify, Coltart was a correspondent cut from the vintage cloth of Dickens or Freud: someone who always seemed to answer by "return of post", and whose letters were eagerly anticipated "events". Extracts from Coltart's letters are quoted by Mona Serenius in "The silent listener", as well as by other contributors, so the reader can at least get a flavour of her gifts in this domain. Although limitations of space precluded us from accepting Neville Symington's proposition that we publish his correspondence with Coltart—running to some fifty pages of single-spaced type—in its entirety, I hope he will execute his plan to bring out a book that contains his epistolary dialogue with Coltart along with those with other analysts.

Probably the greatest treat in store for the reader is Coltart's trilogy of travel narratives, with the "Hotel drama in New York" that I have placed at the end of this sequence like an ancient satyr play. In each of her diaries, whether aboard the Trans-Siberian Railway or on holiday in Tuscany, Coltart vividly displays what Gill Davies terms her "gift of experiencing an event, being part of it, and yet watching it as though she were separate from it". The *pièce de résistance*, "The Grand Tour of New England", written in November 1986, allows us to see Coltart, with Christopher Bollas in tow as her cicerone, "after years of humdrum slog", astonished at being greeted as "an extremely distinguished individual" both at the Austen Riggs Center and at the Boston Psychoanalytic Society.

As it turns out, apart from the travelogues, and the 1989 *curriculum vitae* I unearthed among her papers, only one of Coltart's essays, her 1996 Winnicott Centenary Lecture at the Squiggle Foundation, "Ingredient X"—a major find—and at most one book review, of André Haynal's *The Technique at Issue*, had not been published in any venue. Still, I think there is incontestable value in being able to survey the full range of Coltart's achievements as a writer, including her nine reviews and two obituaries. This breadth reflects her manifold complexity as a person. The reader can contemplate, in turn, Coltart the eagle-eyed observer of manners and morals; the connoisseur of food; the acclaimed diagnostician; the philosopher of the end of life; the Buddhist aware that the "self" is merely an illusion; the judicious critic; the inspiring eulogist. Above all, both in her own writings and in the tributes proffered by others, Coltart comes through in this book as she was in life: not only an exceptionally rich and fascinating human being but also—her own disclaimers notwithstanding—one of the greatest figures in British psychoanalysis, and indeed of psychoanalysis *tout court* in the twentieth century.

Our title derives from the same poem by W. B. Yeats, "The Second Coming", from which Coltart took the phrase "slouching towards Bethlehem" in the paper that made her reputation. First and foremost, "her hour come round at last" is meant to convey that, here, Coltart is finally being given a measure of the recognition that has long been her due. She never received an obituary in the *International Journal of Psychoanalysis*—an omission that can only partially be explained by her decision in 1994 to resign from the British Society—and, as I have noted, even now Gillian Preston and I have not always met with success in seeking to persuade the analysts who surely owe the most to Coltart to acknowledge their debt to her in our pages. But this brings me to a second level of meaning to our title, one that gestures towards what both Neville Symington (in a personal communication) and Muriel Mitcheson Brown have characterized as Coltart's "darker side". As Anthony Molino and I discuss explicitly, and other contributors approach more obliquely, Coltart ended her life in suicide—a supremely mysterious and disturbing act, whatever its ethical justifications. Thus, if Coltart counsels us in "Slouching towards Bethlehem" to have the faith in the psychoanalytic process that allows the "rough beast" of the patient's trauma to be born in its own fullness of time, we cannot escape the realization that Nina herself can also be likened to a "rough beast" whose resolute iconoclasm, culminating in the shock of her death, has had a traumatic impact on the world of British psychoanalysis.

The circumstances not only of Coltart's death but also of her life were indelibly marked by tragedy. As she made public in her interview with Molino, and revealed to close friends privately, both her parents died in 1940 in a train crash, when both she and Gill were still very young. This catastrophe perforce affected both sisters profoundly. I mention these "darker" matters here to pay my own respects not only to Nina Coltart but also to Gillian Preston, for whom it must not always have been easy to revisit in my company these memories of her past. While fiercely loyal to her beloved sister, Gill has been heroic in rendering her own best tribute to Nina Coltart by joining forces with me and serving as the indispensable co-editor of this book.

Reference

Molino, A. (Ed.) (1997). *Freely Associated: Encounters in Psychoanalysis with Christopher Bollas, Joyce McDougall, Michael Eigen, Adam Phillips, Nina Coltart.* London: Free Association Books.

And what rough beast, its hour come round at last,
Slouches towards Bethlehem to be born?
        [W. B. Yeats, "The Second Coming"]

PART I: TRIBUTES
(A) PATIENTS

CHAPTER ONE

Nina-isms

Susan Budd

I was one of Nina Coltart's analysands.

It is difficult to write about a relationship that is both so intimate and yet so remote; for example, I never, either during my analysis or after it, ever called her "Nina". But it is inevitable that, during a long training analysis, the patient comes to know the analyst pretty well, and the training analysis is the central part of an intensive apprenticeship by means of which we are turned into analysts and members of the same profession. After I had finished my analysis, I used to write to Nina, and go to see her from time to time, and I took over from her as the analytic consultant to a psychotherapy training in Birmingham. During these encounters, and in the latter stages of my analysis, she told me quite a bit about her attitude to our rather odd vocation, and I have tried to record here some of her various aphorisms and what I think she meant by them. (I did think of calling this piece "The wit and wisdom of Nina Coltart", but I can well imagine just how indignant that would have made her.)

"You are there, and you are doing it"

When I began working with patients, I often used to feel baffled and discouraged by how little help psychoanalytic theory was and how little it enabled me to understand. Nina, like John Klauber, my first analyst, was delighted by this. At the time, I found it pretty irritating, but after many years of supervising psychotherapists myself, I can now see what they meant. Both of them believed that psychoanalytic theory is essentially unfinished; that there is a great deal about human life that it does not encompass, and maybe never will encompass. Therefore, it behoves us to remember that none of us knows it all, and there is a lot that we can learn from our patients. At the same time, too much anxiety is crippling to the beginner, and it does not help to wish that we could send our puzzling patient to Winnicott, Klein, our supervisor, or anyone else whose acumen we admire. Just remember, Nina said, that someone else might well be better than you, but you are there, and you are doing it. It is to you that your patients look, to you that they have formed an attachment, so you just have to get on with it, and allow them to show you what sort of an analyst they need.

She also told me that, being childless herself, she thought that it was especially important not to intrude herself when patients talked to her about their children; she did not want to imply that she had any kind of special knowledge. Having winced through quite a few seminars where the seminar leader seems to have either never known or forgotten what it is like to be a parent, I can only applaud her abstinence. In general, times change; sitting in our consulting rooms, we have to be alert to just how rapidly sexual and personal mores, and reproductive technology, have changed since the Second World War. We do not have to change mindlessly with the times, but we do have to remember that each generation approaches the universals of human experience in its own way.

"Don't be wonderful"

Nina was a very experienced assessor, and both in her private practice and as Director of the Clinic at the Institute of Psychoanalysis she had ample opportunity to observe how patients reacted to being assessed, and how they moved on, with varying degrees of success, to their analysts. When I started to work in a psychotherapy unit where we both did assessments and took some patients into therapy, I could see what a valuable experience it is to go on hearing about how those patients whom we have assessed actually do in therapy. It is very easy for us to get into a *folie-à-deux* with some people whom we assess, or for them to idealize us; they only meet us once or twice and our pronouncements can seem rather Jehovoid. Nina was not entirely free from enjoying how much she could be idealized; perhaps none of us is. But she was very aware in her more sober moments that the first duty of the assessor is to hand on the patient to his or her therapist in such a way that they have a good chance of settling down with them. If you allow yourself to be seen as rather lovely and magically insightful, this impairs their chances.

No therapy or therapist is just like any other. At the same time, what really helps patients is not our wonderful selves, but our skill in using a remarkably powerful and effective technique. Another analyst might have done it differently, but, on the whole, the outcome would be much the same. I think that therapists who were previously doctors or have worked for a long time in clinics are much better at remembering this than lay therapists, and, therefore, are better at handing patients on. This is equally important when for some reason a patient has to change analysts. Sometimes, the experience with the second analyst really is very different, but all too often the same snags and impasses reappear, though a second time around we may have a better chance of working them through.

Nina had thought a lot about what makes a good analyst or therapist, and in the end seemed to conclude that it is largely that ineffable thing, psychological mindedness. One of the most difficult aspects of training psychotherapists is that we cannot really predict who will develop this and those for whom it will always remain inaccessible, as if they are tone-deaf. I could see from the voluminous files that she handed on to me about the students at Birmingham, and her lengthy reports to both the committee and the students, how hard she had worked to help them to develop as therapists. She also told me that, in her view, giftedness as a therapist is simply not related to how nice, or neurotic, someone is;

some therapists are thoroughly nice and sane and some definitely are not, but the former may well not be neurotic enough to understand their patients, and the latter, if they can keep their difficulties in check, can be very empathic therapists. However, there does have to be a basic core of truthfulness and reliability in the personality.

"Once your analyst, always your analyst"

Just as patients can want to get very close to their therapists, sometimes therapists succumb to the neediness or charm of their patients. The obvious cases are where they go to bed with them, but there are more subtle betrayals of the basic analytic contract. We may find some of our patients very pleasant company, share many of their tastes and interests, and enjoy hearing about their creative work. Paradoxically, Nina thought, it is not the patients whom we like the most with whom we can do our best work; if we end up chatting to them, or inviting them to tea when the analysis is over, we have failed them in some way. Above all, if we have turned them from patients into friends, they cannot come back to us if life deals hardly with them and they need us as analysts again for a time.

She also believed that we do not necessarily have to like our patients to do our best work with them. Some people, she believed, draw analysis out of us, and can use it; others, however likeable, never do. I have thought a lot about this one, and feel that we inevitably tend to like patients more when they like, rather than love or idealize, us, when we can understand them and feel that we are helping them. It is a desperate struggle to work well with the others, and, on the whole, we come to like them more when we succeed with them more. But the liking has to be linked to clarity about what we are there for, which is to help them if we can and to stop if we cannot. Nina pointed out how fundamentally unlike all other relationships the therapeutic relationship is. If a therapy has been successful, the analytic couple generally end up getting on well with each other. In life, the relationship would continue and grow closer; in therapy, that is when it is time to stop.

"All cures are transference cures"

How long should we persist with an analysis or a therapy that does not seem to be working? This is a very difficult issue, but I agree with Nina's view that, in the end, we are charging patients money, and using their time and our time on therapy. Going on doing this implies that we think that we can do something for them, and that if we find we cannot, there may well come a point when it is we who should call it a day. Partly, we need to give them the opportunity to move on to another therapist with whom they would do better, and also not everyone is suited to or can benefit from psychoanalysis or psychotherapy. It is bitter but true that those who have failed at every other aspect of life are probably going to fail at therapy as well. Because of the way that the referral system works, it is often beginners who end up seeing the most difficult and intractable cases. One of the things I vowed that I would never do in teaching clinical seminars was to say, "You shouldn't have taken this patient on; you can't succeed with him". The problem is that the student was pretty much told to take the patient on, and passionately wants to succeed with him. Like other analysts, Nina had noticed that sometimes beginners can succeed with patients where the more experienced would fail; she attributed it to the sheer force of the student's wish for the patient to get better.

She said to me once that she thought that all cures were transference cures; that is, that the patient introjects some of the qualities he attributes to his therapist, and can make them his own. I have thought a lot about this since; I think that what cures people is ultimately rather enigmatic and difficult to spot, not least because we do not know what happens to most of our patients after a therapy or an analysis is over. Both Nina and John Klauber talked to me about the aftermath of analysis: Nina warned me that post-analytic patients often go through a period of disliking their analysts; John thought that the patient has to recover from, and shed, the imprint of the analyst's personality before his analysis becomes his own. This is something that is rarely discussed, but it is why I welcome hearing from patients after they have left me; I want to know which parts of their analysis continue to work for them, and which do not. And many patients cannot let us know until after they have left that their lives have improved; they fear that we might negate or steal their hard work.

"Women make better therapists than men"

I was surprised when Nina said this to me; I had always thought of her as rather a man's woman, and individual analysts whom I knew that she admired mostly seemed to be men. She thought that women were less conventional than men, braver at staying with the patient and walking out into the dark. At the same time, she was sympathetic to the plight of male analysts and therapists in relation to their training organizations. As she pointed out, a reasonably successful middle-aged male psychiatrist or social worker could expect to be in charge of a department, have secretaries, research grants, and other public and visible sources of power and gratification. If they decide to become psychoanalysts, their working lives just are not going to be like that, and this social invisibility is something that women are more used to than men. She thought that men were more likely to seek compensatory authority within training organizations, often with unhappy results. I think that women also look for support and esteem, but rather differently, and can equally become destructive within the profession if they feel that their emotional claims are being ignored.

Nina became increasingly concerned with the tendency within the British Society to gerontocracy. She helped to initiate discussion of how and when analysts should retire; previously, all too often it seems to have been assumed that we are going to die in harness. She had several times, she told me, been called in by the family when this had happened; an analyst had suddenly died, and the family were going to have to face a series of patients ringing the doorbell with whose distress they were going to have to deal in addition to their own. Because the practice of psychoanalysis lies so close to the core of the personality, and we keep in touch with it by doing it, retirement can feel like death. I am only sorry that her own retirement was so short, as her letters to me were full of lively accounts of the things she was enjoying.

It was a pleasure receiving a letter from Nina. She answered by return of post, and, considering the number of letters that she must have received, this was remarkable. She had a very characteristic graceful hand, and an amusing and insightful turn of phrase. I remember a vivid description of a lantern-jawed spinster chatelaine of a National Trust property where she had thought of working as a guide.

"To tell the truth, laughing"

I quoted this Latin tag to Nina once, because I thought that it summed up what she often tried to do. She thought that her patients should enjoy their analyses; I think I would hope that they could come to be able to laugh at themselves, and at life. Analysts from Freud on have been well aware that humour can be used defensively and destructively, but there is a less well-known paper by Freud on gallows humour where he points out that much of human life is really pretty intolerable, and that our best defence against what we cannot escape is being able to laugh at it. How we use humour in analysis is a large subject, and I do not think that Nina always got it right as far as I was concerned. But the birth of a sense of humour seems to be a good diagnostic sign that things are going better and life feels less crushing than it did.

At the same time, it meant a lot to me that both of my analysts were able to laugh. They gave me a lot; they made me into an analyst. They both died too soon, and I miss them both.

CHAPTER TWO

Ways of knowing

Muriel Mitcheson Brown

I knew Nina for a good many years, from 1975 until her death, and I am delighted to have the opportunity to write about her. I can say that with confidence, although I am aware of a degree of hesitation in my claiming to know her. I feel I knew her well, although there is much that I did not, and do not, know about her life, and I did not have an ordinary social relationship with her. "Knowing" someone has a context, and the defining context of our relationship was that I was in analysis with her for ten years. I was first a patient, an analysand, and then, after a break of a year, I went back to her for my training analysis. After qualifying as a psychoanalytic psychotherapist, I moved out of London and then saw nothing of Nina for many years, although we maintained a sparse correspondence. It was more than a decade after the ending of our analytic relationship that we again met, in a professional context, and had what might be called some ordinary conversations. So my knowing Nina is particular, constrained, and boundaried, but also curiously intimate.

I believe that Nina certainly knew me, in the strange, deep way that an analyst comes to know her patient over time, despite the absence of ordinary social interactions, but I also came to know her.

What I know and knew of Nina is a mixture of knowing that is ordinary, based on conversation and encounter, albeit mostly in the consulting room, knowing that is transference-dominated and fantasy-led, knowing that is derived from the general, publicly accessible information about her life and work and ideas, and knowing that is based on a reading of her written work and correspondence. This is a potent and complex mixture of "knowings" but probably, in the end, not that different from the more conventional knowing a person through kinship or friendship or professional acquaintance. It is certainly a knowledge that I value and one that, to some extent, I am happy to share.

In order to write about my knowledge of Nina and say something of why I appreciate her as an outstanding psychoanalyst and a warm and wonderful human being, I will have to say something about myself. I did not know *of* Nina before I met her. Back in 1975, I was extremely ignorant about the world of psychoanalysis, although I had some acquaintance with psychoanalytic theory. My interest in analysis was not new—indeed, the idea of my becoming a psychoanalyst had been formulated back in my teens—but, since I had moved away from a clinical career to an academic one, it was for personal rather than career reasons that I decided to seek analysis. I was cautious in my approach to finding an analyst, but once I had the opportunity and means, I went to a very well-known and respected London analyst for assessment. He directed me to Nina with enthusiasm, observing somewhat mysteriously that I was lucky in her having agreed to take me on but that we would be just right together. I recall that at the time I did not really understand his comment. Moreover, I was disappointed that he had not wanted me to continue with him and was unsure about seeing a woman. Both the disappointment and the uncertainly evaporated once I met Nina, but it was some time before I could appreciate his grasp of the analytic fit!

Why was I seeking analysis? At the time, I was (on the outside) a fit and healthy young woman in my mid-thirties, reasonably successful in my academic career, the proud mother of a beautiful son. I had a good circle of friends and relations and I was sharing my life with a loving partner. That sounds good, and indeed I was not unappreciative of all that I had in my life, but it did not *feel* good. On the contrary, life felt difficult and I felt on the edge of coping. I felt overwhelmed by anxiety, guilt, and a profound sense of failure. I did not like myself, and I hated the way I worried and was miserable and critical when I longed to be calm and gracious and loving. I struggled to be honest with myself, but then found myself full of unacceptable feelings of misery and meanness. I lived in fear of my destructiveness and was exhausted with the effort of being alive. I was aware of internal conflict, but quite unable to cope with it. I was full of neediness, but terrified of expressing it for fear of losing what loving support I had. When I read over some of my journals of those pre-analytic days, they present a sobering picture of profound neurotic unhappiness. I repeatedly listed the good things in my life, castigated myself for my discontent, and resolved to be a better person, but the sheer misery of my feelings dominates the picture. Reading and discussions with friends gave me some insight into my condition, but I did not seem able to make any internal changes and could not break the endless, vicious circle of misery and self-criticism.

Despite this neurotic state and despite my having an established career, I had embarked on therapy with the vague notion, or excuse, of maybe heading towards a psychoanalytic training. However, once I had arrived in Nina's Hampstead consulting room, I first made use of the opportunity to talk through an immediate, preoccupying dilemma. When this was wonderfully clarified and resolved, Nina indicated that we should get down to an analysis and quietly but firmly led me there. She allowed me to discover for myself the folly of contemplating training at that stage and, while she continued to allow me to sort out practical and relational problems, she made it possible for me to explore my internal world and focus increasingly on my own needs without crippling shame. I had tried therapy before, and it had seemed well-meaning but ineffective. From the start, analysis with Nina was a totally different experience: she made it seem natural, desirable, and, above all, full of potential for change. She gave me a new experience, a wonderful sense of optimism.

Nina was very patient with me. At the outset she allowed me to embark on what she called my narrative, my detailed life history, which I tenaciously outlined. She heard my pain in the face of the loss of my mother through cancer and my guilt at the confused mess I felt I made of love relationships. She attended to my embarrassments and shame, to my insecurities at work, to the doubts and discontents of my current partnership, and to my agonised concern for the happiness of my son. I was immensely comforted in the first few months of being with Nina. I developed a profound confidence in her judgement. There was no sense of textbook interpretations, no clever theorizing, no pathologizing, just what I would eventually know as a steady, attentive containment. I recall how, in the early days, when I would often get into a familiar disparaging tone about what I had felt or experienced, she would quietly rebuke me and show me how to listen to myself. Through the listening, she taught me compassion and respect and she gave me hope.

Analysis is a long and complicated journey, but Nina had the gift of making it a pleasurable one: the process was as important as the outcome. She had not written "Slouching towards Bethlehem" at that stage, but I can now see that the capacity to wait and not to hurry the patient on to some premature conclusion was already a part of her approach. It would be many years before I understood this, but, looking back, I can see how important it was for me that, early on in the process, she gave me such hope in the possibility of therapeutic change. Once I had embarked on analysis proper, my recourse to my journal writing was greatly reduced, but I made the occasional entry to record my progress. A few months into analysis, I wrote of this hope and noted how exciting it was to have "the sheer, bloody potential, the joy of it, that not only life is good but maybe I am too". I wrote that I wanted to communicate to Nina that "you have made me wild with a laughing, weeping joyfulness that something will be done, that I can be happy and make others happy".

Analysis with Nina was a fascinating mix of a very correct, classical approach to technique and an intensely real personal relationship. The sessions were often hard, timing was impeccably accurate, the transference was interpreted over and over again, but there was a flexibility that allowed for the interplay of humour, shared experience, practical advice, and a good dose of common sense. I felt both held and contained and, at the same time, that I had the space to move around. But if I am to convey the quality of the relationship, what it was like at the time, I need to get into the detail of the process and hope that through the focus of my analytic story something of Nina's therapeutic skill can be revealed.

Nina had her consulting room in her modest Hampstead apartment, the upper floors of an old terraced house. Patients rang the front door bell and were admitted to a narrow hallway, then up a flight of stairs to a small, beautifully furnished waiting room. This room and the stairs that continued up to private rooms were always bedecked with flowers and plants, and I used to wonder how she managed to keep so many in such a thriving state. The consulting room was comfortable, with functional furniture and some interesting paintings, which I always assumed were the gifts of grateful and talented patients. There was a bathroom on the same level (though I hardly ever had the courage to use it). In her reception of her patients, Nina managed to combine being dignified and even formal in her manner with the assurance of great warmth. Despite my initial anxiety about the whole enterprise, I soon settled into the curious, stylized routine of the analytic hour and my regular trips to Hampstead became a part of my life.

When we began our work together, as I have written, I did a lot of talking, explaining my preoccupying dilemma, which was, on the surface, a simple matter of choosing a holiday hotel. I had tried to please too many people and become mired in confusion and indecision, prey to all kinds of ridiculous fears. It was such a relief to articulate this problem and to have all my fears and fantasies about the trip taken seriously. Unlike friends, who simply told me not to be silly, Nina listened to the dilemma, sifted my mix of feelings about it, teased out the transference implications, and helped me to understand the conflict of needs, the pattern of projections. As a result, I was able to move forward and enjoy my holiday, but, more importantly, through the analysis of my conflict, I had begun the process of understanding my internal world and of owning my prejudices and needs. I had a real sense that a crucial, life-changing journey had begun.

Looking back, I can see that our discussion of the immediate dilemma of the holiday plans had revealed many of the sources of my neurotic conflicts and psychic pain. Over the next months and years we explored my internal world, as well as my history and my ongoing struggles in the external world. In the process, I came to a better understanding of the origins of my anxieties and guilt-ridden miseries. We had to dig deep and probe behind and beyond the surface of my unhappiness in the face of difficult life events.

Eventually, I came to understand the force of the Oedipal conflict and the role of sibling rivalry in my development. I explored the convoluted history of my sexuality and grappled with my guilt and with my sadism. I re-experienced the intensity of my primitive neediness and the awful pain of exclusion. Much of the material I brought related to the events of my life as I strove to cope with ongoing responsibilities and relationships at home and at work, where, as I gradually came to understand, I re-enacted deeply established patterns of object relations.

This is the standard stuff of analysis and it is never easy. Telling the miseries of the past or exploring the conflicts of the present are comparatively straightforward activities with a sufficiently sympathetic therapist, but, though they may be comforting, they do not lead to psychic change. Facing the shadow side of one's personality is a harder thing, and what was so important about working with Nina was the way in which the unbearable aspects of the self became bearable through the steady containment of her therapeutic love. I not only disliked myself at the start, I was deeply ashamed of myself, and I anticipated criticism and rejection. Nina did not just tell me about the superegoic origins of this self-hate and interpret the transferential aspects of the projections I tried to lay on her: she actively demonstrated her separateness, her independence of my ideas of her, in countless ways. She allowed herself to be real, to have responses and feelings and prejudices. She would delight in my increasingly successful challenges to my narrow-mindedness and then give me examples of her own independent-minded views and actions. For example, I can recall my cautious attempts to disentangle myself from the critical judgements of a close friend and Nina saying bluntly, with refreshing clarity, that he was a self-righteous prig and should be ignored!

Nina's mix of analytic skill and human warmth was never more apparent than in our work around my longing to have a child with my new partner. I knew I had her support, but I needed her skill to work through complex fears of sexuality and minefields of Oedipal guilt before I could assert my desire and act on it. I would never have got there without her. My darling daughter arrived at a weekend, rather earlier than expected, and so I was able to turn up to my next analytic session carrying her in my arms. Nina was astonished, delighted, utterly *ordinary* in her warm response, saying how long it was since she had held a tiny baby. What I experienced that day with Nina was her extraordinary agility, her flexibility in relationships. In our interactions she could play many parts, and all were authentic aspects of her complex, rich self. She could be steady and rigorous in a traditional, boundaried way, but she could allow herself to be surprised and moved and to act from the core of her being when she needed to. For me she could be an ally, a friend, sorting out a problem, sharing a triumph, and also the fantasy figure, idealized or terrifying, eluding my grasp. She moved with confidence around and within the many aspects of the analytic encounter, and over the years I was encouraged and enabled to follow her.

In the deeper work with the unconscious, dreams were a hugely important source of information and inspiration. I had some great dreams in those early years! I write that with the satisfaction born of Nina's delight in my dreams. She valued them, said they were rich and wonderful, took them seriously, and managed to make me feel that I had achieved something in having them. With Nina, my dreams were not just something to be interpreted, something to access the unconscious by; they were creations, gifts, something to be proud of and be attached to. In an early dream, after a break when I had been away on a lovely holiday in Tuscany, I came to a session to find that Nina was hosting a party in her large and beautiful garden. She welcomed me, and I was able to make myself useful serving tea to the many guests enjoying the spring sunshine. Nina was so lovely, serene and gracious, and she was approving and reassuring of me. I wandered around happily, and was not altogether surprised to find Freud himself among the company. He was old and frail, but still able to pace gently in the garden, and somehow it was understood that I was in analysis with him and Nina did not mind this. I felt pleased and privileged. A further dream was darkly violent: I was both victim and murderess in a grim, remorseless tragedy. The stark, shocking power of my fear and of my cold, castrating rage was deeply disturbing but also revealing. As we grappled with the associations, Nina noted that the access it provided to deep unconscious processes had been heralded, made possible, by the first dream. With Nina as my gracious ally, I could dare to penetrate the darker recesses of my mind and face the primitive, Freudian monsters there.

Over the years, many more dreams allowed us to explore deeply unconscious and split-off feelings. Looking back, I am amazed at how much we tackled, how much movement there was in the analysis that came about through talking through my dreams with Nina. I experienced real benefits in life and relationships as well as new insights as I grappled with archaic fears. The dreams and the themes are too numerous to narrate, but one further example is illustrative of the process. In the dream, I was on my way to join my partner at the airport, taking my baby daughter with me. On my way, I heard of some party that I wanted to get to and I needed to take a present. I knew I should concentrate on getting to the airport, but thought it would not take too long to buy a gift, as there was a toy factory nearby. I set off in search of some balls that I thought it would be easy to find there. I knew it would be so clever to arrive with them, but I could not find them. The toy factory was chaotic, the layout very confusing; I searched in vain, using antiquated lifts to access various floors and making numerous trips to the basement, but all I found were snooker balls on a huge table. The baby was happy enough, but heavy to carry as I rushed around searching. I finally gave in, abandoned my search, and asked someone to phone for a taxi to the airport, but there was endless procrastination and discussion and it became less and less possible to get there. Suddenly, I realized that I had put the baby down somewhere and I was distraught that I might not find her or that she might wake—and all because I was so stupid and stubborn.

Nina was delighted with the pun on "balls". She helped me to understand how I had tried so often in life to find the ultimate gift to the internal parents, the brilliant, impressive masculine cleverness I thought they would value. In searching for my male self I not only risked missing the plane, but also had lost the baby me. Gradually, we unravelled how the conflict between my masculine solution to the Oedipal struggle had resulted in my repressing my female, sexual self, which could then only find a guilt-ridden, masochistic outlet in painful, rejecting relationships. Nina allowed me to find the meaning myself, but the sense of her involvement and enthusiastic concern was enormously facilitating.

As I said at the start, I was initially relieved to find there was no formal theorizing or pathologizing from my analyst, but in time I did dare to wonder more about the theory. Nina was reassuring when I queried whether it would help the analysis if I were reading psychoanalytic theory. She told me I did not need to, literature was probably of more use to me, but if I felt impelled to read then stick with Winnicott. In retrospect, I could understand this. As the work deepened, we moved back to the early, preverbal years, and I felt safe enough to experience a deep regression. Finding my early self, deprived and needy but also greedy and destructive, was a terrifying experience. I could not have faced that without Nina being able to maintain a steady warmth and acceptance of the whole of me. She could speak of therapeutic love with quiet confidence and total authenticity, and I knew that I could never have been able to bear the re-emergence of either the intensity of early libidinal longing or the shattering power of infantile rage without her containing presence.

Alongside steady containment, dream interpretation, classic transference work, and the capacity for spontaneity, Nina also brought imagination and originality to her work. In my analysis this was often evident, as I will try to illustrate with one example. In deciphering the transference relationship, Nina became aware that it was sometimes difficult to know who was being experienced, as the transference did not fit with the historical object relations that we had explored. Unsurprisingly, there was a familiar maternal transference, which had been very revealing of the painful reality of my early years, and father and maternal grandmother also figured in various guises. However, Nina detected a different relationship, which she came to see as the introjection of my mother's experience of her maternal object. My mother was the only surviving child of a woman who had not only been widowed in the First World War, but who had lost virtually all her male relatives. My mother was brought up by her mother and grandmother and had never been allowed to grieve the loss of her father and uncles. Her need to deny her pain and attend to the other had become a defining aspect of her personality, together with a very split-off hatred of the feminine. So much of my mother's experience had been projected into me, as a way of placating *her* mother, that Nina could see a part of me was totally merged with her. Nina unravelled the intergenerational dynamics of my internal world in a way that proved extraordinarily liberating.

It is impossible to do justice to the richness and complexity of an intensive analysis over several years, and I have been very selective in my use of material. My aim has been to show something of Nina's way of working from a patient's perspective, but I am aware that I can do so only clumsily. I retain a lively sense of the work, and marvel at how much I learnt and how much I changed over those years. There were sobering aspects to the learning process but, as I said before, there was great optimism and much liveliness and humour. The external gains were of enormous value. Before analysis I had achieved many things, but the price had been high: neurotic guilt dogged my enjoyment of motherhood, fear and depression were constant companions, I opted for difficult love relations, and struggled against a sense of failure at work. In time, as I understood the unconscious processes better, I was able to celebrate motherhood with a loving partner supporting me and to operate more fully and joyfully in the world. I was able to make an important change of career, leaving the academic world to train as a psychoanalytic psychotherapist. But these changes needed more than an understanding of my internal world: Nina provided the essential "facilitating environment" that Winnicott talked of, the space in which I could discover and nurture my self.

What I hope I have conveyed of the experience of being Nina's patient is that I encountered in her that rare mix of rigour and spontaneity that her writing subsequently revealed. I have not expanded on the experience of her classical technique, but she was most thoroughly grounded in that. There were whole sessions when I was in such a dark rage I said nothing, and was not rescued, and at one stage I became bitterly angry over her "refusal" to change session times that were difficult for me. But such battles only took place when Nina knew I was ready to bear them: her grasp of the right moment was impeccable. Long before I read of her scorn for the redundant "you mean me" interpretation, I realized I was comfortably able to distinguish the Nina of the transference from the Nina of the therapeutic alliance. What I valued was the freedom to move between intense experiences of regression, with frantic greed or lethal rage, into experiences of real support and understanding. Because Nina had the agility to make herself available in the many, many ways I needed her, I was able to grow. Most importantly, because I had the experience of being valued and understood and enjoyed, I was able to be a better person in the world, in my personal and professional life.

* * *

I ended my personal analysis with Nina after five years of profound change. I then returned to her for a training analysis. I feel very privileged to have had the luxury of both a personal and a training analysis. I was astonished how much there was still to learn about myself while training, but the context of my deepening immersion in the theory and practice of psychoanalysis was challenging and we were never bored. I realize that the "we" there may sound presumptuous, but Nina had a great capacity for involvement and I believed her when she said at the end that she had found the whole thing thoroughly enjoyable. Such generosity of spirit was hugely valuable. She understood the importance of the wholehearted involvement of both patient and analyst in the analytic encounter. A decade after my analysis had ended, Nina responded to a letter from me—in which I had written a spontaneous tribute to the enduring importance of my years of analysis with her—with a wonderful, affirmative summary of the process. She wrote,

> It pleases me so much, Muriel, nothing could please me more than what you say in your long, thoughtful and enormously important paragraph at the end of the letter. I see you have sustained "my introject" in you, and the powerful effects of an analysis with a "successful outcome" in the most marvellous and, to me, moving way. Of course there is nothing "maudlin, sentimental or dependent" about it; it is a unique form of inner friendship between two people who came to know each other in a unique and incomparable way over a long, hard working and sometimes difficult and painful time, and deeply appreciate each other to their very depths.

It was important to me, after I had ended analysis, to continue to communicate with Nina in the external world as well as in my internal object relations. Nina was always quite clear that an analysis should end, that endings were important, but she also made it clear that, after it did, she would welcome letters. I got into the habit of a yearly letter, sent just before Christmas, in which I told her what had been happening to me and my family and something of how my professional work was developing. Nina always responded promptly and warmly. She loved to hear news of my children, of my chaotic but talented son ("one of my favourites"), and of my lovely daughter, whose very youthful appearance in her consulting room she often recalled with delight. She was thoughtful, concerned, and wise in her response to my telling her of some marital difficulties, and full of praise as I reported that we had struggled out of the storms and the doldrums.

Over the years, we wrote more, and very gradually Nina revealed more about herself: her plans for retirement, her delight with the garden, her enormous pleasure at being asked to lecture abroad. It could be said that, even at this stage of the relationship, there was too much self-disclosure but Nina had a very clear sense of the importance of the analyst's becoming real for the patient in the later stages of the work and in the post-analytic period. She had delighted in the detailed account of Guntrip's analyses, edited by Jeremy Hazell (1996), and valued his ideas on this. She was, of course, remarkably self-revealing in her interview with Anthony Molino. She was never doctrinaire in this, and her sense of timing and of what was appropriate for the other at any given time remained acute. She understood the tyranny of idealization and the need to work it through to a more measured appraisal. Whenever, in the course of my analysis, I was clearly putting her on a pedestal as the epitome of wisdom or goodness, she would dryly remind me that the flip side of idealization was contempt, and she would rather avoid being the object of that!

As we corresponded, I was able to use her extensive knowledge of therapists and courses to obtain advice for people who were seeking analysis or training in various parts of the country, because she was always pleased to help with referrals. I was delighted to be able to reciprocate to some extent with contacts for my part of the country, albeit apprehensive the first time she referred a patient directly to me. My own practice developed and, in addition to my clinical caseload, I became increasingly involved in the training and organizational aspects of the work. I could write to Nina of the difficulties and stresses of the institutional side of psychoanalysis, sure of a perceptive and supportive response. She was a staunch ally in the face of conflicts with the doctrinally rigid or the bureaucratically bound, and was a shrewd adviser on ethical dilemmas.

Most importantly, I wrote to Nina about my internal world and of my own continued growth as a person as I encountered more of the joys and difficulties of life and coped with loss and change. The wonder of being heard, understood, and taken seriously, so valuable throughout the years of analysis, remained important in the years of our correspondence. I so appreciated the deepening and the increased reciprocity of our communications, and it was great to have, on paper, confirmation of the inner dialogue.

Nina loved the travel and the touch of celebrity that she enjoyed after her books were published. She wrote of the opportunities for travel and lecturing and teaching as the "perfect combination". Although she enjoyed herself hugely, she could be wickedly critical at times; for example, in 1986 she wrote, "I've just had a wonderful fortnight's working trip to the States—like being on an intravenous drip of ego boost, apart from the sheer fascination of it all. Although analytically they are dismally old-fashioned, have hardly got into object-relations at all, still on old ego psychology". She was very pleased to be asked back to the USA, and delighted to do part of the tour in dialogue with Kit Bollas, whom she enthusiastically described to me as "the best thing to emerge from British psychoanalysis for many years, and hugely readable and congenial". She loved the lecturing, but found the pace of some of the trips pretty exhausting, and she wrote of how she needed to retreat a little and be by herself to recuperate. One letter contained a great diatribe about the conspicuous consumption and waste she had experienced in America, because she knew we shared an attachment to a degree of frugality and simplicity in lifestyle. But she loved the enthusiasm for her writing and ideas that she encountered abroad.

Nina's dislike of the stuffiness and rigidity of the analytic world was often expressed. The freedom she enjoyed as a clinician to move around in the analytic space was a quality that rendered the institutional hierarchies of psychoanalysis very irksome to her. In my professional life, I took on more responsibilities with various institutions, both locally and nationally, particularly in the area of training, which gave me some challenging situations to deal with. When I wrote of them, Nina sympathized with the problems I faced and commented,

> It's worse than the academic world because, in the therapy world, one has (justifiable) expectations that people should behave better

and with more kindness, sensitivity, insight and love. But do they? Do they heck! Let me tell you that I am so absolutely fed to the teeth with the sort of thing you are describing, and which I recognise instantly, that I am withdrawing from this world on all fours, and in fact, cutting the practice down to two and a half days a week in September and going to spend a lot of time in my new wild garden and tiny bungalow in the Chilterns. The analysts are the worst of the whole bunch, and a lot of idealisation of them/us, and the Institute, means that envy, identifications and acting out take on similar forms across the therapeutic-organisations-board as they do with us. . . . The inner workings of the Society are a shambles, and if I hadn't already made my Resolve, the iron would have entered finally into my soul at our AGM [Annual General Meeting] last Wed., when the glaring sectarian politicisation of the Kleinian vs. Independent chronic volcano erupted into a really unbelievable mess over a supposedly non-Group matter.

She ended her explicit letter, "Keep well, and keep a little Detachment in you about the shenanigans, life is too short and precious to sink under them!"

Nina also wrote in a very encouraging and affirmative way about my clinical work, pleased that I was now "a round peg in a round hole". She commented, when I had noted it was ten years since I had qualified, that her analyst would confirm that I could *now* consider myself an analyst: she had often said that one needed a decade of practice to find one's own style and the confidence to stick to it. She often conveyed that she took real delight in my enjoyment of the work:

> And more than anything I'm glad that you are happier and still growing and "remain fascinated by the psyche"—it *is* endlessly fascinating, and if ever there were someone who ploughed her way through to where she rightly had to be, it was you. The process doesn't stop, believe me.

Once she commented,

> Yes, of course you over-work, and I expect it's a bit neurotic but I do have to say that your analyst didn't give you an introject that was *different* from that, so there's no hope for either of us sitting back with our feet up—or not for long. I do a *bit* of that now.

In due course, Nina wrote more of her move towards and into retirement, and of some of her health problems, and I found myself shifting dramatically in my perception of her: the residual transference weakened and I could begin to acknowledge her frailty and glimpse her defences. As more of her books and papers appeared I had, of course, already learnt more about both her ideas and her life. As I noted in our correspondence, however, her published writing was never a surprise to me, but only a confirmation of what I already deeply knew. But, through our correspondence, I became more aware of a darker side of Nina, and could sense something of her fears and of her loneliness. I could also appreciate her profound courage.

In the spring of 1997, I was moved to write a long letter to Nina that was not just the usual update of family and professional news. I did write about work and about her latest book, but I also tried to put into words what I felt about my analysis with her and say what it had meant to me. I had a deep urge to communicate my gratitude and my love, and also my concern. I felt a certain urgency about this task and a slight apprehension that it might be intrusive. Nina, of course, responded promptly and at length. She told me more about her recent, dramatic illness and hospitalization, and was very pleased that I had enjoyed her latest book.

> I will tell you—because who else will—that in January . . . a very clever, very cool, very laid back young man rang me and said: "I don't want to be hyperbolic about this, but your book has sold faster than any other book we have ever published." . . . Of course, I was thrilled to the marrow, and deeply flattered and grateful.

Answering my query about her work, she wrote, "No, I don't want to go on forever, mouldering and dementing behind the couch". She then contrasted herself with some powerful elderly Kleinian analysts who were still working and, rather wickedly, noted that "it is a Religion for them, as I long ago decided, and they are the Repositories and messengers of the Only Truth". In response to my tribute to her she gave the thoughtful and loving affirmation that I have already quoted. She then added, "I can conjure you up and talk with you very much as you describe, though obviously the relationship is, as ever it was, 'equal but asymmetrical' and I do not need to do that so often". She recalled our "converse about the need to be loved and *to love* and to feel lovable", and recommended Jackie Gerrard's paper on "Love in the time of psychotherapy" (1996). The letter ended, "Dear Muriel, it pleases me more than anything else could that you say you 'feel content inside despite your ingrained pessimism'. Thank you for telling me something so rich. Much love, Nina".

That was my final letter from Nina. The next communication from the bungalow in the Chilterns was from Nina's sister, briefly reporting that Nina had died, suddenly but peacefully, letting me know, with characteristic sensitivity, before I had read of it in the papers.

I think it was very appropriate that there was so much about love in these last letters. A description of Nina would have to cover many things. My knowledge of her includes knowledge of her strength, her integrity, her intelligence, her humour. I have testified to her fine intellect, her independent spirit, and her powers of imagination and creativity, all of which I experienced directly in the years of my analysis and our correspondence. But what is most enduring and most important to me was her warmth and the kindness and dedication she brought to the task of healing. She worked with and through love. She was not afraid to use the term because she had the confidence that comes from really knowing what it means. There was nothing sentimental about her kind of love, and it came from the core of her being.

The other defining attribute of Nina was her delight in the unconscious. She worked hard to access and understand the unconscious, in herself and in others, but she knew what she meant when she referred to the "sheer unconsciousness of the unconscious". There was nothing sentimental or facile or arrogant about her familiarity with unconscious process: it was a talent she possessed and she put it to use. I am sure I am not the only person, privileged to have known her, who remains profoundly grateful for that.

References

Gerrard, J. (1996). Love in the time of psychotherapy. *British Journal of Psychotherapy*, 13: 163–173.

Hazell, J. (1996). *H. J. S. Guntrip: A Psychoanalytical Biography*. London: Free Association Books.

CHAPTER THREE

Nina and the parcel

Alex Douglas-Morris

I first met Nina in 1970, when I was twenty-three, and I still see that date as the most significant in my life. From that day, everything changed.

Nina invited me to talk about myself and my family, listening carefully, and when I had finished, she said, "You have presented me with a wonderful parcel, in exotic wrapping paper and richly coloured ribbon, but the contents are muddied and distorted".

In many ways, over the next twenty-seven years, we sat in her room with her Vermeer postcards, black and white rug, and gentle lighting, unpacking that parcel. We worked through some parts, and of those contents that could not be removed she named them and said, "See them as unwelcome friends. Stand at the top of your staircase as they make their way up towards you and warn them, 'You can stay for ten minutes and no more'".

Seeing Nina was always on a professional level, but, over the years, our friendship developed and began to flow into other areas. My mother knew Gill (Nina's sister), Nina met my two sisters, my husband David, and our two daughters . . . so, I embraced Nina into my family.

We mutually recommended books, plays, and films to each other. She felt Eugene O'Neill's *Long Day's Journey into Night* perfectly summed up my family and said I would feel entirely at home in one of Ivy Compton-Burnett's books.

We both adored the colour pink, and agreed on the EXACT shade. She gloated that the bath, basin, and front door of her new home were all in that colour.

At the end of each session, Nina would shake my hand, and it was only many years later that she explained this was an unusual practice for a therapist . . . but she had understood my need to have physical reassurance.

One of the moments I remember with amusement was one soaking wet day, when I had sloshed my way to her house minus coat and umbrella to find her waiting, armed with a black bin-liner, which she merrily placed on my chair. It squeaked throughout our session, and from that time forward, whenever it rained, Nina had a sturdy bin-liner on hand! That small event sums up perfectly for me Nina's sense of fun and lack of pomposity.

Nina and I travelled a long, gusty road together. She held my hand and steered me through the buffeting winds, celebrating my highs and holding me tight through the lows. The colour and creative energy in my present life are due to Nina's guiding light . . . her love, compassion and wisdom opened doors and carried me from the shadows into the light.

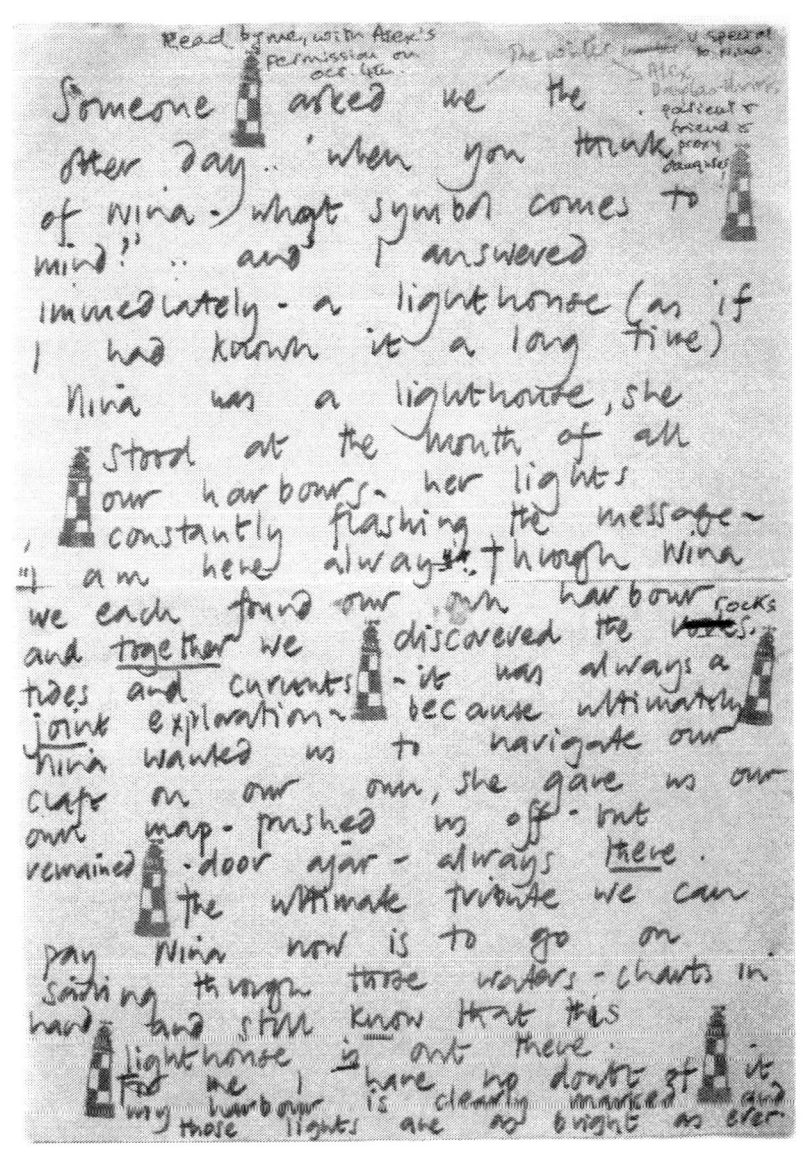

Figure 1. Alex Douglas-Morris's "Lighthouse letter".

CHAPTER FOUR

A Buddhist way of seeing*

Barbara Hopkinson

I met Nina Coltart in Spring 1968 and our paths crossed like this.

In the mid-1960s the marriage of a relative was in a bad way. The husband's infidelity had affected his wife to such an extent that her previously confident, bubbly personality had changed to one of depression and apathy. I watched the whole family deteriorating for some time until, quite suddenly, between one month and the next, there were distinct signs of *joie de vivre* returning. At an appropriate moment, I enquired as to the cause, and was told that my relative had been given the name of a wonderful doctor in Hampstead who was showing her how to deal with her despair in a new way.

Something made me ask the name of this remarkable person— it was Nina Coltart. The name stuck in my mind. I think I knew unconsciously that I might need her one day, as my second marriage was becoming a repetition of the earlier disaster.

---

* Previously published in 1998 under the title "Warm-hearted, witty, wise and the most tremendous fun" in *Interbeing: Journal of the Leeds Network of Engaged Buddhists*, 16 (Summer), 26–28.

Several years later, I had reached the end of the road: I found Dr Coltart's number and rang her. In those days she answered her own telephone, and I was lucky enough to find her at home. She made it clear that she was not willing to accept new patients, having more than she could manage already. Desperation made me persistent, and eventually she agreed to see me.

She sent me a map showing her house. I printed instructions to myself in large block letters as to train times, underground train routes, my appointment time, her name, my name—my zombie-like state made all this necessary. I did not tell anyone where I was going.

Arriving safely, I sat in a small, charming waiting room in terror! I was afraid that she could not, would not, help me, and then what was I to do? The door opened exactly at the time arranged and there stood this tall, elegant woman. Her face showed both kindness and strength, and I knew instantly that I had found something I had sought throughout my life—a powerful, compassionate ally.

She greeted me in a friendly but reserved way and we sat opposite each other in her consulting room. On later occasions I was conscious of flowers and pictures, but this time I only saw her. We gazed at each other for long minutes. I did not know where to begin, but I only had fifty minutes, so I had to say something. All I can remember of that encounter is her drawing my attention to my continual self-denigration and, at the end, her instructions that I was very ill, that I had been ill for years, that I must go home, go to bed, and permit myself to be ill. She gave me a prescription for anti-depressants and from that day onwards I followed her advice on all matters—not immediately, perhaps, but eventually. She was never wrong.

Within two years I had recovered enough to start work again, not in our hotel, but as a part-time assistant in a book shop. Suffolk was a great Transcendental Meditation centre at that time and I learnt to meditate. Dr Coltart was delighted, saying that I could not have done anything better. I was seeing her regularly, but at intervals of months, and around 1970 I reported that I had completely lost my Christian faith and no longer believed in God. We talked about this, and she said, "I am not trying to turn you into a Buddhist but here's a reading list. See how you get on." Among the titles were *The Way of Zen* and *The Way of the White Clouds*. The moment I began the former, I knew I had found the spiritual path for which I had long searched, and from then on my analyst became my Buddhist teacher and, eventually, my dearest and most special friend.

I saw her infrequently over the years, as I had recovered from depression, but we kept up our friendship through enormously long letters in which she continued to teach me. I had found my way to various Buddhist groups, none of which seemed quite right for me. On hearing this, she advised me to approach the Theravadan centre, to which she belonged, the Amaravarti Monastery at Great Gaddesden, which I did. There I felt completely at home and have followed that path ever since.

Now that she has gone, I value even more the spiritual teaching that went from Ajahn Chah, to Ajahn Sumedho, to Nina Coltart, to me; I am not a teacher, but I have Nina in my mind constantly, so that many of my friends feel that they know her, too, because I refer to her and her teaching so often. Her wise and benign influence has not ended with her death.

I spent an afternoon with her in the summer of 1996, the last time I saw her. She helped me accept the loss of a dear younger brother in a way that stood me in good stead when she died, so that I can remember them both with joy. In our last conversation, she described my response to Buddhist teaching as "cathectic". I only know that without her guidance I should not have survived into contented and fruitful old age; I should not have survived at all. My only regret is that she was not able to enjoy her seventies, too.

What set her apart from analysts in general and gave her the extra quality of compassionate, loving wisdom was her Buddhist way of seeing life and her troubled fellow creatures. She was warmhearted, witty, wise, and the most tremendous fun.

CHAPTER FIVE

A one-off visit

Kathleen Murphy

I first met Nina Coltart about 1980, when my doctor referred me to her, as a one-off visit. She quickly put me right on one point on which my thinking was at fault. She came across as a very kind person and one felt at ease with her.

At some point, possibly a couple of years later, and I cannot now remember how it started, after I had written to her, and she replied with a long friendly letter, and to that I replied, and, hence, a long and interesting correspondence began, and I looked forward to her letters coming, and to quickly responding.

Some time after this her housekeeper was taken ill, and I offered to do the vacuuming, if it would be of any help to her. I felt her life and her work were of so much help to others that to try and fit in housework seemed such a waste of Nina's precious time. So I did the vacuuming and a few small errands (for which she paid me handsomely!), and I hope was of some help to her.

I might add that her housekeeper accomplished far more than I ever did!

Then Nina retired and invited me over to her house in Leighton Buzzard on several occasions, always making me feel welcome.

She had been very ill on several occasions, but I only knew of this through her letters. She never actually spoke of being in pain, or feeling unwell. She was a very brave woman, modest, humorous, and very attached to her sister and her family. I suspect that aspect of her life made her the warm and understanding woman that she was, never mind about her profession!

(B) SUPERVISEES

CHAPTER SIX

A whole attitude to life and work

Michael Brearley

Many people influence our work and thinking. Often we can forget, or not fully allow ourselves to know, how much someone has influenced us. And one reason for this can be that someone's ideas become so central to our thinking that we lose touch with their source in that other person. Nina Coltart was an influence on me of this kind, one who was so close that I risk taking her for granted. It is also hard to know what comes directly from her, quotably, as it were, and what comes more indirectly but pervasively by means of assimilation and identification from a whole attitude to life and work. In just such latter ways, I think, we also take things in from our parents and our analysts.

Nina was the supervisor of my first training case. This was a difficult but ultimately rewarding experience, and her help with it, for an inexperienced candidate, was immense. The help was also, as I came to see more clearly with hindsight, subtle, tactful, and given with a light touch. Nina was able to take a back seat, refraining from forcing stuff on me beyond my capacity to take it in. She knew that too much information would overload and confuse me, and too much criticism would inhibit me. She recognized the centipede in me—if one asked a centipede to think about the movement of each leg, it would fall into a ditch. Like General Kutuzov in Tolstoy's *War and Peace*, she refused to get drawn into meretricious ventures for personal glory, and had faith not only in the process of psychoanalysis, but also in me and the patient.

She was, however, quite capable of being forthright, as we know from her writings, and as I found in professional contacts with her on more than one occasion. She could, I think, be over-active on behalf of a patient, and boldly and appropriately supportive of her supervisee (me).

Nina often wrote about our "impossible profession". We are on a "tightrope", having to try to keep our balance between contrasting errors or over-emphases. For instance, we often have to walk narrow tightropes between focusing too much on transference and not enough, between receptivity (silence) and activity (interpretation), between engagement and detachment, between spontaneity and careful reflection. All this is very much what I think, too, and is an important part of what I would include in the notion of the analyst's neutrality.

An even more important theme that Nina Coltart conveyed to me, personally and in her writings, is her use of the concept of love in psychoanalytic work. She stresses in her papers and books that by "love" she means agape rather than eros. It has little to do with falling in love. Her notion of love in its role in our work has nothing to do with sentimentality. As she says, one may dislike a patient, indeed, dislikeability may even be a presenting and important symptom. The love she speaks of involves a sense of what the patient might develop into, or what the patient cannot allow, and gives room for the whole gamut of emotional responses (as indeed does our love for, say, our children). Components of this loving attitude include patience, kindness, courage, and humour, as Nina demonstrates. Above all, there needs to be a particular kind of loving attention. She ends her paper "Love is not enough" with the following sentences:

> Unless this whole extraordinary and recurring phenomenon, which constitutes our working life, can be called the work of the capacity to love, then I would agree that love is not enough. On the other hand, if you consider that I have justified my argument, I might—at risk of being misunderstood—even dare to say: then "All you need is love".

CHAPTER SEVEN

Charisma*

Mary Twyman

"Charisma" is a word often used—sometimes overused—in describing outstanding figures in their fields. However, I came across a recent gloss on the term from Chris Patten, currently Chancellor of Oxford University, Nina Coltart's *alma mater*. He defined charisma as a combination of grace and authority. This, I think, captures exactly those qualities that Nina brought to her thinking, her writing, and her relationships with friends and colleagues ... and in my case (and in Mike Sinason's), to those she taught. We were both fortunate to have Nina as a supervisor for our first training cases. For myself, the foundations of my nascent identity as a psychoanalyst were firmly and robustly nurtured by her teaching, and my gratitude for the quality of her *attention* to my early stumbling efforts with my patient remains constant.

"Attention" is the title of the paper she gave as the Arbours 20th Anniversary Lecture, and is a lasting marker of her interest in, and support of, the Association.

---

* Remarks delivered on 8 July 2008 at the Institute of Psychoanalysis on the occasion of the Fifth Annual Nina Coltart Lecture, given by Dr Michael Sinason and sponsored by the Arbours Crisis Centre.

CHAPTER EIGHT

Nina Coltart the consultant: hospitality conditional and unconditional

Pina Antinucci

The home of the Sybil

In the photograph of Nina Coltart I retain firmly impressed in my memory, the expertise and acumen of the diagnostician go hand in hand with her hieratic demeanour; a kind of mystique, which she played on, with wisdom and self-irony, as she declared that her stance was in the service of the in(tro)duction to the mysteries of the unconscious. The neophyte—the prospective patient—had to go through a momentous initiation process, as he was ushered into her consulting room, to meet the priestess of psychoanalysis.

I have used the terms "mystery" and "neophyte", employing a language that connotes an initiation process, and this is what I recall my encounter with her to have meant—an initiation into psychoanalysis.

I encountered Dr Coltart the consultant from a variety of perspectives, as an analysand-to-be, as a practitioner receiving and welcoming her referrals, and, later on, even as a member of the Directorate of the London Clinic. In these different capacities, I had the opportunity to reflect on her philosophy and attitude regarding assessment interviews. There are many themes I could and will pick up, many things I could say, the most important of which, however, is her capacity to capture the person's need to find an internal place to belong to, and a language of his or her own. This is certainly what she elicited from me, as I am more and more aware, as I circle back to that encounter repeatedly in the course of time. And I will start from there.

In 1981, what is now the distant past, I started a psychotherapy training with the Arbours Association, and Nina was on their Training Committee, with the specific task of carrying out consultations with the prospective students, so as to refer them on for analysis. At that time, Nina was also the Director of the London Clinic, the consultation service of the British Psychoanalytic Society; consequently, she had a vast knowledge of her colleagues, their trainings, interests, capacities, and experience. She had also gained a very broad experience of diagnostic consultations, both in the public sector and in her private practice. Within the psychotherapy milieu, Coltart had gained a reputation for being the best Director the London Clinic had ever had, and certainly she has left a notable mark on that institution.

I wish, however, to return to Nina the Director, not of the Clinic, but of herself, as "the character" she scripted and performed on the psychoanalytic stage. When I first met Nina, I was a foreign young woman, not quite settled in London and in adult life; therefore, I felt rather intimidated when faced by a tall, well-built, middle-aged, elegant woman, who gazed at me with her large piercing blue eyes and a knowing smile on her face. I do not know whether she captured the meandering of my associations, slowly moving towards the metaphorical representation of a Sybil's lodgings, or whether she herself put forward that self-representation. What I did feel, anyhow, was that her words aptly described the impression she was aware of making on her interlocutor when, with her self-ironical stance, she invited me to enter her Sybil's "cavern" and to tell my history, at the end of which she would pronounce her judgement, undoubtedly in a truly cryptic mode, which would require an interpretation.

Memories from my college days jumbled together in my mind, and I recalled the ambiguity of the sibylline pronouncement "*ibis redibis non morietur in bello*"[1] Would she make similarly ambiguous utterances? And, furthermore, would she make them in her foreign language, which at that time sounded to me less familiar than Latin? I found myself wondering with some trepidation.

Needless to say, the encounter with Nina Coltart represented a transformative event in my life. One of the most significant moments occurred when, after having listened to some of my story, she exclaimed, "Oh, you and your Roman Catholic superego!"

Some powerful lesson in cultural relativism that was! By simply focusing my attention on the adjective "Roman" put before "Catholic", she aided me in experiencing the possibility of listening to my own discourse as other-than-familiar. I was getting the taste of the other foreign idiom I would begin to hear coming from the nooks and crannies of my mind, all yet to be discovered.

Today, if I try again to listen to the voice of the London Sybil who taught me how to listen to the "mermaids' song" of my unconscious mind, what emerges as the most significant occurrence is that I started then to dream in a foreign tongue. In Borges' words, I "came to dream in a language which was not that of [my] parents" (quoted in Flegenheimer, 1989, p. 377).

With these words, I like to pay homage to a prominent thinker of contemporary British psychoanalysis, highlighting what could be defined as the *mythopoetic spirit* which inspired her, and which consists essentially in the possibility of becoming a subject through a narrative of one's self. The word *mythos* in Greek means, in fact, at once a narration and a myth; it is also a story that is supported by a temporal dimension where, paradoxically, there is a reconciliation of the "never" of the real event with the "always" of human truths to be rediscovered, time and again, and reinterpreted. Likewise, there is a reconciliation of the subjectivity of intuition with the relatively more generalizing objectivity of science.

Similarly, a paradoxical convergence of personal tact and intuition with systematic, rigorous reflection characterizes Coltart's approach to diagnosis.

---

[1] The ambiguity turns on placement of the invisible punctuation, so that the sentence can mean either: "You will go and return, and will not die in war", or "You will go and not return, and will die in war".

In 1987, she published in the *British Journal of Psychotherapy* a short paper titled "Diagnosis and assessment of suitability for psycho-analytical psychotherapy", which begins with the following statement:

> In day-to-day work, one draws on principally unconscious skills, knowledge and intuition. But the situation in which you need to be consciously in touch with a whole range of ideas and concepts is the diagnostic interview. Here I would stress *diagnostic* in conjunction with assessment for analytic psychotherapy; we have to be getting at some sort of diagnostic picture, in order to think about the patient coherently and, if necessary, to be able to discuss him with colleagues to whom we may be referring. This picture has to include, of course, what the patient is *not*. [p. 1]

Psychoanalysis has gone through complex vicissitudes and still struggles with the notion of diagnosis, redolent with the flavour of scientific taxonomy. Qualifying it as a *psychodynamic diagnosis* is meant to differentiate it from the traditional medical interview, yet some uneasiness remains to this day, as is testified, for example, by a recent essay by Rossi Monti (2008), titled "Diagnosi: una brutta parola?" ("Diagnosis: a bad word?"), which addresses and reopens the discussion on the necessity and usefulness, from both the theoretical and the clinical and technical points of view, of coming to formulate a diagnostic evaluation upon the conclusion of the first encounter with the patient.

On this age-old question, Nina adopts a clear position, making unambiguous statements suffused with pragmatic and, at the same time, poetically evocative spirit, so much in keeping with her character. She compares the psychoanalytic consultation to a happy marriage between the exquisitely idiosyncratic idiom of (poetic) intuition and the more conventional, objective language of scientific—in her case psychiatric—communication. Nina, in fact, claims to be entitled to speak about psychoanalytic diagnostics, the discipline she practised for decades both as a psychoanalyst and a psychiatrist in a variety of settings. And in her reflections on the role of the diagnostician, she emphasized its twofold significance, the real and the mythological, which is clearly present in people's imaginary, albeit as an only partially conscious fantasy. It is understandable that a mythological aura should surround a professional whose mandate is to issue a "prescription" that is certainly not ordinary, but rather momentous, and which, according to Nina, quoting Diatkine, involves "the patient in an adventure which is not comparable with any other medical treatment (and yet which curiously falls somewhere in the outer boundary of that category) . . ." (Coltart, 1987, p. 2).

With regard to the link with the medical model, Coltart is explicit, as she maintains that the training and experience acquired in psychiatric departments is undoubtedly—if not essential—a great advantage in diagnostics. So much so that, from the 1970s right through to the 1990s, almost all the consultations to establish suitability for analytic treatment were carried out in London by colleagues with a medical training.

It is desirable, according to Coltart, that the diagnostician not be looking for patients to fill his own vacancies, so that, freed of that pressure, he can use and rely on his intuition and his knowledge of his colleagues' work and availability to make appropriate referrals.

To be able to make an accurate diagnosis, it is essential to have developed one's own well-informed and coherent point of view on clinical aspects, such as, for instance, trauma, and the specific and characteristic sequelae of certain traumatic experiences, or psychosis, or the possibility of working with transference psychosis.

Furthermore, it would be advisable to have a good working knowledge of various forms of psychotherapy, so that psychoanalysis is not seen as the last resort for desperately ill cases. The latter, a rather distorted picture at that, is often the characteristic, ill-informed view of those who are afraid not only of psychoanalysis, but even more, of the possibility of capturing the emergence of their own unconscious mind. To convey Coltart's thought more effectively, I let her speak:

> The mythical assessor, who does not exist, has an omniscient knowledge of all possible criteria of analysability, a peculiar capacity to predict the full course of treatment, a clairvoyant power to read the whole personal history and potential, both conscious and unconscious, of someone whom he is meeting once in a lifetime for two hours, and a God's eye view of the details of this person's therapeutic relationship for the next five years. This may sound ludicrous when spelt out, but if you examine your own half-conscious

expectations, I think you will find that this creature exists somewhere on the fringe of them. [Coltart, 1987, p. 2]

Hyperbolic style, a taste for irony and paradox, are certainly undeniable, as is Coltart's courage in shedding light on, and making explicit, the not-so-easily verbalizable messianic expectations which people's imaginary locates in diagnostics and in its practitioner. The diagnostician, however, must practise in a very realistic and responsible manner his task of "matching" patient and therapist, bearing in mind that the best fit is not based upon a sort of "twinning process". It is, rather, a question of allowing the representation of an analytic couple at work to emerge from one's preconscious. Nina's favourite term to indicate the end result of this consultation work was "match", which belongs to the semantic realm of marriage and nuptial erotics. Its corollary is a theory of the talking cure as founded on transference neurosis and its treatment. I wonder, however, what she might think, were she alive today, about the alternative word "fit", and whether she would willingly adopt it so as to encompass the semantics of the maternal care given to the newborn, which we have more and more come to see as a prototype for the analytic couple, incorporating the language of infant research, as has now become so fashionable.

Still, Nina availed herself of the marital metaphor, and this gave a slant to the representation she favoured of herself as a kind of Godmother of analytic couples, carrying out a function akin to what is conferred by traditional Armenians on older women, who bless the pair newly engaged or reconstituted after a separation or bereavement. She had, in fact, instigated a peculiar form of personal mythology based on her exquisite capacity to match analysand and analyst.

I remember quite well how, after a consultation, she would part from the prospective analysand promising, tongue in cheek, that she would let her unconscious work in search of an analytic match which, short of being ideal, would certainly prove to be "the best possible".

Could one say that Coltart liked to surround herself with a peculiar mystique of diagnostics? Perhaps. What is certain, however, is that she had, and consciously made use of, a notable talent for eliciting the patient's wish and capacity to entrust himself to an analyst's mind, and this experience had a beneficial outcome on the treatment. She was also very gifted in drawing out the patient's interest and curiosity, which, together with her match-making mystique, very quickly opened up a variety of imaginary hypotheses about the essential and constitutive ingredients on which the analytic couple would be based, a sort of foundation myth. But, here, we are already quite clearly on the stage of transference love and its vicissitudes.

Diagnostic criteria

What constitutes the focus of Coltart's thought is the psychoanalytic consultation, a hybrid creature in the service of two contrasting needs: on the one hand to arrive at a nosographic definition as the outcome of the encounter with the patient, while, on the other, being a stopover on a long journey to be mapped out, moment by moment, as a *going concern*.

For over two centuries, since the age of Kant, psychiatry quenched its thirst for knowledge by naming a mental illness and describing it, as though the taxonomic effort sustained the illusion that the disturbance could and would then be knowable. Psychoanalysis, on the contrary, feared that a diagnosis would do no more than flatten, or even deaden, the psychodynamic dimension of the interview, preventing the clinician from being curious about and surprised by the phenomena he could participate in and observe personally in the consulting room. A psychodynamic diagnosis, in fact, is always provisional, subject to the reaching of ever deeper layers of the mind and its functioning, and can only be obtained, with any luck, at the end of the analysis. Diagnosis, then, or work in progress?

Coltart's reflections on the criteria for the assessment for suitability for analysis are mainly based on the state of the London Clinic in the post-war years, when the small number of colleagues able to carry out psychodynamic diagnostic consultations was compounded by a distorted vision of psychoanalysis as a sort of panacea for all kinds of psychological malaise, which resulted in an extraordinarily long waiting list of over 400, while candidates looking for training patients lived in a state of chaos and confusion. Coltart shows her command of the diagnostic tool, which provides her with the co-ordinates of a grid aimed at satisfying the requirements of a systematic approach. However, alongside the criteria useful to the clinician to assess analysability, she goes into territories that are generally left unexplored, as they pertain to the more universal domain of human attributes. These are aspects the literature does not address, and, consequently, they remain out of the general discussion. Therefore, going back to Freud's technical essays and advice on beginning treatment, she draws out three aspects—*intelligence, character,* and *money*—that are usually neglected, seemingly because they are considered to be unworthy of a political, idealistic, utopian, or high-minded discourse.

With regard to payments, leaving aside the issue of private fees, Coltart maintains that Clinic patients should contribute whatever small amount they can afford to their analyses, even though at that time—hard as it may now be to believe it—the NHS subsidized up to ten treatments per year! She thought that only patients whose unemployment was deemed to be a temporary condition should be taken on, because the inability to hold down a job was a very negative indicator of their capacity to sustain and complete the treatment satisfactorily.

As far as *intelligence* is concerned, it is certainly not so easy to define it. By intelligence, Nina does not mean intellectual brilliance, which could even turn out to be a powerful defensive bulwark. She seems to have in mind the quick thinkers, those individuals endowed with a keen and sharp verbal intelligence. Yet, the diagnostician should not be too categorical in his assessment, because people who take their time to mull things over, and appear to be slow, in the long run often make good patients. In conclusion, verbal intelligence and articulacy cannot be evaluated on their own. Intelligence, which perhaps should be qualified as "analytical intelligence" and associated with "psychological mindedness", is linked to the "will to be analysed" (Coltart, 1987, p. 3). In her exploration of this criterion, Coltart quotes Namnum, who, in a 1968 paper, put the *will to be analysed* in relation to the capacity to develop a *treatment alliance* whose function is to carry the treatment along in the phases when the emotional turbulence of the transference neurosis shows all its might. She agrees with Namnum that the *autonomous ego* is the carrier of the will to be analysed, while the "wish for recovery" is supported by the drives. Nina, however, departs from the American ego psychologist by interpreting the will to be analysed as, in Winnicott's term, a "going concern" for the analysand, just as the baby is for a good-enough mother. In this sense, Coltart truly is an independent thinker who draws on different psychoanalytical traditions and puts them together within a personal frame of reference.

Alongside intelligence and money, one has to consider other human aspects of the patient, such as "ethical development" and reliability, to a degree that should elicit the diagnostician's human sympathy and emotional participation.

I would like to point out how Coltart steers away from technical language—she could, in fact, talk about intact ego functions, or superego development—but prefers to talk, instead, about ethical qualities, human sympathy, tact: all attributes that ordinarily well-educated people can understand. Coltart comes across as a sophisticated and rigorous clinician who shows directness, honesty, and tact. (She would sometimes report, with her knowing tone, her concluding remarks to a patient, along such lines as: "You know, you are in a mess". Strong, unequivocal statements that patients would take seriously, with care, while—one could surmise—trying to recover from the surprise at the use of such strong, down to earth language.)

Indeed Nina loved languages and literature, and she could speak with the poetic simplicity which results from complexity and capacity to tap into the polysemy and evocative power of language, putting into practice the teachings of Winnicott.

Psychological mindedness is perhaps the single most important aspect of suitability for analysis, as it is predicated upon the patient's capacity to be surprised and curious about himself, to question the meaning and motives of his actions, feelings, fantasies. Needless to say, psychological mindedness is not a monolithic entity, but, rather, a spectrum of psychic functions which can be compromised to a certain degree by pathology, though not necessarily. And it is this openness to self-enquiry that can support the therapeutic project, notwithstanding the seriousness of the disturbance.

Diagnostics today

One could legitimately question how useful these concepts might still be and whether they are applicable to our contemporary view of diagnostics, which needs to address the lamentable condition we come across more and more often in the consulting room, when the individual has recourse to action and acting out, instead of self-reflection and self-enquiry. The malaise is intense, and these patients clamour for a form of help which can relieve their suffering and seem to demand that the analyst should venture forth in search of their mind in the interstitial spaces where it withdraws, imprisoned and fragmented, hidden from the subject himself. Personally, I believe that to give due attention and consideration to Coltart's thought on diagnostics, especially in its more systematic aspects aimed at providing us with a powerful tool for a psychodynamic exploration, can only enrich our modern perspective. Needless to say, we cannot abdicate our critical function. Yet, what is alive and extraordinarily modern in her vision is the consistent focus on the encounter with the patient as an opportunity for the analyst to learn something new, even in those cases that do not come to be referred.

To return to psychological mindedness, I would like to suggest that it might be useful to view this quality as an *inclination or passion for psychological reflection, coupled with the capacity to feel curiosity for the potential signification of one's own mental contents and functioning.*

Psychological mindedness, as such, requires further and detailed exploration of its constitutive aspects, maintains Coltart, which should form a sort of checklist for the consultant analyst to keep in mind:

1. Is there the capacity in the patient to take a distance from his own emotional experience? This must be nicely judged, as obviously it should not be such a distance that one senses there is a great chasm, as in very severe denial, splitting or repression.
2. If one listens beyond the full-stops in a narrative can the patient go on, and begin to reflect on himself, perhaps in a new way, *as a result of* being listened to in this particularly attentive way? If there are no signs of elaboration or extension by the patient on trains of thought, there may be severe inhibitions and/or anxieties, or extreme passive dependency, and a valuable capacity for free association may never develop.
3. Are various memories brought forward with different charges of affect? And are the affects, so far as one can tell, more or less appropriate? If not, a flat and uninflected history may bode ill

for analytical therapy and indicate severe affective splitting and blunting. In other words, a lot of memories with no feelings are suspect.
4. Is there a capacity to perceive relationships between sections of history, and between details that are recounted, and the patient's prevailing sense of discomfort? If the patient starts by complaining of one or more symptoms or states of mind, but shows no sense of related significance when he goes into his history, then again there should be a warning signal in the assessor's mind.
5. Is there some capacity to recognise and tolerate internal reality, with its wishes and conflicts, and to distinguish it from external reality? You will see that this connects up directly with the continuing judgement in the interviewer's mind about the possibilities of maintaining a therapeutic alliance in conjunction with a transference neurosis. Does the patient show some facility in interview to move between the two, that is internal and external reality, in a way which shows a certain cathexis for the value, and the enjoyment, of interpretation and the taking of psychic responsibility for the self?
6. Does the patient show a lively curiosity and genuine concern about this internal reality, if he has already shown that he got a good glimpse of it? This is a crucial point. Psychoanalytical therapy has nothing to offer a patient who only wishes to be relieved of his suffering. If he can make even a tenuous link with the idea of relief from psychic pain, with an increase in self-knowledge, and if he then shows some real pleasure in finding out some tiny thing about himself in the initial interview, this is one of the best criteria for the analytical approach. This kind of drive and interest about the sources of pain in oneself is the greatest possible help in therapy, and is a sustaining tributary to the therapeutic alliance. It can help to counteract even very severe, including acting out, pathology.
7. Is there some capacity for the use of imagination? Fantasies may be presented in a diagnostic interview, but even small signs, such as a striking use of metaphor, or the voluntary report of a dream, are positive indicators.
8. Are there signs of a capacity to recognise the existence of an unconscious mental life? Is there some acknowledgement that in some ways the patient is in a state of involuntary self-deception? Are there some signs of a willingness to undo this state of affairs?

9. Does the patient show signs of success or achievement in some, even if limited areas of his life and some degree of proper self-esteem in relation to this? It is an important truism that he who fails at everything will fail at analysis. Here I would emphasise the areas of study or work and one or more important relationship. [1987, pp. 4–6]

The reason for reporting this lengthy passage in its entirety is essentially to convey the accuracy of Coltart's vision. It moves dialectically from an overall perspective to a search for the smallest signs of awareness the patient might evince of his internal world.

The subject emerging from these markers, at first sight, could appear to be a healthy neurotic. Such a person would surely make a good candidate for a control analysis. Yet, a closer reading discloses a minimalist's approach to the psychodynamics of consultation, in the sense that the focus is on the microscopic transformations that occur in and through the interview. It is the encounter with the analyst and his capacity to access the world of psychic phenomena, to transform them by thinking about the patient in a new way, that represents the mutative event in the patient's life; as such, it can mobilize curiosity and the capacity to link past and present, internal and external life. Obviously, the consultant needs to look for any glimmers of this capacity to use and respond to the experience of being thought about. This implies that, for Coltart, *taking psychic responsibility for the self* does not mean the same thing as saying that the patient has reached the depressive position and is consciously intending to make reparation to his damaged internal world. Rather, it seems to indicate that he can recognize a nuclear experiencing self at the core of his inner reality that needs attending to.

Concluding remarks

To set into a broader and appropriate historical context Coltart's formulation on diagnosis, it may be worth mentioning briefly that, after Freud, Glover (who enquired into character disorder), Zetzel (who attempted to differentiate along a wide spectrum the multifaceted presentations of hysteria), Knapp, and Limentani had further developed this topic from the 1950s through to the 1970s.

Often, the research had been spurred by pragmatic aims, such as to arrive at nosographic and diagnostic psychoanalytic categories as an aid to establish criteria for analysability, thus guaranteeing, as much as possible, that treatment would prove to be feasible and be carried out to a satisfactory conclusion.

The British Society, unlike other training institutions in Europe and in the USA, guided the candidates through the selection of control cases through the London Clinic, whose effort, naturally, was to minimize the incidence of drop-outs, with the negative effects on the candidates' morale. Losing a patient, even after many months, set candidates back in their training, and this had repercussions on their supervision and training analysis, and even on the institution as a whole.

In the USA, by contrast, the psychoanalytic establishment was under pressure to prove the scientific value and therapeutic effectiveness of the talking cure. This state of affairs stimulated research such as, for instance, the longitudinal study carried out by Knapp, Levin, McCarter, Wermer, and Zetzel, "Suitability for psychoanalysis: a review of one hundred supervised analytic cases" (1960). This essay listed "psychosomatic states, delinquents, psychotic signs or behaviour trends, adverse life situations, schizoid borderline psychotics, too long periods of previous treatment, very high levels of anxiety and tension, and some patients older than the analyst" (quoted in Coltart, 1987, p. 7) as conditions that could render analysis very difficult, if not impossible.

At the same time in Britain, the psychoanalytic developments initiated especially by the group of Independent analysts coalesced from the 1970s onwards into formulations freer from excessively rigid schematizations that, while still abiding by the necessity to establish criteria for analysability, moved the focus more and more on countertransference and the person of the analyst. To a certain extent, these developments had been ushered in by Winnicott, whose specific contribution on classification (1959) had advocated the usefulness of a psychoanalytic approach to the field. Winnicott's influence, however, was far greater, in that his emphasis on both the pathogenic and reparative factors contained in the environment, as well as his perspective on psychosis and delinquency as developmental deficit disorders, not only made these disturbances thinkable within the parameters of the psychoanalytic cure, but also cast a new light on the function of the setting, the mind, and the personality of the analyst. Tending in this direction is Limentani's theorization (1972), when he invites the analyst to move freely across different areas of his own psyche in the consultation with the patient, who would, thus, have the chance to access and experience the internal mobility and use of self which represents the foundation and the hallmark of the analytic adventure.

Coltart goes back to, and takes further, Limentani's critique of the diagnostician as a rigid and silent analyst who seems to adhere to a scholastically and fideistically idealized behavioural model of the practitioner who, in the name of neutrality, ends up having an inaccurate and skewed picture of the phenomena that he should be able to observe. This is the professional whom Coltart defines as a "caricature of the analyst", who offers no help to the patient in the course of the interview, does not utter a word, does not intervene or give back what he has been able to understand of the subject's psychic functioning, and yet, at the end of the consultation, refers him to a colleague whom one can legitimately imagine to be a carbon copy of the model of the silent consultant.

With the courage and directness that gained her the appellation of "maverick", Coltart states that the analyst who puts on a coat of opaqueness and mystery, who remains impassively seated in silence, succeeds only in giving the patient a demonstration of his narcissism and even a taste of his sadism, while, on the contrary, he should work hard. Such a form of reticence would be justified when treatment begins or is under way, whereas in the assessment interview the analyst needs to be able freely to make use of his personal capacity to relate, should have access to various aspects of his personality, with sureness, interest, and solicitude towards the patient, for whom the encounter is a memorable and emotionally highly charged event.

The analyst should be able to understand the significance of this encounter for the suffering person and how intense might be his anxiety, which should be contained and relieved. Moreover, the practitioner should make his own mind available for the patient to use, so as to try to have a view of the internal world of the stranger who is sitting in front of him and to whom the analyst needs to give back a concise representation of what he has comprehended of the patient's pain as well as of his functioning.

Coltart closes her paper with a statement formally clothed in simplicity, though it carries the intensity and passion of a conviction which might come over as irreverent, or even transgressive, when set against a form of knowledge imprisoned by rigidity and schematization:

> It should always be remembered that if you are prescribing psychotherapy on a long term basis you are making a powerful statement, and your respect for the patient should entail that you give him your own insight into his needs and character, and your own reason for making the prescription. [1987, p. 8]

The fate of diagnosis; diagnosis as fate

Coltart's paper on diagnosis and assessment was written over twenty years ago. It responded to theoretical and clinical needs very much alive and felt at that time, and, thus, a contemporary reading is bound to highlight its historical value and significance. At the same time, *we moderns* cannot be exempted from expressing our gratitude, perhaps in the form of annotations in the margins. I will attempt to put forward some minimalist notes on the usefulness and modernity of her view, by drawing on contributions from authors as diverse as Umberto Eco and Christopher Bollas, who both focus on destiny.

In an unpublished paper, Eco (2009) analyses the logical and ontological status of fictional characters such as Anna Karenina or Madame Bovary, characters he defines as "fluctuating semiotic objects". They are located in an intermediate state of play-like reality, where their existence is anchored to essential "diagnostic features". One such feature is that Anna Karenina throws herself under a train, and this cannot be changed into something else: an escape to Siberia, for instance. As the fixity of such essential diagnostic traits is not amenable to historical or theoretical revision, the literary character—maintains Eco—belongs to the domain of myth, and, therefore, it keeps us closely connected to the very human sense of Fate.

Bollas (1989) also familiarized us with the individual's sense of being fated, of having his freedom of choice curtailed by the internal constriction of that which he has not thought about or understood and which prevents his talents and constitutional endowment from coming to fruition.

Could we then imagine Coltart's philosophy of consultation to be a tool by which to gain access to the essential "diagnostic features" (Eco, 2009) of the fixed repetitive internal scenarios of the patient, so as to begin to transform these structures through the encounter with the analyst and in the service of the greater mobility and freedom of the patient's internal world?

Nina might be intrigued by this interpretation and the link between psychoanalysis and literature I have proposed: I can just see her knowing smile.

References

Bollas, C. (1989). *Forces of Destiny: Psychoanalysis and Human Idiom.* London: Free Association Books.

Coltart, N. (1987). Diagnosis and assessment of suitability for psychoanalytic treatment. *British Journal of Psychotherapy*, 4: 127–134.

Eco, U. (2009). Why it is not true that Anna Karenina lived in Baker St. Unpublished paper given at the Milenesiana Festival of Literature, Music, Cinema and Science.

Flegenheimer, F. A. (1989). Languages and psychoanalysis: the polyglot patient and the polyglot analyst. *International Review of Psychoanalysis*, 16: 377–382.

Knapp, P. H., Levin, S., McCarter, R. H., Wermer, H., & Zetzel, E. (1960). Suitability for psychoanalysis: a review of one hundred supervised analytic cases. *Psychoanalytic Quarterly*, 29: 459–477.

Limentani, A. (1972). The assessment of analysability: A major hazard in selection for psychoanalysis. *International Journal of Psychoanalysis*, 53, 357–361.

Namnum, A. (1968). The problem of analyzability and the autonomous ego. *International Journal of Psychoanalysis*, 49: 271–275.

Rossi Monti, M. (2008). Diagnosi: una brutta parola? *Rivista di psicoanalisi*, 3: 795–803.

Winnicott, D. W. (1959). Classification: is there a psycho-analytic contribution to psychiatric classification? In: *The Maturational Processes and the Facilitating Environment* (pp. 124–139). London: Karnac, 1984.

CHAPTER NINE

My Nina

Maggie Schaedel

My Nina belongs to no one else! I am, of course, paraphrasing the words of one of Winnicott's patients when I emphasize that the Nina I knew and remember, and about whom I am about to write a brief personal memoir, may be also recognizable to others who contribute to this volume, all of whom will have their own unique and personal Nina Coltart.

I was assessed and referred by Nina for my training analysis over a quarter of a century ago. Seventeen years later, I found myself in a crowd at the 100-day memorial ceremony at the Amaravati Buddhist monastery where I met, for the first time, her family: her sister Gill with children and grandchildren with all the resemblances, and the extended tribe of colleagues, supervisees, and ex-patients. Some of us have corresponded since and met at various memorial events, including a series of lectures now held in her name at the Institute of Psychoanalysis. I recall the first such memorial lecture, which I chaired in March 1998, organized by Arbours Association and held at the Amadeus Centre in West London. The subject: "Psychoanalysis and religion"; the two speakers: David Black and Joseph Berke; and the discussion was of matters close to Nina's heart. At the time, her death was still a raw pain for many of us, and while the ideas were important and interesting I felt the event was empty, desolate, and lacking a sense of Nina's (absent) presence.

Many times I had seen Nina address a new audience with her characteristic, very English, no-nonsense manner, in which there was discreetly couched a sometimes unnerving, straight-talking, yet alchemical spirit. She was a popular teacher. I had seen her address lecture theatres of mainly training psychotherapists with basic advice on such things as "how to furnish a consulting room" (including such details as a plastic bin "in case of vomit"). She spoke of the essential ingredients in the making of a psychotherapist (including "Ingredient X"). She had talked about the necessary foundations (grounding in theory, personal analysis) as "lavishing attention to details which one can later forget". In 1998, I had forgotten details, and felt the emptiness which her death had opened up.

I missed her encouragement, her humour, her wisdom, and her original thinking. I missed her sense of fun. I remembered how she would not balk at opportunities to encourage her audience, her readers, or supervisees and colleagues to survive and learn through bleak states of confusion, struggle, and the blank, wordless emptiness that sometimes governs the experience of the unbearable, the experiences which lie "beyond words". (Once, when planning a conference where she was to provide "goldfish bowl" supervision *in vivo*, she wrote to me, "it would be handy if there was a cock up ...".) She was not too afraid to talk about times when she would not always know what she was doing, and I had longed to reach that kind of maturity in which not-knowing was a prelude to learning something new. But I remember the 1998 memorial lecture, with its vast audience, as a cold event, and one which lacked playfulness and spirit. Maybe it was too soon after she died for the sort of creativity we had associated with her. In re-reading her letters to me, I have reflected on those qualities which made her life, her work, her retirement, and her loss quite remarkable.

My relationship with Nina spanned twenty-five years as her role in my work-world broadened and included supervision of clinical work and encouragement for my clinical and academic teaching. Against her advice, I moved away from London. She had fears for the professional isolation I might find: "It's a desert", she warned. But I was committed in this direction, and Nina then agreed to help me if she could. She referred patients, offered supervisory consultations when I could get back to London, and was always prepared to think with me about the issues involved in teaching psychoanalysis and psychotherapy within a university. Nina came down to Kent several times to help and to teach herself. She shared in the struggles of the times, many of which revolved around the challenges of introducing psychoanalytic thinking to professional arenas in which either a medical or a humanistic model prevailed.

Nina first read her paper, "Blood, shit, and tears", to an audience in the University of Kent in 1983, and since then she has spoken to Anthony Molino of the ironic nature of her title (a parody of Churchill's "Blood, sweat, and tears"). Maybe this was too close to the heart of rural Kent. While clinicians and some academics were receptive, others on the periphery found the ideas quite difficult and the tensions bubbled into an administrative dispute.

Nina loathed the politics and bureaucratic dimensions of institutional life, while she was also quite interested to listen from a distance. But on this occasion in October 1993, she fell afoul of the university's fragile bureaucratic structures and, in particular, crossed an about-to-be-retired administrator who had reached an obsessional frenzy. Two issues perplexed this woman: she refused to type the word "shit" in memos and brochures advertising Nina's lecture "Blood, shit, and tears". Also, in order to process the paying of Nina's fee, she insisted on "evidence" that Nina was as old as she said she was! In addition, a senior lecturer had wondered aloud whether the title might "offend".

Nina fell upon this issue with derision and sharp sarcasm. She wrote to me that she was "horrified that the secretaries can't even say the title of BST! It's like 'the girl who was so pure, / She could not say the word manure . . .'. And as for the psychology lecturer who finds it so offensive—put me on to him/her—do!"

Nina was having fun, helping me transcend the embarrassment with an enthusiasm to take on the forces of bureaucratic darkness. This is very much how I remember her support. She was possessed of a fierce protectiveness, courage, forthrightness, and, of course, had a wonderful humour. We ended up laughing on so many of those occasions in which I had arrived strung out with yet another professional knot. She refused to allow me to be so rattled by the minor narcissistic differences of the psychoanalytic community and would respond—often immediately—with an unsentimental, wise, and sometimes witty suggested riposte. At other times, she would recognize the deep significance to me of such splits and exclusions.

When I first met her in 1980, Nina told me after three consultations that she would wait until the identity of the right analyst for me would "swim up" into her consciousness. She said that it might take another three weeks. I settled into the next few years of analysis, as had so many of my peers, with an uneasy sense of having already met the one I really wanted, which was Nina, and, of course, Nina recognized this phenomenon, writing later of how we all possess internally an ideal therapist, one in whose reality we might long to believe.

When I heard Nina present her paper, "Slouching towards Bethlehem . . . or Thinking the unthinkable in psychoanalysis", I felt that I had recognized in her grasp of the *something* that is "in all of us . . . which will never be in our reach . . . a mystery at the heart of every person . . ." an intuition that held much meaning, and I pursued the possibilities of seeing her as a supervisor/consultant. I had moved away from London, and had developed a clinical practice and an academic/clinical post in psychoanalysis and psychotherapy. I felt I could trust in her attention to my work, and this conviction survived through the remaining years of her life. Wherever I was working, in whatever capacity, a consultation with Nina was reliably useful. She had the capacity to "recognize" me and my work, sometimes without the necessity (or burden) even of remembering. Once, having forgotten, but diarised, an arrangement we had made, she wrote, "Actually, I don't even *try* to remember anything I can write down". Once this was so disconcerting to me, but now makes complete sense.

Nina has written on attention, and, in her interview with Anthony Molino, she speaks of a particular sort of attention: a bare attention, a thoughtless state of mind which can exist alongside, or become integrated at some points within, a psychoanalytic attitude and frame of reference. This was what I felt I could rely on.

She became the one in whom I had lodged the multiply invested narrative of a professional journey, and she was also a travelling companion who I felt might help me think and explore "the mystery of things". I associated this with a kind of mutually shared recognition of the sort where the experience of self and other has catastrophic loss at the core. I felt that she and I belonged in a shared world.

After I began to work in Kent, I got to know Nina as one who came and went on trains. This often involved my waiting at stations in Kent, sometimes at the exact location of her early childhood home. Meeting her off an arriving train usually felt optimistic—a warm reunion. But leavings and partings on station platforms were marked for me as empty times, and she never wanted me to wait with her. Once, I felt I really could not leave her before the train arrived. By then she had begun to limp; she seemed vulnerable and alone. This was the last place we met.

Shortly after this, Nina agreed to the recording and publication of a conversation with Anthony Molino, in which details emerged of her own catastrophic loss of both her parents in a train crash. I reflected that it was after my own experience of station panic that she had decided also to tell me. I felt this information to be a much needed piece of reality; it made some sense of my anxiety and the particular way we had managed to recognize something of each other in our working worlds.

I have since discovered also that while our consultations and informal meetings had felt so significant and unique, I was, in truth, one of many "siblings", or distant cousins, who, having met and shared memories, have became part of a surviving tribe, some of whom may be contributors to this volume. It comes as no surprise to read an interview or to speak to a colleague and discover that we share some significantly similar intimate memories of time spent with Nina. At one memorial lecture at the Institute of Psychoanalysis, someone spoke publicly of the impact of discovering that Nina seemed to know him quite deeply after only a brief time. If I remember correctly, he recalled how she replied, "I am an expert at intimacy"!

The experience of developing a profound connection with one whose capacity for such intimacy is shared by many has become the familiar framework of the psychoanalytic method in which transferences to the analyst take shape as relational phenomena that are felt to be authentic, real, and current, while being rooted also in past events. And so, I cannot really know now quite how completely shared was my feeling that Nina wanted me to continue to need her, to seek out her opinion, to update her with my latest personal and family news, tales of politics and adventures in institutions and groups. She used to greet me enthusiastically: "Oh do tell!". And so I did, through many years of university or NHS work and struggle. She was such an ally in those days when psychoanalytic thinking was rather London-centred. She was intrepid and forthright, and I drew strength from her commitment at times when professional betrayals could leave me shattered.

This was the background world in which I knew Nina Coltart, a world of which she eventually grew tired and longed to relinquish. She decided to retire, and talked to me about her decision to leave psychoanalysis behind. She said she could bear the idea of her own death and lost no time in urging me to get on working and living without her, as she knew she could now live without it (psychoanalysis). I wrote back, "How do you know when you don't have to keep on?" I wanted to know how she knew when it was possible to stop.

By return of post, Nina replied, "I think if you lose an analyst after you have officially left him/her then it is not counted as true loss. . . . I expect most of us to grow beyond needs (real ones) for analysts or therapists. Of course there are a number of people who never do or become recidivists for the analytic nipple . . ."

As I reread these letters, I am reminded of one who was neither afraid of her own death, nor of emptiness or aloneness, one who also had loved to link and bridge and play. She was preparing me for the ending of a relationship. I knew how much Nina had achieved in terms of respect and love within the psychoanalytic community, but she was preparing herself also for leaving this and for a time when she might exist in the world in ways which had thus far eluded her. I sensed her irritation at those who might not wish to let her go: "Loss of the analyst is not real loss".

Nina's penultimate letter to me read, in part,

> I retired because my life-long vocational love of psychotherapy was burning out, and I wasn't as intuitive, sharp, or interested as I used to be, and have lots of other things I want to do plenty of before I grow too old, stiff or demented. It is a lovely liberated feeling to be gone—and to have resigned from the Analytic Society, which I'm

sorry to say was greeted with shock, amazement, protest and incredulity that I could Live Without Them and It, from many quarters! Some of the wiser, maturer ones saw the point completely . . . .

I took note of what I felt to be a caution to not pursue her—"the wiser ones saw the point completely". I also thought that she may have been positioning me to accept her eventual death, which was also prefigured in the final chapter of her last book—". . . as I come to the close of my writing life . . ."—and the message to those who had "stayed with me to the end" was that she had enjoyed her work.

In 1996, one of my children had become ill, and it was characteristic for Nina to want to know details, particularly of medical concerns. I often thought that Doctor Nina Coltart was enquiring on such occasions, and I did also value her medical knowledge. On that occasion, Nina said, "When it is your own child who suffers, you want to feel the pain on her behalf, so unbearable is the helplessness." I have wondered about this comment, particularly in light of her childlessness. She was profoundly empathic, she longed to free herself of a world that she said had "staled on her", and I also imagine that she may have been attempting to free us also (those who loved and valued her and those who might have clung possessively) from the possibility of a too-traumatic rupture. So many individuals, groups, and institutions seemed to want to claim her as theirs—mine included! She was wanting to free herself as she might also have been wanting to prepare and protect her extended analytic "family" from the experience of catastrophic loss. Her retirement contained such responsibility. As I am about to enter my sixth decade, and important colleagues are lost from within our community, there are days when I think about the psychoanalyst's particular responsibility in retiring, and I wish she were still here to think with us again and to write about that now.

The last written communication from Nina was late in 1996. It had been my sad task to let her know about the death of a mutual friend and colleague. He was young and his death sudden and shocking. In hearing from her again, I suppose my concerns might also have been unyieldingly self-centred, and I regaled her with my take on the latest fragmentations within the psychoanalytic organizations with which she had been previously connected. In relation to the pains of organizational politics, Nina wrote to me, "I think it's something to do with what Neville Symington has said that having an analysis leaves one *less* ego-structured and more narcissistic, with which I profoundly agree and think we all need to work on . . .". I, too, agree with this.

In relation to the death of our friend, she wrote simply, "Whom the gods love, die young". A few months later Nina also died, aged sixty-nine.

This brief personal account of my connection to Nina illustrates the integrity, the seriousness, and the concern of a psychoanalyst whose words and work were an inspiration to me. She was warm and friendly, and with a verve and a wit possessed of the sharpest candour. She was not too afraid of doubts and uncertainties, which became the precursors to her own thinking and writing. She was brave in her sometimes controversial commitments, and she enjoyed her work in which playfulness and fun formed an intrinsic part.

CHAPTER TEN

An "internal supervisor"

Elizabeth Wilde McCormick

Nina was my clinical supervisor for my private psychotherapy practice from 1989 until 1994. I owe her much. She lives on as an "internal supervisor", and I often hear her voice saying things such as, "Are you really sure about that my dear?", or "What an extraordinary story!" I also draw on her as a strong role model, for a lot of my therapeutic work today is supervision of experienced practitioners from different orientations.

I wrote to her initially to ask if she would take me on because I had heard of her work and I wanted to understand something of the Freudian approach to psychotherapy, which had been missing from my training. My background was in social psychiatry, humanistic and transpersonal psychology, and cognitive analytic therapy. At our first meeting, she asked me to explain what it was I wanted from her. I must have done this adequately, because she beamed and her eyes sparkled as she said, "Yes, dear, no one really understands sex and power as well as Freud!"

She taught me to be a lot more robust and challenging in my interventions, always from the basis of a compassionate heart and when the timing was right. She was very good at assessing timing of interventions after a period of endurance, a skill she writes about in *Slouching towards Bethlehem* and *The Baby and the Bathwater*.

We shared many things during the five years. She became interested in the work of Dr Anthony Ryle and cognitive analytic therapy; we explored the interface between clinical practice and spiritual discipline; we discussed energy exchange between therapist and patient, and about the shifting into fifth gear.

There is one story that stands out in all the work we did. This involved a young woman who was unable to speak of her emotional life but communicated with me through stick drawings. As I became more interested in the drawings, they increased in number and in their content, and I took them to supervision. This was unusual for Nina, because her work was mainly with practitioners who used the analytic couch, and she was intrigued to see how the process of using drawings as transitional objects and a mode of expression would work. When this patient contracted cancer, we both felt a very deep sadness and Nina feared that she would not survive it, given her psychopathology. But the drawings started to tell us a different story; they heralded something both heroic and deeply spiritual in nature with this young woman. So we marvelled at the process and shared the understanding that we never know where someone might take us, and should always be open to surprises. This young woman did indeed live on for another fifteen years. In these years, she learnt to love and accept herself and was reunited with her estranged family.

Nina was particularly helpful to me when I became ill with meningitis and in the months following this when I was unable to work. I continued in supervision, often only by telephone, and I learned the great value of flexibility and belief in the other person that a good supervisor can offer. She also encouraged me to bring my own material into supervision when this had an impact on the work with patients, and we discussed my own dreams and my journal-keeping, which I have found to be an essential tool as a writer. I also talked to her about the books I was writing and my plans for them.

It is since her death that my interest in Buddhism has flourished. I do not know whether Nina's own practice influenced me subtly as we sat together for all those sessions, but I wish that I had had my own practice then, as there are so many questions I would like to ask her!

Just last Christmas, and thanks to the kindness of Nina's sister, Gill Preston, I visited Polstangey, their home on the Lizard Peninsula in Cornwall, and sat on the slate bench with the beautiful name carving and discovered that Nina also had my name, Elizabeth. I knew, for she had told me, that Cornwall was always a haven for her and her sister, particularly after their parents both died in a train crash during the war. So I sat for some time, thinking about Nina and the girl she had been on those lawns, walking the Cornish lanes, listening to the crash of the ocean on the granite rocks, and I celebrated her and all that she had given to me and continues to give.

> May all beings be well
> May all beings be happy
> May all beings feel at ease

CHAPTER ELEVEN

Baby Peter*

Mary Leatt

Sunday 3rd Aug. 1997

Dear Gill and David,

I am writing to you to let you know how sad my family was to hear that Nina Coltart had died.

My husband read a reference to her obituary in the *Guardian* yesterday. We tracked down the issue of 28th July and there it was in black and white . . .

We first met her when she needed a baby to study on a weekly basis for a year, while studying psychoanalysis. A nursery mother asked me if I would allow her to come and see Peter, our son, born 1961. I did not realise that there was to be more than one visit and was a bit taken aback when told this. We then lived near Gospel Oak Station, Parliament Hill Fields.

Our domestic circumstances were a little fraught. We had a mortgage on a narrow Victorian house, the top floors let on a

---

*A letter of condolence to Gillian and David Preston, written upon learning of the death of Nina Coltart.

controlled rent. My husband's first wife had died of diabetes shortly after the war while he was in Egypt before being demobbed. On return, he had a baby son, 16 months!

His father died, so his mother had brought up his son [Michael], now aged 11 years. We thought she should come and live with us, as she could not really afford to run her home on a widow's pension. When Nina first came to visit us, Peter was a few months old, [our daughter] Pam about four years and suffering a huge "baby" reaction, and John crossing London on an uncomfortable bus journey, teaching in a school he did not like—keeping us all . . .

When I first saw Nina I was greatly relieved. She seemed so charming and friendly, not a bit like a doctor. In those days, I was rather in awe of doctors. She seemed much younger than me. I only realized recently that there was barely three years' difference in our ages.

Nina used to come at about 5.00 or 5.30 in the afternoon. Michael would be coming in from school, John coming in harassed from school and expecting tea straightaway, Pam showing off like mad because Nina was coming to see Peter, not her, and Peter sitting in his highchair eating whatever came his way—all in the kitchen!

After about a year of this, Nina was just like one of the family—everybody loved her.

She visited us long after she need have done. She joined us on our walks to the nearby children's playground, bought the children ices and was even visiting us when our youngest child, Jeffrey, was born in 1963. She bought Pam and Peter two fabulous Norwegian sweaters that they passed down and kept for years!

We left London in 1966. From that time Nina and I corresponded on an annual basis, both relating family news and trying to condense a year's experience into a letter.

She was always particularly interested in Peter. Although never achieving much academic success in school, he achieved a 2 grade in Sports Science at Liverpool Polytechnic, then managed to get sponsorship from the Canadian Sports Council to get an MSc. working on a team that was investigating whether glucose taken before a match improved the performance of individuals playing football. When he returned home he surprised us all by saying he wanted to study medicine and was able to get a mature student's entry to Leicester University.

Nina seemed really pleased that he had taken this course. She gave him £500 towards his course which helped enormously. He had to write to many organisations for gifts and loans to help him through. Luckily, Kent funded his last year. Of course, I helped him so he did not have too many debts to pay off!

He has now started a job in charge of Sports Medicine at his old college, now a University, where, he said, sports has taken off in a big way. He will have to help setting up experiments with 60–70 students under his instruction. It's only a .5 job. He will do Locum work as well.

Peter and his girlfriend, Karol, a midwife, are both mad on climbing, like [your son] Jonathan whom they could even meet one day.

We have lived in Broadstairs for thirty-three years. Throughout that time, Nina's friendship has meant a great deal to me, especially her continuing interest in our family, particularly Peter, "my baby", as she called him in her last letter.

She also wrote of all your family and their children and Naomi Tara ("the first grand-daughter hurrah!").

I was always amazed and really grateful that when Nina became so important, influential and active in so many ways, writing books of her experiences giving lecture tours in America and still helping patients through analysis, that she could still keep in touch with me through our annual letter.

Her death must be a tremendous loss to you and your family. Also to the many other friends made through her life of compassionate caring for all those people with problems whom she helped.

I was particularly impressed by her becoming involved in her local school, especially on her accompanying a swimming group. She will be missed by so many people.

She mentioned to me, in her last letter, that she had a perforated ulcer. I presume this is what, ultimately, caused her death.

I thought she would have had many more active years. As well as being saddened, I was very shocked to read about her.

If there is to be a financial contribution to any organisation in her memory, I would be glad to contribute on behalf of our family.

It's hard for me to believe that her life and work have ended. But it must be so much more difficult for you, your family and her close friend Vicky [Plumb], whom she mentioned continually in her letters.

I do extend to you my very great sympathy in this loss. I will never forget Nina. I loved the photograph in the *Guardian*.

Sincerely,

Mary Leatt

(C) FRIENDS

CHAPTER TWELVE

Homage to a valued friend*

A. H. Brafman

The death of our dear Nina Coltart took me by surprise. I was aware that she was facing serious health problems, but somehow I did not expect she would die. I have found that many others were equally shocked and pained. I heard of different emotions, but above all, most people felt immense sadness at the loss of such a valued person.

I am pleased that our Society has decided to pay this tribute to Nina tonight. She well deserved this. Personally, I welcome this opportunity to describe my picture of her and recount some of the experiences we shared. Nina was an exceptional person and I was fortunate to count her as a friend and colleague. She always seemed full of life, facing people and tasks with endless concentration and seriousness. Her smile was irresistible and her laughter was warm and ample, almost childish in its spontaneity and innocence. The

---

*Originally presented at a Scientific Meeting of the British Psychoanalytical Society, 15 October, 1997, and published in November of that year under the title, "Nina Coltart (1927–1997): An Obituary", in *The British Psychoanalytical Society Bulletin*, 33(10), 15–17.

predominant impression was of a person determined to deal with the task in hand: friendly and encouraging, but not one who indulged in wasting time or effort. She could not suffer fools and she expected people to be honest and respectful as a matter of course. Privacy was as much a right as it was a duty. Discussions involved issues, never the private life or motives of the person concerned.

I first met Nina when we started our psychoanalytic training. We were a large group and not a particularly homogeneous one. Some colleagues seemed to have memorized all of Freud's writings and many spoke as if fully conversant with the principles of the analytic group they had just joined. They behaved as if they were not so much students as soldiers fighting for their side. Nina was eager to learn from every lecturer; she was interested in the new subject, rather than in group dogmas. On the whole, Nina did not volunteer comments during lectures or seminars, but when a lecturer went round asking a question, it became clear that she had done her homework on the reading lists and she was one of the few who always knew the answers. When we had seminars on baby observation with the cherished Mrs Bick, Nina's reports were outstanding and the whole group always savoured the life and movement of the mother–baby interaction she described (it is a tribute to her warmth and devotion that mother and "baby" remained in touch with her ever since). When we started clinical work, again we found that Nina's accounts of sessions not only conveyed her sensitivity and empathy, but also they were written up with a richness, depth, and sense of humour that eluded most of us.

After we qualified, Nina and I had the idea of organizing meetings where we might discuss our experiences, and we started our "Group 64", the year in which our lectures and seminars came to an end. I remember visiting Nina's house in Well Road for the first group meeting; it was virtually impossible to see the wall lining, since bookshelves and pictures covered all spaces. She showed us the first floor, where she had her consulting room and waiting room, both furnished rather sparsely but warmly and tastefully. We then proceeded to the second floor, where we sat in her lounge. Coffee and cakes were part of a welcoming atmosphere that helped us in our search for support and enlightenment. We had members of all three groups of the Society, but we managed to create a climate of friendship that enriched us all.

Nina's private practice flourished and she joined the small elite of analysts who seemed to receive endless referrals from all sources. She soon became the Patron Saint of most beginners in private practice. I have heard from many analysts and therapists of their gratitude to Nina for sending them patients at the time when they most needed them. In her consulting room, Nina did not see patients at dawn (as she put it), since she enjoyed going through her post and the papers early in the morning, but, once started, she would work through a punitive schedule, ten or more hours without any breaks, after which she had evening lectures or various meetings to deal with. Food never seemed to play much of a role in her life, and I suspect that "meal-times" was a notion that existed only as part of her social life.

Nina obtained full membership of The British Psychoanalytical Society in 1969, and in 1972 she became a training analyst of the Independent group. In 1972, she was appointed Director of the London Clinic of Psychoanalysis. The Clinic meetings were an enjoyable and exciting experience, due to the atmosphere of camaraderie that Nina managed to create. She had a commanding presence, encouraging the discussion of cases, as if never holding views on the patient under discussion, and invariably leading the group to a decision that seemed to satisfy all participants. Nina clearly had the ability to make referrers trust that she would do her best for their patients at the Clinic and we had no shortage of cases in those years. We had the inevitable complaints from supervisors of analytic candidates who felt that we had accepted patients who were not really suitable, but Nina seemed to know how to satisfy them. I believe it was Nina who first had the idea of inviting students in training to attend the Clinic meetings, and they greatly valued this experience. Years later, in the 1980s, Nina convened a group to conduct a research project on cases referred to the Clinic; our planning discussions went quite far but the formal application was turned down.

Along with the Clinic work, Nina was very involved with the life of the Society. Not counting committees where she had ex-officio participation, Nina was a member of the Education, Membership, Clinic Liaison, Admissions, Executive, Rules and Procedures, Benevolent Fund, Student Progress, and Archive committees, as well as being Vice-President of the Society and Chair of Board and

Council between 1984 and 1987. She was also a member of the Liaison committee in the discussions with UCH/Middlesex hospitals, and chairman of the Working Party on the Scientific Life of the Society, in 1987. And then we all know how active she was in the teaching programme of the Society, giving theoretical lectures and clinical seminars, besides training a good number of analysts and being one of the most sought-after supervisors.

Nina's command of language and the lucidity of her thoughts owed a great deal to her pre-medical life: she went to Somerville College, Oxford, where she qualified in English and Spanish Literature. Only the other Saturday, at the Memorial in her honour, we heard of her reading Cervantes' *Don Quixote* in the original! And books remained a first love for her. Nina would never boast of her knowledge, but whenever some author was mentioned she was found to know his work quite intimately. The same approach was applied to psychoanalysis, and even though Nina was not one to quote authors in every sentence, she had a thorough knowledge of the literature.

Nina had a small group of close friends who played an important role in her life. Agi Bene was one of these; she had been a member of our class, and Nina visited her often after Agi moved to Israel. When Agi died, still young, Nina was very shaken. She often visited New Zealand to meet a colleague and friend of whom she was extremely fond. I also knew of a school friend of Nina's who lived in the West Country and seemed to be the person closest to her; when she developed lung cancer, Nina was quite devastated, and her death was a major blow. When Nina mentioned one of her friends, I was struck by the depth of feelings she seemed to attach to that kind of relationship; she definitely did not use the word loosely.

Talking to Nina was always a pleasure, since her intelligence, sensitivity, and wide knowledge meant that a wide range of topics would be covered. Her visits to my house marked lively and happy occasions. Nina took a great interest in my children, who admired and loved her. She would discuss literature and Buddhism with one and music and ethics with another. On another level, smoking was a recurring subject, since cigarettes and wine constituted pleasures that Nina did not succeed in either eliminating or adopting permanently. Nina had a large number of people that she looked after. I knew of cases where this involved financial support, but this was only a detail. Nina had the rare gift of knowing precisely what help each person needed and she would then send a letter or have a meeting that kept quite a few people leading their lives on the basis of this "topping-up" that they could obtain from her.

Nina's interest in Buddhism at first puzzled our group. She had told us of her interest in bio-feedback and we thought that here was another example of Nina's intellectual curiosity. Some of us still saw religion as a matter for analysis, and it took us some time to understand Nina's feelings about this. She clearly operated on a level of thinking and feeling that eluded most of us. But it was typical of Nina that she was prepared to discuss these problems and that, as ever, she commanded immense respect.

The world of psychotherapy had great support from Nina. She gave lectures and seminars to many groups and institutions here and abroad. A group of therapists in Sweden had the privilege of Nina's regular visits for quite a long period. Her knowledge, her capacity to gauge the needs and capacities of individuals and groups, her sense of humour, her ability to make the precise comment that proves helpful, all combined to create admiration and gratitude.

Nina's three books have been very successful. Readers have valued the richness of her clinical experience, her independence of thought, and her capacity to convey the complex in simple language. She derived immense pleasure from learning that her writing was thought to contain the same attributes that people attached to her living persona.

With such an appearance of spontaneity, it can seem a contradiction that I still think of Nina as a very private person. Nina was sincere at all times, but her candour was somehow combined with an ability to preserve her privacy. Nina enjoyed a good exchange of views but she seemed to recognize when objectivity was substituted by personal motives, and this usually led to the end of the discussion, though always in a manner that preserved an amicable atmosphere.

There were times when I felt that "my" Nina might be quite different to everybody else's Nina. Gill, her sister, must have known a Nina that none of us ever met, much as Eve [Griffiths], her school friend, shared with her a language that none of us knew to speak. The important point is that I valued knowing Nina and I am sure that this feeling is shared by all those who knew her—in whatever capacity.

CHAPTER THIRTEEN

A recollection of friendship

Nina Farhi

I contemplated Nina as she sat, body erect, neck curved, eyes closed, a handsome and imposing woman, in the midst of a throng of people. And I watched these people as they moved eagerly towards her, then hesitated, then, somewhat bewildered, moved away.

She had made herself the centre of gravity within her complete inner stillness. She had also created a space around her that was hers and hers alone. Utterly personal.

This was her preparation before lecturing. Always in touch with her uncertainties, aware of her need to gather her resources, while deriving her power through the meditative practice of emptying herself of her Self.

However, I was very shortly to be chairing her talk (I now forget which), and it was time to rouse her. Lecturing, I know, was the world which she both loved for the freedom it gave to live out her mastery of her subject and for the opportunity it presented to perform with that charismatic presence, which, nevertheless, was always bounded by a silken skein.

Her papers, written in immaculate prose, spoken in forceful or graceful and intentionally colloquial English, abjuring jargon, delighted her audiences.

On the podium, through the singularity of her connectedness to thousands of people, she emanated a power that, far from being cultivated, was entirely innate. At the same time, she was able to convey the particularity of her person, both deeply serious in intention and, equally often, immensely funny, without either detracting each from the other.

This impressionist memory contains for me some of the polarities I discovered in my deep and still enduring love for my friend whose forename I shared.

Our professional relationship scarcely lasted more than a few meetings. I had come to her, a seasoned psychotherapist myself, drawn, I think, by the complexity I sensed in her personality, contrasted by the practised simplicity of her writing. Here, in the latter, was clarity—a clarity that had drawn countless thousands to find in her idiom what they themselves were searching for.

A woman of a sometimes intimidating aura and intensity, she would let no one, prior to any engagement with her, evade her so acute powers of observation, both intellectual and visceral. But, once through her conscious and, certainly, unconscious perceptive and apperceptive sensory internal antennae, you were (or you were not) there.

Initially on guard, like an Olympic fencer, and ready to lunge, riposte, and parry, the foil would be immediately lowered, mask and gloves would be off, and there we two would be, sitting on the floor, seemingly having known each other all our lives and prepared to live off this fantasy with delight.

This image of the Olympic fencer came to me as I was struggling to capture the paradox that was my friend, Nina Coltart. I have, of course, become more aware of this as the decade of her absence from my life has passed.

Perhaps many people outside my own constrained profession experienced her otherwise. Or perhaps that immediacy, certainly passing through the same prism which never left her, was evident from the start with these others, and Nina and they feasted off what together they most enjoyed: literature, philosophy, opera, religion, travel, gossip, a riotous sense of humour, a delight in absurdity and a wickedness that might pitch each into a children's playground.

Yes, and psychoanalysis, about which she was as committed as she was to anything else in her life, and to which she gave everything—to patients and to any other who came to speak or to hear her. She assiduously distilled her brilliant intellectual ability and sophistication into that most difficult task of any communicator: clarity and directness that come from the need to reach others and to be reached by them.

Perhaps, enigmatically, this confused some of her senior colleagues, with whom and about whom she had a quite individual view. She cut to the middle. If she encountered a lack of personal truthfulness, pomposity, posturing, unbounded self-interest, the cold blade would descend. They would become subjects of indifference. Ridicule, however, suggested that she was also vulnerable.

And she was vulnerable at her core. How could it have been otherwise? She was at once dismissive and, I know, deeply hurt at the British Society's lack of respect or recognition for the ten years she had spent as Director of its Clinic, creating a prodigious network of contacts between psychiatrists and analysts—a task not seriously undertaken previously by any other psychoanalyst.

There was no obituary for her in that august body's journal, *The International Journal of Psychoanalysis*. There are some colleagues, no less eminent than she, who have declined to add their personal memories to this recollection and celebration. I remain puzzled by this, as is Gillian Preston, her sister—a person outside The Profession. (Nina loved to use capitals in her letters.)

Nina and Gillian shared a rather striking aesthetic calligraphy. Long after Nina's death, letters from Gillian would create that same thrill of excitement and sense of anticipation that Nina's extensive correspondence always elicited from me.

Nina's letters were so entirely like our conversations: a mixture of playfulness, mockery, seriousness, competitive reading speeds (who had read which new and seriously good novel first), an exquisite delicacy concerning my chronic illness, a darting miniature of something seen, heard, or thought. She loved writing letters. Indeed, it was something of a passion. Again, a truthful and palpable need to meet and to be met before relaxing into intellectual matters or fun. And always there was that aesthetic sensitivity combined with her intellectual strength and absolute individuality.

Nina, of course, was pre-technological. The rapidity and frequency of her correspondence make me think nowadays of e-mails—with a massive caveat. She would have been appalled at the liquidity of that form. Her letters to me were through and through communications from the core of herself. That core was deep, and today it remains, in my own psychic awareness, just as painful—and yet joyful—as when she was alive.

The unique contribution to her profession, no doubt, had its origins in the search for her Self, which continued until the day she died. She became increasingly interested in the pre-symbolic experiences of early childhood, and earlier still. In this, we were more nearly equal. It was to this area that I was most drawn and to which she was entirely open. I never quite lost my sense of awe that I had been allowed so close to someone who had such a greatness of spirit.

At the same time, she lived and worked on precarious foundations. This pre-symbolic vulnerability inevitably was used in the service of her vocation—an important word for her in defining what made a good therapist.

Nevertheless, it was from this core that she influenced thousands of lives, either through direct contact—be it a single consultation at a critical moment in someone's life, or through her assessments of perhaps more than three thousand potential patients, as well as years of psychoanalytic endeavour with her own patients and in supervision—or through her books, her ideas, her capacity for delight, for laughter, for friendship.

Perhaps, most of all, she was sustained at many levels by her curiosity. It was virtuoso in its range and utterly clear-sighted. It resembled certain gifted young children who combine extreme sensitivity with outstanding intelligence. Sparked by that innate originality of vision, the world, for them, creates and recreates itself anew. That precious quality endured in Nina.

She was there to be met. She was both recognizably singular and also an exemplar of life in all its dimensions.

After she had resigned from The British Psychoanalytical Society and left her house in Hampstead, she would come and stay at the top of our house, room suffused with smoke and books plucked from our very considerable library. This became, in her words, her "London pad".

She left The Society with no regrets. It became a silent subject that revealed much.

She spoke of the pleasure she took in her house in Leighton Buzzard, Bedfordshire, as the beginning of an adventure. I experienced a new, if unanchored, vitality in her. All, as ever, was before her and I looked to the future with her as a potent presence. Her death remains a painful loss. But after this jolt of memory, I find a smile emerging from deep within me.

CHAPTER FOURTEEN

My pen pal

Gill Davies

In truth, I only met Nina once, and that was in the late 1980s. I was struck by her appearance and demeanour. She was handsome, but seemed quite austere—the kind of person who, I felt strongly, would do things meticulously and correctly. She struck me as a particular type of English woman, upper middle-class, clearly well read, radiating personal authority, neither a taker nor receiver of liberties. Faced with such a seemingly perfectly-formed person, one wondered if there might be possibilities for "difference" just below the surface. Was she what she seemed to be?

Some years later, I had become the managing director of Free Association Books. I wrote to our authors to explain my arrival and to outline some of my intentions in relation to the administration of their "affairs" (at the time, paying their royalties was our most pressing need), my approach to managing the list, as well as the kind of publications I was seeking to contract. It was the usual kind of letter a publisher sends out when joining a company. I did get a reply from Nina, short, polite, wishing me well, and so on. Things might never have developed further from that first exchange of letters, but one day I wrote asking if she could advise me on a synopsis for a book that an author had sent me.

I fully expected to be told she was far too busy to help me (a fairly common response from analysts and therapists), but, to my surprise, I got a quick reply, and not only did she agree to examine the synopsis, but she even gave me a date by which she would return her report. This is rather unusual, because often "delivery" can be as difficult to prise out of an adviser as it is with an author. My perception of Nina was that she was so important that she must be grand and very busy, so I had put in my request with some hesitancy. The report she wrote was a model for the kind of advice the publisher needs: it was clear about content, it was clear about the market for the book, it was helpfully critical where possible weaknesses had been spotted. There was no point-scoring at all. Furthermore, she wished to brush aside the usual niceties of anonymity. I could tell the author who had written the report and she would be happy to have direct contact if it would be helpful. There was almost a complete absence of the usual signs of ego, which to me is usually an indicator of a very strong person.

Having had such a happy experience using Nina as an adviser, I sent her a number of such synopses while I worked at FAB. During that time, however, another kind of letter-writing emerged. I cannot remember now when it did, but one day I received the usual kind of fairly formal letter from her but within which there was a nugget of something else. There were a couple of throwaway remarks marked by very dry humour, and just a hint of dissension about her own profession. These remarks made me laugh out loud, and they contained a strong hint of a rather different person to the one I had first encountered. As a pleasant change from the usual grind of the working day, I decided to reply immediately and took up the ball she had presented in her amusing remarks and ran with it. I enjoyed it. I wondered if she would reply. She did, and the reply marked the beginning of a long and fairly active exchange of letters between us.

In sum, we became pen pals. I received a letter from her about once a month. Some time later, I discovered she was a very active letter writer and I have no doubt that there are many others out there who were much closer and more important correspondents. But her choice to write and entertain me was the gift that she had bestowed on me.

The letters would arrive and were immediately recognizable. Both the envelopes and the writing paper were, I am sure, made from a wonderful paper called Conqueror! Did she choose it for the name or for its lovely, creamy, robust elegance, I wonder. Everything was handwritten. There was no mistaking Nina's clear, open, characterful writing. It was a pleasure to look at. The arrival of these letters always raised my spirits. After a while, one of the young people who worked for me, and who would bring down my mail when it arrived, would say with a twinkle in his eye, "I think this is another one from Nina!". The fact is that, after some time, I began showing the young staff the letters. I enjoyed them so much that I wanted to share my pleasure, as we did not have that many opportunities for a laugh at the time. Eventually, a group expectation of the imminent arrival of humour along with her letters emerged.

So, what did she write about? Seldom anything very personal, unless I raised something about myself. Being of a particular age at the time, I mentioned in one letter that my doctor was very keen on hormone replacement therapy and, as she had been medically trained, what did she think of this? The reply came back, "I'd just as soon throw it over the lawn". She also wrote on one occasion, and I found it very affecting, of the time when she and her sister Gill (still children at the time) were told that their parents had been killed. She went to meet them at the railway station, only later to learn crushingly that they would not be coming back, and she explained how that terrible event had affected her for the rest of her life. But, by and large, what I never heard about was whether she was happy or sad, or disappointed, or bored. Yet she had a tremendous gift of seeming personal, chatty, confidential, close.

What I did hear a lot about were ordinary, mundane events, which she managed to transpose into highly entertaining anecdotes. She had a gift of experiencing an event, being part of it, and yet somehow recording it as though she were separate from it. There was the day she took a group of school children to a kind of theme park, and every ride or "exciting experience" this theme park offered, and the ways in which the children coped with them, had been remembered in such detail and so vividly that I might just have well been watching a film of it all. Then there were her various days as a room attendant in one of England's grandest, aristocratic, country estates. I think it was Woburn Abbey. When I am visiting such a place, or a museum or art gallery, I wonder how and why these people do not start screaming with boredom. Yet, rooted to her spot, Nina had watched the world go by and captured on paper that crushed silence and induced awkwardness that is so characteristic of people in places that we are expected to appreciate for their beauty, rarity, or privilege. The English are particularly good at this, of course, looking almost embarrassed at the ease of their adaptation to creeping around a hallowed hall. Her account was as good as Alan Bennett's might have been.

Possibly my favourite was the account of the day she had tons of what I shall politely refer to as a form of fertilizer delivered to her house. She had had raised beds made in the garden. It was quite a big job, I seem to remember, but once the rich, nourishing stuff had been delivered and raked in, she was going to set about planting. Clearly, she had not anticipated the obvious (neither would I), and arrived back to notice an unmistakable whiff in the air. She could smell it from half way down the road. She knew and feared where it was coming from. Its full glory burst on her as she entered her garden. Her description of her realization that she had created a stinking hell in her own back yard, the rapid and furious succession of anxious thoughts about angry neighbours bearing down on her and where should she hide, was a brilliant, and hilarious, account of a full-blown panic.

The penultimate time I heard from her was via an uncharacteristic postcard telling me that she was rather ill, and depressed by it, and she doubted if she would be able to write again. I replied immediately saying that I could come and visit if she would like some company. She wrote again on a postcard to thank me but discouraged me from the idea. I knew instinctively to back off, but I had no idea what was coming, and when it did, I was rocked by the news. The launch party for *Freely Associated* turned out not to be the highlight of my time at Free Association Books that I had so looked forward to. Her absence was terrible.

So, I lost my pen pal. I have dealt with a number of very distinguished writers during my career in publishing, but she was one of the really memorable ones whom I could count on the fingers of one hand. They shared a few characteristics. Not only were they exceptional writers, they were all very amusing. No one (from their professional writing) would have expected them to be a bundle of laughs, but when off duty, they were the embodiment of the saying that life is a tragedy for those who feel and a comedy for those who think. Each of them, although quick to praise those they respected, could be bitingly funny about charlatans, and psychoanalysis has its share of such types. Nina's views were such a relief to a publisher in daily receipt of too many self-important, yet inhibited, letters from those who had appointed themselves to the High and Mighty and the Precious. They made me grind my teeth. She told me I had reason to.

There are other characteristics, too, that Nina shared with them. She had the ability to teach without appearing to: the odd phrase just gently dropped parenthetically in a letter, that made one sit up and think hard the next day. Finally, the greatest gift of all: to make one somehow feel interesting, knowledgeable, amusing, when one was not necessarily so. The ghastly expression "life-enhancing" comes to mind, but that is what it is. She was stimulating and she was fun!

If she had lived longer, I would certainly have tried to persuade her to become a novelist so that we could all have enjoyed her brilliant talent for narrative, characterization, and the absurd. None of that could happen, as it turned out. I remain privileged for being allowed to have a glimpse of another Nina. Not "just" the utterly distinguished and admired analyst, but someone who was one hell of a good companion and entertainer. Grounded solely in letter writing, it was all the more remarkable for that. I hate to close this piece with a cliché, but I am bound to say I do not think we shall see her like again.

CHAPTER FIFTEEN

The silent listener

Mona Serenius

I never actually met Nina Coltart in person. Nevertheless, I came to regard her as one of my most intimate friends. She was, for me, a role model and a mentor, ever since 1994, when our correspondence first began, up to her tragic death in June 1997. Even now, when so many years have passed, I can feel her powerful influence on me and on my life. I also have reason to believe that in the last two and a half years of her life she considered me a close friend and came truly to enjoy our correspondence. In the beginning, she ended her letters formally: "Kind regards. Yours sincerely, Nina Coltart". One of her last letters ends, "Yours ever, with much love, Nina".

How, then, did this intimate relationship come about?

To begin with, Nina Coltart was certainly not prepared to become so involved with me. I can think of several reasons why. She had been asked by the Editor in Chief of the *International Forum of Psychoanalysis*, Jan Stensson, to read and comment on the first draft of my article "The silent cry. A Finnish child during World War II and 50 years later" (1995). She showed rather clearly that she was irritated and reluctant to do so, especially since she was under the misapprehension that I, the author of the draft, was a psychoanalyst by profession—quite understandable, since I was supplying my article to a psychoanalytic journal. My article did not include a discussion on psychoanalytic theory, nor did the draft include a reference list. I had been in psychoanalysis for six years and had read a fair amount of psychoanalytic literature by the time I wrote the article, but obviously did not think it appropriate for me to theorize on the subject.

In fact, I was the managing editor of the *International Forum of Psychoanalysis*, and Jan Stensson had encouraged me to write an article about my personal experience of being a Finnish war child. He supplied me with a frame, within which I felt it might be possible to speak out in writing about my childhood memories from a child's perspective and how I thought they had affected my adult life.

It had to be written in English, which suited me fine. Having to use a foreign language was a way of detaching myself to some extent from the overwhelming emotions that had, up until then, prevented me from getting started on my story. Possibly my way of writing, English not being my mother tongue, also disturbed Nina, with her solid education in English literature and modern languages and her own undeniable stylistic talent. My unobtrusive way of speaking of some of the existing studies on Finnish war children, although in fact I disagreed strongly with the results, may have been another source of irritation for her. But, paradoxically, Nina's comments and corrections of my language were actually the starting point of our friendship.

In my first draft of "The silent cry", I was afraid of speaking out regarding my own experiences and those of other war children: "these stories may seem unsignificant ...". Nina corrected me in her vigorous style:

> '*in*significant' (not un . . .) Incidentally, I think you are doing something psychological here—these stories are *not* 'insignificant' by any standards—the 'comparison with the horrifying experiences of war children today . . .' is a false use of 'comparison'. There are *no stories*, which are worse or more horrifying than what you have told us here—*different*, maybe, but not worse. To lose one's family (even for a few years)—mother, father, siblings *and* home *and* language—in fact all elements of one's life experience, 'history' to date, true

self, in fact, is almost unthinkably horrifying to the reader and *was 'unthinkable'* to you 'children' far into adulthood, and perhaps forever for some.

I also mentioned that most research reports so far published seemed "biased and controversial", without expanding on why I thought so. Nina commented:

> 'biased and controversial'—in which direction? Who are these people, making these evaluations? . . . This is *such an IMPORTANT point both politically and psychologically*, that I think you should *expand on it*. It is a shocking paragraph, and right at the heart of the ghastly traumatic happenings. If you leave it as such, a bare skeletal statement, it almost looks as if what you go on to say in your next paragraph is still operating up to a point.

Later, in a letter of 24 August 1994, after I had included a section on the "scientific" studies, she wrote:

> I don't think there is much risk that you are manifesting bias; those papers are or are not as you describe, and the authors have to take responsibility for them, and if necessary be challenged. The fact that your own personal experience is part of the ground from which you criticise them does not by any means necessarily indicate 'bias'.

Nina had unerringly found my weakest points. For me, her comments were infinitely valuable. Not only did I feel she gave me the right to speak out and speak loudly, but she provided me with a platform to speak from: she told me that I had a right of opinion as much as anybody else and that it need not be inferior to that of others. Whether I was "right" or not was not all-important; I had the right to defend *my* point of view and my truth. Up to that point I was still very confused, and seemed to think that my ideas and opinions carried less weight than just about anybody else's. I did not really trust my own senses. In that respect I was still like a small child "whose will was in my father's pocket", as the saying goes in Swedish. Nina authorized me to become not only audible, but also visible. I received the right to take my place among the grown-ups, to occupy some space.

But I can think of other reasons why Nina did not want to engage too much in me and my writings.

In 1994, she had decided to leave the British Psychoanalytical Society. "I'm glad to be away from it all, to tell you the truth; I worked faithfully for the Society in many capacities, but always kept my inner self detached from the gossip and politicking and general shenanigans", she later wrote to me (30 June 1995). In her interview with Anthony Molino, she describes herself as "the most independent representative of the Independent Group" (1997, p. 177) and also as "an eccentric" and "quite a recluse" (p. 180). "I was", she tells Molino, "actually turning my back on my identity of a psychoanalyst" (p. 171). Nina was sixty-six at the time and felt (after one of her closest friends had died of cancer) that she "suddenly wanted more time . . . to visit friends and see more of them" (p. 181). She also confessed to feeling that her "memory [was] failing pretty rapidly . . . the ordinary memory loss of old age" and, more importantly, "I found I was getting bored. I was decathecting the whole process. I wasn't so good at it any longer" (p. 181). "And the sense of liberation, of real liberation that came upon me almost as soon as I'd gone, was wonderful. I didn't regret the decision at all, and I haven't since—not for one second" (p. 182). Of all this I knew nothing at the time; I only learnt about it later. But in spite of Nina's valuable comments, I had sensed her reluctance and detachment. I respected her highly and did not want to impose on her. So, our interchange might have ended there. In the meantime she had, however, been invited by Jan Stensson to become Editorial Reader for the *International Forum of Psychoanalysis* and had gladly accepted.

In April 1995, my article appeared in print, together with Nina's comments and my reflections on them. I sent her an issue of the journal and, in my accompanying letter, told her that although I was happy to see it in print, it had caused me quite a bit of emotional turmoil, and that I had been hesitant about exposing my vulnerability in public. Interested as I was in psychosomatic phenomena, I could not help but tell her that almost exactly at the time when I realized that my article would in fact be accepted for publication, I developed an "adenoma or a possible tumour in my thyroid gland", which needed surgery. The surgeon informed me that I would have to remain *silent* for some time right after the operation. Some months later, on the very day the article appeared in print, I caught an infection which affected my vocal cords and stopped me from using my voice altogether! "These events may of course be mere coincidences, but to me it seems that speaking up is not entirely without dangers", I told Nina. She answered, by return of mail, that she had "realised it would cause me 'emotional turmoil'", but nevertheless thought it "*was so well worth doing*" and said she wished "that more people would not be so afraid of self-exposure, and would write more personally". She then went on to comment on the tumour:

> I think your story of your lump in your thyroid, and then your laryngitis is extraordinary! It strikes me that not only have you been put in a position of being only capable of a Silent Cry, but also you have given yourself a 'lump in the throat'; is that an expression for crying, in Swedish?
>
> I do believe the body tracks the mind closely, and I have no doubt whatever that you were showing the dangers of speaking out, and also underlining the seriousness and intense reality with which you did speak out.

In May the same year, I briefly met Christopher Bollas, who was lecturing in Sweden, and he told me that he had read and liked our exchange in the *International Forum*. I knew that he was a good friend of Nina's. He asked me if I intended to go on with my own writing and also if I meant to continue my correspondence with Nina. This encouraged me to write yet another letter to Nina, commenting on "the lump in the throat" as an expression for crying, or, rather, "silent crying". The same expression exists in Swedish. "I had not thought of it in that way myself, but it really makes sense", I wrote. "Makes me wonder what will happen when it is being removed".

Nina answered (30 June 1995),

> I was delighted to get your 'real' letter of May 11th. It is one of the great advantages of doing things like read your paper(s) [referring to her task as ER for the journal]—one makes a new friend. What a pity I did not know you when I used to come to Sweden regularly—I came every 6th weekend for about 6 years, flew out on a Friday night, stayed in the Seamen's Hotel, did one supervisory group all day Saturday, went out to dinner at someone's house on the Sat. night, did another group all day Sunday and flew home on

Sunday evening. It was lovely and I loved all 'my people'. In the summer we had a long weekend up in Biskop's Arno, in a special big house for that sort of thing, and one summer I taught them "the whole of Freud" in 4 days! Goodness, I had to work hard for that— I made notes on about 30 Freud papers; but they had to work hard too—I expected them to have read them all, and one person presented each paper. I was/am so shocked that 'analytical' trainees don't seem to read Freud any more. And it's *all there*.

And later on, in the same long letter:

Let me know more about the removal of the Lump in the Throat. *There's* your next paper perhaps? I'm *quite serious* about you writing more, from your unique angle; and I am sure Kit was too.

The letter ended "Keep in touch! All the best—Yours—Nina".

In my letter of 11 May, I had also quoted a passage from Milan Kundera's *The Book of Laughter and Forgetting* (1983). I had recently finished reading Nina Coltart's first book, *Slouching towards Bethlehem* (1992), including the chapter titled "Attention" (pp. 176–193).

Tamina serves the customers their coffee and Calvados . . . There is almost always someone sitting on a bar stool wanting to talk to her. They all like her. She is a good listener.

But does she really listen? Or does she just look on, silent and preoccupied? I can't quite tell, and it really doesn't matter that much. What does matter is that she never interrupts anybody. You know what it's like when two people start a conversation. First one of them does all the talking, the other breaks in with "That's just like me, I . . ." and goes on talking about himself until his partner finds a chance to say, "That's just like me, I . . .".

The "That's just like me, I . . . s" may look like a form of agreement, a way of carrying the other party's ideas a step further, but that is an illusion. What they really are is a brute revolt against brutal force, an attempt to free one's ear from bondage, a frontal attack the objective of which is to occupy the enemy's ear. All man's life among men is nothing more than a battle for the ears of others. The whole secret of Tamina's popularity is that she has no desire to talk about herself. She offers no resistance to the forces occupying her ear; she never says, "That's just like me, I . . .". [Kundera, 1983, pp. 79–80]

I have often wondered what made me seek out Nina as my "good listener", my Tamina. She was equally puzzled to begin with. And what made her let me "occupy her ear" for so long?

Of course, there were some obvious reasons why I felt drawn to her. From the contact we had already established, I had formed an image of her as a vigorous, independent, and honest woman with a good sense of humour and no tolerance for pomposity and hypocrisy. Energetic and colourful: this showed clearly, I found, in her beautiful handwriting, covering every inch of the paper she wrote on. She sometimes excused herself "for using old fashioned methods like handwriting. I've just got so disenchanted and fed up with my prize computer and all its tricks, and colour and this and that, that I'm about to give it away to a friend who fell in love with it. An expensive mistake". I was pleased that she wrote by hand—I recognized her handwriting from afar and was delighted to receive her letters.

She was the kind of woman I deeply admired and wanted to be like. And she had encouraged me to go on writing—"there is a lot more in and behind your story, the paper you have already written is only a start". She had left the door open for me, ending her letter with "Keep in touch". Besides I knew she was bound to be a "good listener", having worked as a psychoanalyst, and a famous one at that, for such a long time. But there was something more.

* * *

When I started this essay, I hesitated between saying that "I never met Nina Coltart *in person*" and *"in real life"*. But what, then, is real life? Do you know a person less if you have never met or seen her, or is there a way of knowing someone deep down, that has nothing to do with socializing on a more superficial level? And how, then, does this come about? I knew almost nothing about Nina's everyday life, and about her own history. She disclosed hardly a thing about her own traumatic experiences in her letters to me. There was just the occasional hint. Only after her death, in the interviews she gave Anthony Molino in September and December 1996, published in 1997, did I learn about her own tragic losses and how they had affected her life, including her decision to live on her own and refrain from having children. I had read her first book and enjoyed her very personal and literary style of writing, but it only confirmed the image of her I had already formed. I cannot really explain how I "knew" she would understand my deepest, inmost self, and why I trusted her as my silent listener when I wrote down my story about the "Lump in the Throat".

Robin Skynner, in a book entitled *Families and How to Survive Them* (1983), co-authored by his famous patient, John Cleese, describes an experiment used at the Institute of Family Therapy in the education of family therapists (pp. 18–26). When a group of new students first meet, before they get to know or even talk to each other, they are asked one by one to choose one other person in the group that they feel would fit into their own family or fill a gap in their family. They are asked to do so only by looking at the other persons in the group; talking is not permitted at this stage. Subsequently, each couple should choose one other couple, still without talking. Within each group of four, they should then decide which role each individual plays in the "family". Finally, they are allowed to start talking and discussing their personal histories and family backgrounds.

It turns out, Skynner goes on to say, that in some strange way each person has chosen three other individuals who have very similar family histories, or families functioning much like their own, just by looking at them! Even the ones "left over", the ones last chosen, have something in common. They are often adopted children, or foster children, or children raised in institutions.

Skynner finds an explanation for this astonishing phenomenon in the unconscious information each person constantly transmits about who he is, and our equally unconscious ability to read another person's body language and be sensitive to signals we recognize. But what if one has not even seen the person in question, not even a photograph?

My story about the "Lump in the Throat" was meant to be a reasonably short account of the events in my life that occurred around the time when the tumour was discovered and the subsequent operation, and of several strange dreams I had in this connection, where a dead or very sick baby played a part. Apart from the actual publication of "The silent cry", which, for some reason, had thrown me off balance, several other life events, such as helplessly witnessing the Estonia catastrophe, where over 800 people died at sea, from another ship close by; my youngest child moving away from home for good; and my own move from a big house to a small, temporary apartment in the city, where I was to live all alone, had severely disturbed my emotional equilibrium. I will not go into any further details. But once I started writing, I got lost in all sorts of associations to previous stages in my life, even my very earliest years, dreams from far back, etc. What was to be a short account turned out to be a lengthy story in several parts, which I wrote with Nina constantly on my mind, as the silent, benevolent listener. I sent her the first parts at the end of April 1996. In my letter I wrote:

> I don't know what you can make of this, or whether it is of any interest to you. However, I am ... hoping (as you mention in a passage in *How to Survive as a Psychotherapist* [1993] as one of the joys of the profession) that you might find the story of the process worth reading.

I also told her that I was not expecting any psychoanalytical interpretations from her, that I had written it mostly for myself and with no intent of getting it published, as it was much too personal. I then went on to ask her if by any chance she would have time to meet me in London, where I would be for some days at the end of May.

Nina replied (5 May 1996):

> I am hesitant to say anything very much at all about your three pieces of writing—largely because of feeling I understand you better as a result of reading them. ... I will only say I read them with absolutely absorbed attention, there was no difficulty in concentrating or imagining them, you have a remarkable gift for a sort of deep simplicity of speech which takes one right into what you are describing, and makes one—me—feel that I know more of what it was/is like to be you than you have actually put in words. This must be a connection with the inner and silent person who is so protected, even aggressively, by your own person.
>
> And it is for this very reason I must try to explain why I do not think it would be a good idea for us to meet when you come over to Oxford and London at the end of May. I don't in the very slightest way want to seem rude or hurtful, or slighting, or neglectful, and if you can listen from your inmost Silent Cry self, I don't think

you will think it is, but will hear what I mean. It is much clearer to me than before that you have formed a very important relationship with me; you say that I was constantly on your mind during the process of writing, and your silent and patient listener. I feel very honoured by this and proud to understand that I have become such a significant Other deep in your inner world; particularly when I read that you could not call out, from early on to say anything about what you were feeling . . . nor ask for comfort for yourself. I perfectly agree when you write 'To make the effort and endure the pain of growing on must be recognized by an Other'. . . . For some reason that I don't really grasp, nor do I have to—it is not the point—I have become an Other for you who is present at the extraordinary and vigorous and soul-searching process you are going through, in examining your life, recent and far, and putting down the essence in words. Probably I recognize the secret and searching inmost you within the reasonably well-adjusted, smiling, socialised self, because it is not at all unlike myself—our histories are different, but that again is pretty irrelevant.

. . . This brings me back to your friendly and courteous suggestion that we should meet; I think it would be misguided; on the wrong level of relating. We are both nice, interesting, socially-skilled, friendly people, who, partly out of our own needs, know a lot about 'relating' and all that stuff. But it would get between you and me, like deliberately building a perfectly rational, well-planned wall between us. I bet you would then find that you had deprived yourself of the Other who has been with you and listened and in some sense watched over you while you write and journey on. It would be wrong to spoil that, perhaps destroy it—it could well be the unconscious aggression which destroys what is most needed, out of fear, and to protect the inmost self. The true intimacy, which has extraordinarily flowered between us, could be ruined by jolly chat about your conference in Oxford and how nice my garden is, and what I did in Paris, etc. . . .

In a note at the top of this letter, she wrote, *à propos* a paper she had evaluated for *International Forum*,

> The death myth paper is *appalling*! I have said so pretty firmly, but I suppose the author will only be hurt, *not* take the points—but '*tant pis*', one must not be soppy or sentimental, say it is good if it is BAD.

I was very moved and also relieved (11 May 1996) by her reply:

> I must confess that in fact I was ambivalent myself about actually meeting you in person, though I did not quite understand why. I thought it had to do with some shyness on my part, which I ought to fight. This may sound like an afterthought, but it isn't. Reading your letter made me understand and accept the real reason for my hesitation. . . .
>
> You say you don't really grasp why I have chosen you as the Other, the one I am telling my story . . . I did not quite know either. . . . Then it struck me that you seem to have something I badly lack, still. You seem to have access to your aggression (which is in my experience also linked to sexuality) and to allow yourself to use it whenever necessary; which does not prevent you from being both kind, considerate and tactful when that is needed. I find that very attractive . . . I still tend to place my aggressive feelings outside myself, as becomes obvious in some of the dreams I had after my operation last year.

She answered (22 May 1996):

> I was so glad my letter made such sense to you. In fact, after I had written it, I was sure that it would, and furthermore, I was more sure than ever of the accuracy of the 'interpretation' I made, namely, that it was the underlying, aggressive streak that goes against your own true best interests, actively at work, and trying to destroy something good that had come into being for you. I very rarely 'make an interpretation' these days, but there was a feeling of lightness and clarity about having done it, in me, that I remember from when something had been fished up, or come up of its own accord, from deep within—the sort of thing that Bion calls O, and which is in fact quite rare, and confirms that 2 people are communicating from a deep level, and very straight. I agree it is not really at all *necessary* to locate why I had become the Other—but equally, I think you are absolutely right in what you go on to say; that I do have access to my aggression and have it harnessed to my affections so that when I am in deep communication with someone who is really wanting to show me something of themselves (nothing exhibitionist about it, that's just your deferential self unnecessarily apologising!) I can be very tough if necessary, in complete confidence that it will not go amiss—or that if it does

temporarily, it will sort itself out very quickly. Let me say that I think this is something that can really be worked on, and that one can see and feel it changing in oneself. I began to get clearer and tougher in my late forties. It is certainly connected with one's sexuality. And I think the thing to work on is any of the anxiety in oneself that it may raise. . . . What *is* one afraid of after all? It's a sort of omnipotence or conceit to think one is all *that* powerful.

And then, a note on top of the letter:

The critique of that death-myth paper was certainly aggressive! But I felt someone had to tell this man he's up the gum tree, or else he'll just go vacuously and pompously *on* and *on*!

In the summer of 1996 Nina and I exchanged small notes and postcards—I told her that I was temporarily too busy to continue the story of the "Lump in the Throat". My son was getting married, I was travelling quite a bit, both in my work and privately, and I was once again moving to a new apartment.

While I was in Ghana for two weeks, my mother, eighty-four years old, who lived in Finland, had a cerebral infarction that left her demented and unable to walk. She also had severe heart problems and could no longer live at home. I sensed that the end was near and wanted to visit her as often as I could. She recognized me and was happy when I came to see her, but I could no longer communicate with her in any sensible way. She lived in her own world of fantasies and distant memories, more and more detached from the outside world. I was terribly sad, but remember thinking "I still have Nina, though". In this situation she was my consolation. In fact she had filled a gap—she had become the "mother" (although she was just twelve years my senior) who actually cared about my true feelings and my inmost self. My real mother was certainly a caring person, but she had only been able to express her affection by worrying about whether I had time to eat, or got sufficient sleep, or wore warm enough clothes as protection against the North winds! She was indifferent, on the other hand, to my own concern about the tumour. "Don't worry, it will probably disappear by itself", she wrote. "I am sure it is not dangerous". (In fact, it turned out to be benign.)

Nina's book *The Baby and the Bathwater* (1996) had recently been published, and I read it during the summer. She had clearly announced that this would be her *last* book. I felt slightly uneasy, especially reading the last chapter, "Endings" (141–166). I remember thinking, "I hope she is not ill too, I cannot bear that". In mid October I got the following alarming message from Nina:

> About 3 weeks ago, out of a clear blue sky, I perforated an acute duodenal ulcer—hitherto completely silent and symptomless, and now thought to have been caused (a rare but known side-effect) by an anti-arthritic medication I had taken for about 2 months.
>
> ... I really feel, as they say, like a limp rag doll, and as if I don't know *where* to look for replenishment. Suppose I feel marginally better than 3 weeks ago, but it is bloody slow, and pretty *boring*, although I am not depressed—trying to put all the Buddhist teaching continually into practice—mindfulness, living in the here and now, detachment etc! ... Let me hear from you and about *you* and how things are—not just sympathy for me!
>
> Looking forward to your story when you have the time.

I answered immediately, and told her about my premonition, triggered by the last chapter in her book. I expressed my deep concern for her health and sent her an issue of *Konsthistorisk Tidskrift, A Journal of Art History* (1993, vol. 62, no. 2), which I edited as part of my job, hoping it would give her a brief moment of relief from the boredom she felt. I also sent her two more parts of my own story and told her, "this period of dreaming and fantasising and putting it all into words has been very rewarding, although I cannot claim that I fully understand the whole process, *how* it has worked and *why* it has helped me".

On 25 October she wrote a long letter in which she thanked me for "the little art journal, every *word* of which I instantly read!" She went on:

> I then with great attention read your two sections. I suppose my overall reaction was one of great admiration of you and your courage and determination—I'm pretty sure you would say, about all the dreaming and therapy and sheer *work* you have been doing inwardly—'I had no choice, it's not courageous, I *had* to do it' but I still stand by what I am saying. There is a sort of courage which is

not willed, or particularly conscious, but a deep resource on which one can draw, and does, when needs must—it comes from a lot of living in which, again, more or less unconsciously, one has lived determinedly and bravely, often maybe anxious and depressed, but just bloody well keeping on keeping on, for the sake of others, children, patients, friends etc,—and also for oneself—just because one isn't going to be *beaten* by life and one's past; one takes no pride in it, it feels inevitable—but it *is* courage, and it is admirable, and highly moral, whatever one would think of it oneself. I recognise it simply because (I say with no false pride or modesty or anything as trivial and *ordinary* as that) I know it in myself, the life-long effects of early traumata, and how they go on needing WORK. I think with the wisdom which arises from those deep layers of ourselves, you picked me out for your Other with an unerring and almost mystical aim.

She ended her letter by telling me, "I'm glad to be able to say, that just *this* week I feel as if I might rejoin the human race soonish!"

I was deeply moved by her words, and also greatly relieved that she seemed to be slowly recovering, and told her so.

In the meantime, my mother's health had steadily deteriorated, and I travelled back and forth to Finland as often as my work would permit to be with her. In early December, she finally passed away. While I was sitting at her deathbed, when she was already deeply unconscious, I wrote a letter telling Nina about how I felt, letting go of my mother. That letter remained a draft, I never actually sent it to her. Instead I told her in a Christmas letter that I felt the whole story about the "Lump in the Throat" had been "a preparation for my mother's death, helping me to face it with open eyes, accepting it, with great sorrow, but as something natural and inevitable".

In her Christmas card, Nina wrote, "I'm much better, almost restored to normal state of good health". And then, in a short note thanking me for another issue of the art journal (1996, vol. 65, no. 3), containing an article called "'They heard her singing her last song': On Pre-Raphaelite paintings of the Lady of Shalott" (Lind, 1996)—"quite apart from the overall interest to me, I was delighted to see the *whole poem* written out, as I hadn't got it anywhere. My sister and I used to know it by heart and chant it in unison as we tramped through the Cornish lanes". She also says, "I had to tell your colleague, that I wasn't, after all, able to review the book she had asked me to do; I just found I couldn't concentrate properly and my attention span is still reduced, or rather, is—I think—doing inner work, and not so available for other. I am a lot better, though, generally".

Mid February I received another short note:

> You were right, I am not so well, but what I've got is a depressive illness, something I've never had before, much though I have known of intermittent depression. I can only think the sudden withdrawal of far too much thyroid, which I was on for years, they discovered, plus the post-operative effects of the insult to the system have lit up a long damped-down bonfire of stuff I haven't worked through in the past. Anyway, I didn't mean to shock or disappoint you, but I thought it better to be truthful with you, my friend.

"Nina, I must ask you", I wrote in reply, "has anything *I* wrote ... evoked memories in you that triggered your depression? ... I have to ask before I go on sending you more stuff ... one tends to regard a psychoanalyst as someone who is able to receive and contain and share with you just about anything and who has worked through all her own traumas. ..."

Nina's very last letter to me, from March 1997, was no longer in her characteristic handwriting. "I'm asking a friend to type this for me, as a drug I am taking for the depression affects my writing badly and makes it scrunched up and rather shaky".

> Thank you very, very much for your extremely nice and kind letter, which said everything I could have wished for in the circumstances. I feel profoundly grateful for your understanding and for all the comments you made. They all made me feel that I was glad I told you, and it certainly was a token of friendship
>
> With regard to your important question: no nothing that you have written in your story or your letters has evoked memories or reactions which have affected my depression at all. I can see exactly why you asked but do please accept my assurances that the above is true. Indeed, I would welcome and look forward to anything you have recently or are currently writing. You certainly would not contribute to making anything worse for me.

I had told Nina that I "was in a strange stage of emotional flatness" after my mother's death, and that I did not get much accomplished for the time being. It took me quite a while to get the last parts of my story written down. Not until 20 July 1997 did I send her the final "chapter" of the "Lump in the Throat". By then I actually felt that I had "come out on the other side" and was beginning to feel "whole" once more. The last part was about handling and trying to integrate my aggression, sexuality, and creativity, but also about death and about a new beginning. I had recently become grandmother of my first grandchild.

Writing down all the events, dreams, fantasies and associations set in motion by the "Lump in the Throat" had been very rewarding, for reasons I cannot quite grasp to this day. The meaning of many of the dreams and fantasies still evades me. The texts were never analysed or interpreted; I had told Nina all along that I did not expect that from her.

I began my letter of 20 July by apologizing to Nina for the long delay and wrote, "I sincerely hope that meanwhile your life has also turned to the better and that your depression has begun to fade away. I so much hope I can go on communicating with you, although I consider this story finished with the part I am now sending you". I quoted Christopher Bollas, who, in a recent lecture on Creativity here in Stockholm, had said, "An analysis has no real end other than the one we decide on ourselves, because the stories of our lives have no ends, life is an ever-ongoing process. The only definite end, the only end we can be sure of is Death".

As it were, this *was* the definite end of our special friendship. Nina died on 24 June 1997. My letter, with the last part of my story, never reached her. When I returned from a short holiday, a letter from Nina's sister, Gill Preston, awaited me, with two obituaries and my returned letter and essay. She told me about Nina's final months, her rapidly deteriorating physical health and her depression. "She faced a life of dependency which she would have loathed and all her spark had gone". But Nina still lives very vividly in my memory and I am truly happy to have known her.

References

Cleese, J., & Skynner, R. (1989). *Familjen - hur man klarar sig helskinnad ur dess famntag*. (*Families and How to Survive Them*). Stockholm:

Månpocket/Bokförlaget Forum [original work published by Methuen, London, 1983].

Coltart, N. (1992). *Slouching Towards Bethlehem . . . and Further Psychoanalytic Explorations*. London: Free Association Books.

Coltart, N. (1993). *How to Survive as a Psychotherapist*. London: Sheldon Press, SPCK.

Coltart, N. (1995). Some comments on "The Silent Cry" by Mona Serenius. *International Forum of Psychoanalysis*, 4: 48–49.

Coltart, N. (1996). *The Baby and the Bathwater*. London: Karnac.

Kundera, M. (1983). *The Book of Laughter and Forgetting*. London: Penguin [original work published by Éditions Gallimard, Paris, 1979].

Lind, C. (1996). "They heard her singing her last song": On Pre-Raphaelite paintings of the Lady of Shalott. *Konsthistorisk Tidskrift (Art review)*, 65: 179–195.

Molino, A. (Ed.) (1997). *Freely Associated. Encounters in Psychoanalysis with Christopher Bollas, Joyce McDougall, Michael Eigen, Adam Phillips, Nina Coltart*. London: Free Association Books.

Serenius, M. (1995). The silent cry. A Finnish child during World War II and 50 years later. *International Forum of Psychoanalysis*, 4: 35–47, 50–52.

CHAPTER SIXTEEN

Nina Coltart: a person of paradox

Stuart A. Pizer

Nina Coltart understood, wrote about, and embodied paradox. As she affirmed with respect to Buddhism (which she practised for decades): "For a Westerner to proceed healthily on the spiritual path which may lead to self-transcendence, and loss of 'the fortress of I', there needs must *exist already* a stable, strong sense of personal identity" (1992, p. 167). Thus, as a psychoanalyst, Coltart remained firmly grounded in the foundations of classical theory, and a crispness of technically practised formulations and interpretations, while also bringing us with her into the realm of ambiguity, mystery, silence, faith, patience, awe, and even joy in working "in the dark".

She advocated rigorous preparation for clinical work and a lifelong dedication to sharpening our conceptual focusing skills. Without a doubt, Nina was secure in her discipline, strictly mindful of her technical frame and acute in her clinical observations. But, at the same time, she recognized that psychoanalysts, along with their necessary responsibilities and their requisite tools, need also to embody and bring into their consulting rooms a larger moral, humanistic, and spiritual perspective. As she succinctly put it, "treatment" begins with how we "treat" another person.

Nina wrote and spoke with the same voice: direct, succinct, literate without gratuitous decorations, but with wit, confidence, and humour. For me, her special gift was for invoking arcane or esoteric terms, such as "faith", or antiquated terms, such as "manners", and rendering them in accessible, straightforward, experience-near defining language that placed them at the heart of our analytic calling. In her conversational writing, with a tonal quality that Matthew Arnold would have called "high seriousness", Nina reminded us of the ethos behind our human encounters in a clinical context. About manners (and here we must read her to mean the manners of the analyst), she wrote,

> The people whose manners we genuinely admire and enjoy are those who, without it being obvious, skilfully enhance our sense of significance and worth. All contact, whether conversational or silent, is accompanied by an atmosphere of warmth and generosity; this promotes trust and openness. As it is said, they bring out the best in us. [1992, p. 137]

I recall my first meeting with Nina Coltart in 1990. My wife, Barbara Pizer, and I had invited her to present a paper for a special evening programme of our institute, the Massachusetts Institute for Psychoanalysis. Christopher Bollas had recommended her to us as *the* analyst's consultant on difficult cases and *the* person to contact for a therapeutic referral in London, as well as a leading voice among the British Independents. When we met Nina at the airport, we imagined that she would be fatigued after her long flight from London. Instead, with vigorous cheer, she requested that we go straight to the Boston Museum of Fine Arts to view a recently opened Monet exhibit. Walking through the galleries with Nina, experiencing her riveted attention to the paintings, I found myself looking at the canvases with an intensified focus. Over tea at the museum, having been with each other thus far barely two hours, we found our conversation both easy and very much alive, and true. It was startlingly possible to feel an immediate, vital, and enthusiastic rapport.

That evening, Nina presented. At the microphone, she riffled through a pile of her papers, saying, "Let's see, which one would you like? Which do I feel like reading tonight? All right, how about this: 'What does it mean: love is not enough'?" After reading her paper, she returned to her seat in the audience, and promptly removed her shoes as she attended to a discussant's remarks. When asked to respond to questions, she marched back up to the podium in her stockinged feet. I was amused, but also impressed, by her unselfconscious naturalness. Nina was a guest at our home and, returning home later that evening, she noticed an oil painting over our living room couch. Wanting a closer look, she once again removed her shoes and climbed up on the couch to take in the details. No hesitation, no pretentions. Although we had the pleasure of extended time with Nina on only three occasions (inviting her for return visits to participate in a symposium and a workshop at our institute), we felt that we had become friends. I believe that Nina and Barbara quickly found and enjoyed a kindred spirituality combined with hard-headedness. For me, it was deeply moving to feel that, in her responses to me, I was incisively recognized, in ways I knew myself, with a breathtaking immediacy and kindness. In continuing correspondence during her remaining years, Nina showed, particularly woman-to-woman with Barbara, but also with us both, a dear and touching capacity for intimate confiding and sharing. In her personal as well as professional writing, she bridged time and distance with her true self.

Nina could be outrageous in the precise authority of her clinical dicta. Thus, at the workshop on technique, she proclaimed, with a wink, "all sociopaths have blue eyes". What a paradoxically categorical declaration from a teacher whose essential message was one of profound respect for the humanity of patients, along with the uncertainties and mysteries of psychoanalytic "understanding" and clinical process, and the leaps of faith that are our acts of love and devotion in therapeutic relationships! She reminded us to hone our disciplined clinical tools and to refresh, restore, and feed our own souls to remain fortified as instruments of our calling. Nina exemplified the kind of "strong personal identity" that supports a capacity for surrender to the dark, a wonderfully paradoxical bridging of certainty and "negative capability". Her writings inspire us to become more of what we can, and should, be, both as analysts and as people.

Reference

Coltart, N. (1992). *Slouching Towards Bethlehem . . . and Further Psychoanalytic Explorations*. New York: Guilford Press.

CHAPTER SEVENTEEN

Cometh the hour*

Brendan MacCarthy

When, in 1994, I wrote as President to Nina Coltart expressing the hope that she would reconsider her decision to resign from our Society, I ought to have known better. In her polite but firm reply, it was clear that the lady was not for turning. This brief exchange of letters epitomized Nina's character—strong, lucid, and fearless. Having lost both parents in a wartime rail crash, as they were travelling to visit their two daughters, evacuated to Cornwall, it would not be unreasonable to think that Nina, then aged twelve, had a special awareness of what it was like to be alone. For all her extrovert manner, and her many friends and colleagues, she was always a very private person, always alone.

Her tragic childhood must have contributed to her forceful and highly independent style. Independent by nature and independent by group.

---

*Originally presented at a Scientific Meeting of the British Psychoanalytical Society, 15 October 1997, and published in 1997 under the title, "Nina Coltart (1927–1997): An Obituary", in *The British Psychoanalytical Society Bulletin*, 33(10): 14.

Nina managed her life in a very efficient way and, when crippling arthritis and intractable pain spoiled her enjoyment of her retiring years, she took control of her own death with no attempt to conceal what she had done. She was strongly averse to the cover-up, never one to turn a blind eye.

It might be expected, as a former Clinic Director, that I would pay tribute to probably the best Director the Clinic ever had. But that much is already well known. It was the job she loved most; indeed, she overcame my reluctance to apply for the Clinic Director post, saying with a laugh, "You idiot, don't you realise that Clinic Director is the best post in the Institute, the only post worth having?" And she loved the Clinic Directorate, that happy band of devotees who perhaps gave her the joys of the family she never had.

But I prefer to speak instead of her main yet little known achievement as Vice President. In the short three years as President or Vice President, the incumbent, if lucky, can manage but one success, be it a major Constitutional change, a successful defence against attacks from outside, or perhaps managing an Institute relocation to a new site. When Nina became Vice President, and for some years before, there was a serious and worsening crisis within our Administration, affecting every level of functioning, damaging morale, and threatening our resources. There had been much soul-searching and hand-wringing, but no effective solution seemed possible, remedial action being judged to be as risky as inaction.

Cometh the hour, cometh the woman. Nina, with great subtlety and determination, consulting appropriately at every stage, brought to successful conclusion the malaise that so threatened us, ushering in a decade or more of remarkable growth and development in our affairs. I know of very few people in our Society who would have had the strength to deal with that crisis as Nina did, and we are much in her debt.

Nina understood that credit and celebration for lancing a boil within a family must be muted, but I know that she also felt hurt that such an exhausting and exacting task, taking such a heavy toll on Nina herself, seemed so little appreciated or valued, and I know for sure that her disillusionment dated from that time. A few years later, she refused nomination for the Presidency and progressively withdrew from our affairs. I pay tribute to her for her role in solving the staff crisis because she became something of an unsung hero in the dramas of the 1985 winter and we ought, if belatedly, express our gratitude for what she did.

There are many things about Nina's life—and death—which make me sad, but I am glad I knew her, and I loved her for her strength. Combative and controversial she certainly was, but then, perhaps every Institution should have a Nina.

(D) SCHOOLMATES

CHAPTER EIGHTEEN

School friends

Janet Mothersill

I first met Nina in junior school, Kinnaird Park in Bromley, Kent, and we became friends there. Her father was a much liked GP in the area. Sadly, after 3–4 years there, war was declared and my father, a senior civil servant, was ordered to move his office north from London to Lancashire. We happened to be on holiday in Devon at the moment, so, at very, very short notice, it was arranged for me to go with my cousin to a boarding school in Dorset, Sherborne School for Girls. When the tragic train accident occurred in 1940 and both parents were killed, Nina and Gill (who had been evacuated to the family's recently purchased Cornish home) were placed in the care of their grandmother. She knew of my friendship with Nina, so contacted my parents to find out where I was at school and arranged for Nina to join me in the same House at Sherborne. We remained good friends and went on one camping trip together, but otherwise lived too far apart to see much of each other in holidays.

Being slightly older than Nina, I went to Cambridge in 1945, reading classics. Nina stayed at school another year and went to Somerville College, Oxford, in 1946. I understood later that the Headmistress felt that she was not good enough in the sciences then to get a university place, and, therefore, she read Modern Languages. In fact, she did extremely well at college and led some committees. After matriculation, she went to stay with a friend, I think in America, and it was only then that she accepted that she had really always wanted to be a doctor. Therefore, she applied to some well-known London hospitals and, having taken entrance exams, Barts (St Bartholomew's) were so impressed by a mature and interesting essay that she wrote that they agreed to take her provided she did some chemistry and physics studies. As a medical student she did outstandingly well, and took, I think, a number of prizes.

I married in 1949 and she was, of course, the bridesmaid, along with my sister-in-law to be. During my married life we saw little of each other, sadly, though I did have a brief holiday in Polstangey when my eldest daughter was very small. We did just keep in touch and she sent me all her published works, which I much enjoyed. Once she retired I did the odd visit to Leighton Buzzard, but not enough. My husband died in May 1997 after three years of illness needing my constant care. I knew Nina was not well, and my great sadness was that after my husband's death I thought at last I would have the opportunity to visit her, but that was not to be, as I got the news of her sad death.

Nina was a lovely person, vibrant, good fun, and highly intelligent. I miss her.

CHAPTER NINETEEN

That sense of awe

Jane Reid

I first knew Nina when I arrived at Sherborne School, aged twelve, in 1945 and she was an awesome eighteen and head of my house, more grown up than the grown-ups, more distant than the staff. Soon, she departed for Oxford to read—languages was it?—and I, in due course, followed her there.

Later, I got to know her quite well and had great delight in her company. We met at her sister Gill's house only every five years or so, but nevertheless we were friends. We had wonderful conversations, picking up topics from the last time, exploring every kind of subject from every kind of angle. It was always stimulating, always fun. But I never quite lost that sense of awe. As a young woman, in the conformist climate of the 1950s, Nina had the strength and determination to be different, to go back to O-levels to qualify for medical school after finishing her Arts BA, and to undertake the long years of study and practice that brought her to the pinnacle of a profession chosen, perhaps, because through it she could help people deal with the trauma in their lives. I admired her for her humour and her humanity, her integrity and her wisdom, but perhaps most of all for her courageous and high-minded pursuit of distinction.

CHAPTER TWENTY

A knock on my door

Antonia Gransden

I must have met Nina in Hall at Somerville College, Oxford, for one day there was a knock on my door, and there she was. She asked me in her cheerful voice whether I'd like to come and have coffee, so I did, with three or four others. After that, I often went and had coffee with her and other friends, usually Linnet Birley (now deceased), Anne Earle, and sometimes Annette Warburton (later Dame!). We had wonderful, hilarious chats; those were delightful times. We had Nescafe with condensed milk ... very delicious in those austere post war days. Sometimes we had cake, or crystallized fruit, which, as far as I remember, Nina got from her uncle in Kenya, or Anne Earle had sent from America. Occasionally, it was coffee in my room, but Nina always tended to be the giver, then and later, in our lives, and I the most grateful receiver, though I did feel rather guilty about that.

About Nina personally, she was beautiful, tall and slim, with a slight stoop. Occasionally, she daringly bought an expensive article of clothing ... I particularly remember a black velvet jacket. Also a beige dress. I can see her with her prayer book, ready to set out for church. She was a regular churchgoer in those days.

She was always cheerful and seemed so self-confident. Once she told me how she had hit some encroaching young man (was he called Hish?) on the head with a tennis racquet . . .

Once, in confidence, she told me of the tragic death of her parents and the difficult time after that, at home and at school. But I didn't learn until much later that her cheerful, self-confident manner hid problems and unhappiness.

To me she was a magic, golden person.

CHAPTER TWENTY-ONE

A very special time

Anne E. Knight

Nina was a marvellous friend, indeed my best friend at Oxford, and we remained close until her death. She made Somerville a memorable experience for me, though what I remember most of all is that we had a blast. She had the most brilliant and enquiring mind I have encountered. She "read" modern languages, but yet knew more about PPE (Politics, Philosophy & Economics—my subject) than I ever learnt! She had a commanding presence, but was never bossy or arrogant; she was generous, with a marvellous sense of humour, and was intellectually ahead of us all. She was a very popular president of the JCR (Junior Common Room, equivalent to a Students' Union). An unforgettable three years, including haunting tobacco shops for cigarettes, in short supply in those post war years! And what was the pub we frequented regularly? I forget! She introduced me to squash and chess (and regularly beat me), and her home in Cornwall was my home during my time in the UK. One long vacation was spent bicycling through the Highlands of Scotland in some appalling weather; never shall I forget the Moor of Rannoch. We went climbing on the Isle of Skye. Another vacation, we worked for a travel agency (run by the husband of the Principal of Somerville, Janet Vaughan) escorting schoolchildren across Paris, putting them on trains to join French families . . . or, for all we knew, the white slave traffic. I don't think we lost any.

It was a very special time in my life.

(E) FAMILY

CHAPTER TWENTY-TWO

Little Christmas

Mary Nottidge

N ina was my godmother, or Buddha-Mum, as she referred to herself. Having studied medicine at Bart's with my father in the 1950s, she had been part of the same group of devout Christians known as the St Augustine's Society. My father introduced her to my mother before they were married and the three of them remained great friends until her death in 1997. She once told my father, "I've come to the conclusion that God for me is an interval between lovers". When my parents approached her to be my godmother she was already exploring Buddhism and my mother was concerned that she might not want to accept the role. Their hope was that a godparent might give their children an adult friend, an alternative to the parents, rather than testing them on the Ten Commandments. Ever quick, Nina's reply was, "But of course I shall constantly be asking Mary if she's committing adultery!" By the time I knew her she was a Buddhist and the most fabulous godmother you could wish for. She had a marvellous ability to make one feel incredibly special and was adored by the whole family.

From the age of about two or three she and I developed a game where I would call "Nina!" and she would reply "Mary!" and this would be repeated again and again with increasing speed until we were both tongue-tied and giggling. We must have carried it on for years until I became too self-conscious to play. Not that you needed to be self-conscious with Nina.

Nina was always interested in what I was doing or what I was "into", and from an early age we had a special and affectionate relationship. She would come upstairs into my bedroom, which visiting adults rarely did, and we would talk about what I was reading or thinking, what was happening at school, or we would pore over magazines together, looking at pictures of the Princess of Wales, of whom we were both great fans in the early years.

She visited us every year in spring or summer and brought with her wonderful presents of books for my brother and me, always managing somehow to catch the mood of the moment, whatever stage we were at. Books that Nina gave me have remained firm favourites. She introduced me to Jane Gardam's *Black Faces, White Faces*, Iris Murdoch with *The Sea, The Sea*, and Ruth Prawer Jhabvala's *How I Became a Holy Mother*, and I have no doubt that my love of literature stems from the delightful journey of exploration that she set me on from an early age. When I was seventeen, she sent me a book entitled *Choices—A Teenage Girl's Practical Workbook for Career and Personal Planning*, by Mindy Bingham, Judy Edmonston, and Sandy Stryker. It was September, but Nina wrote explaining, "An early Christmas present, darling, because it's just out, and it's so fascinating, why should you wait?" My eyes were opened and the world became my oyster.

Those Nina weekends were such fun, my parents happy and relaxed in the company of their dear friend; her humour, her alternative outlook on life (so exciting for teenagers), her menthol cigarettes which I found so glamorous, her ability to tell my father not to be absurd (and his ability, on those occasions alone, to laugh at himself), as well as the fabulous food my mother cooked in Nina's honour. There was a pudding that, according to family legend, Nina had tasted and declared "This is heaven! Can we have this every time I come?" We did, and it was ever more known as "Nina-Pud".

Nina's visits came to be known as Little Christmas, signifying to us how special they were, regular but not frequent, festive eating, and the exchange of gifts. My memory is that the sun always shone on a Nina weekend. The excitement surrounding her arrival was great and the atmosphere was wonderful. On the Saturday evening, the adults would dress up and go out to dinner. One year, elegant Nina wore a brightly coloured long dress slashed up one side to her thigh. I asked her why her dress had a slit and she demonstrated to me how the slit could reveal an enticing section of leg and then be "demurely" covered up if it showed too much. I've never forgotten it. It was more of a lesson on dressing and sexual behaviour than I ever got from my mother.

One year when she was staying I was asked to go up to her room and tell her it was breakfast time. I knocked on the door but heard no reply and, assuming her to be asleep, I decided it would be best to go in and wake her. Nina was sitting bolt upright on a chair just inside the door, deep in meditation. On hearing me enter she must have opened her eyes to see me looking at her, completely astonished. "Are you all right?!" I asked. She nodded, closed her eyes, and went back to her meditation and, although I had the sense that I had barged in on something very private, there was no admonishment and no problem.

Through the eyes of a teenager, Nina brought with her a sense of mysticism, inner wisdom, and exciting alternatives to the status quo. As teenagers she enabled us to ask taboo questions, talk about sex and drugs, try her cigarettes, and think the unthinkable right under our parents' noses. I once asked her why she had never married and she looked at me and said, "I didn't want anyone telling me I couldn't watch the telly because the football was on. Or demanding, 'where's my clean shirt?'" Of course, I thought, why would *anyone* get married?

Nina was the perfect antidote to controlling and old-fashioned parents. After years of pleading with my parents to allow me to have my ears pierced, I know it was Nina who, when asked by my parents, persuaded them there was no real reason to deny me any longer. In true fairy-godmother style she went on to support my heart's desire with Christmas and "Little Christmas" presents of the loveliest dangly earrings of the sort any teenager would die for.

She continued to be supportive long after I had left home; talking me through a time of acute eating disorder where my parents seemed unable to react with anything but conflict, and responding to a bout of angst and depression by arranging some psychotherapy for me in Oxford where I was studying. She invited me to her house in Hampstead just once, when I was working in London during one of my university vacations. She made a fabulous vegetarian meal, which we ate on our laps in her sitting room and talked about sexuality, feminism, euthanasia, and favourite books. In my final year she visited me at Oxford and met some of my closest friends, all of whom entirely appreciated the honour of meeting her. When I got engaged she counselled me closely on my reasons for wanting to get married (how could I not remember the telly and shirt comments?!) and gave her final seal of approval by giving the oration on my behalf at our wedding in February 1997.

One image that she left me I still cherish to this day. At the time I didn't really understand it although I've come round entirely to her way of thinking. My idea of a perfect evening, she once told me, is to be invited to a party with all my favourite friends taking place just next door and to feel I might pop in at any time if I want to, but actually to have chosen to stay at home curled up with a good book.

CHAPTER TWENTY-THREE

A chink of craziness

Penelope Twine

I have struggled to put my thoughts about Nina into succinct words, as she was such an important person to me, in so many ways. Her patience and listening skills were an inspiration. Her intellect and humour could challenge and encourage at the same time. Her astute remarks were so personal and memorable, even years later. And a chink of craziness flavoured all parts of her and gave her that extra edge.

I miss her frequently and am reminded of her in bizarre ways. The internal walls of the WC block above a favourite beach in Cornwall have been painted deep purple and bright pink—colours I immediately associate with Nina. She loved, and often wore, them. A new Jane Gardam book came out this summer; Nina introduced me to this author, along with many others, through her genuine, unsnobbish love of modern literature.

Nina made one feel special and worthwhile, and confident that, if you worked hard, you could achieve. She was such a wonderful aunt, mentor, friend, and person to have known. It's a cliché, but I really do feel it was a privilege to have been her niece.

CHAPTER TWENTY-FOUR

Memories of Neen

Martin Preston

Two great big suitcases, bulging with lots and lots of Christmas presents. That seems to be a major part of my early memories of Nina. Her arrival marked the real start of Christmas, when the presents under the tree would suddenly double in number and the excitement and anticipation climbed up several notches.

As the youngest child in Nina's limited immediate family I had no idea at all as to her professional position. She was just "Nina", or "Neen", as we always called her: "Neen, Neen, beautiful Neen, the beautifulest woman that ever was seen". We would chant the childish rhyme, made up by my sister, I think, and look forward to her visits. There was always something slightly glamorous and mysterious about her. She managed to express an amazing sense of closeness and trust combined with the tiniest hint of aloofness and privacy.

You could trust her, you could talk with her, you could express and explore your thoughts, fears, and feelings. She was a great "accepter" and a fine example of love, tolerance, and generosity. She could also be incredibly stubborn. She lived alone and she had found her own way through her personal traumas and pain. She liked things to be the way she wanted them and perhaps her family, especially her sister, my mother, were the only people with whom she felt relaxed enough to "let go" and show that even The Great Nina Coltart could sometimes be extremely pissed off and petulant. She had a minor obsession about punctuality. Given her early experience of waiting for her parents on the train that never arrived, she would get anxious if people were late. When visiting her, I would always make sure I was slightly early, then ring her doorbell at the exact time that I had told her I would arrive.

Her other strange obsession was her relationship with cigarettes. She was one of the heaviest smokers I have ever known and I am sure that her smoking, combined with the sedentary lifestyle of the academic and psychoanalyst, contributed to her early death. She believed that non-smokers were jealous of the pleasure she gained and she had very little tolerance of anyone who objected to her smoking. Once when I was ill in bed, she came to keep me company and play a game of cards. She smoked the entire time she was with me! It was almost as if she had focused all her personal madness into her smoking, enabling her to be so kind, caring, and generally absolutely wonderful in everything else.

She certainly had a great influence on me and she provided a point of steadiness that helped me mature and come through all my own problems. She had a knack for saying or doing just the right thing to get your thoughts pointing in the healthiest direction. She would never force it or try to push. She would put the information in front of you and let you pick it up and take it in when you were ready. I see this most clearly in her insight into my own sense of spirituality.

Like her, I had been a very devout Christian in my teens. Also like her, I had found Christianity to be increasingly unfulfilling as I grew into adulthood. I found it raised more questions than it answered, it had too many internal inconsistencies, and I couldn't reconcile it with my knowledge of physics and biology. She had gone through a similar process and it had left her with what she described as a "God-shaped hole". For her, Buddhism provided the solution. Somehow she knew that it would not be quite right for me. When I got confirmed as an Anglican (aged seventeen and of my own free will) she gave me two things: a beautifully handwritten copy of the seventeenth-century "Desiderata", found in a church in Baltimore (she was a talented calligrapher), and a copy of Lao Tzu's *Tao Te Ching*.

The Desiderata ("Go placidly amidst the noise and haste and remember what peace there may be in silence", etc.) hung above my bed and I read it every day. The book just sat on a shelf. About seven years later, the universe (or "God" . . .) played a wonderful joke on me. When I told Nina about it we went into uncontrollable giggles together at the scatological nature of what had occurred and at how one sometimes needs a shock or surprise in order to move forwards. I had recently started learning Tai Chi Chuan, or "Chinese Yoga", not knowing that it had any connection at all with *Tao Te Ching*. Simultaneously, I just happened to decide that it was about time I started on this book that Neen had given me. Books that you read by dipping into are often best kept for the smallest room in the house. So there I was, just building up pressure, and opening *Tao Te Ching* for the very first time. It fell open at random. I looked down and saw the words "Empty yourself of everything . . ."!

Thanks to Nina's insight into my nature and character, and her delicate and minimal action in influencing me, I have filled my own "God-shaped hole".

Another big parallel I see between myself and Nina is our interest in medicine and healing. I remember feeling something of a cold shiver when I read her description of how and why she decided to become a doctor. It was because of her father. He had been a GP and, of course, he had been on that train that never came in. Her urge to be a doctor was partly due to her own natural desire to help and heal and largely due to her need to fulfil her father's destiny. I went through very much the same experience. I was aged eight when I decided to become a doctor, and I remember very clearly that it was almost entirely because I wanted to honour the grandfather that I had never known. Years later I realized that in fact I was trying to become my mother's father, being driven by an urge to help her rather than any desire to be an actual doctor. Perhaps this is why Nina moved into psychoanalysis and I went into osteopathy—we both wanted to help and heal, we both wanted to be the missing man, and neither of us actually wanted to practise medicine.

My final link to Nina was spooky and intriguing. I can't explain it in any way except to invoke tenuous concepts of energy fields and patterns of resonance. One day, for no apparent reason, I just couldn't get Nina out of my mind. We all knew that she was fading and my mother had been looking after her. I kept thinking about her and thinking about her. I felt a strong desire to phone her, but knew that she was not well enough to answer or talk to anyone. Nevertheless I even had the exact words in my head for the message I wanted to leave on her answer machine. I dismissed it and got on with my day and I shall always regret not leaving that message: "Hi Neen. It's Martin here. I don't know if you can hear me right now or if you will get this message at all. I just wanted to let you know how much we all love you and appreciate everything you have done for us all over the years and wish you luck on your continued journey".

The next day, my mother phoned to let me know that Nina had died.

Nina was one of the best. She was an extraordinary person, full of love and generosity. I feel privileged to have been part of her life and I am so pleased that her legacy lives on, continuing to bring healing and happiness to so many.

CHAPTER TWENTY-FIVE

Word games

David Preston

I first met Nina in the early 1950s. Her younger sister, Gill, was training to be a teacher and became friends with my sister, Angela. Long before I married Gill, I visited her and Nina at their home in Cornwall in order to fetch Angela, who had been holidaying with them. My dog, Tom, was *not* popular with their wirehaired terrier, and I myself was not particularly popular, as I omitted to bring my ration book. I remember thoroughly enjoying a series of word games, at which Nina naturally excelled. This in a way epitomized my rather jokey relationship with Nina, which reached a high point in the punning postcard I sent—and the post office successfully delivered—to her Hampstead address at 1A, Well Road.

Won, Eh? Well Rowed!

143

Figure 2. Well Road in mid-1980s: lithograph by Matthew Wright.

CHAPTER TWENTY-SIX

A five-minute introduction*

Gillian Preston

A t last I've made it, though I did wonder when a points failure at Redhill station delayed all the trains by an hour!

Thank you for continuing to include me, and thank you for keeping Nina's name alive in this unique way.

For some of you I maybe am a new name and new face . . . I am Nina's kid sister by four and a half years. I could title the next few minutes "101 things you never knew, and could not possibly guess about Nina". One of my earliest memories is of her chasing me round the garden of our house in Kent, where our father was a GP, trying to put earthworms down my neck. I don't think she succeeded, nor do I think it did me any lasting trauma. I quite like them, especially in my compost heap. She also had devious ways of playing on my childhood fear of the dark . . . our Cornish home, at

---

* Remarks delivered on 19 June 2007 at the Institute of Psychoanalysis on the occasion of the Fourth Annual Nina Coltart Memorial Lecture, given by Michael Brearley and sponsored by the Arbours Association.

145

that time being lit by oil lamps and candles, which gave her plenty of scope . . . in retrospect, it seems a little out of character?

She came to medicine late, having read French and Spanish at Somerville College, Oxford, where she was a popular President of the Junior Common Room, and managed to collect a half-blue in squash along the way.

She had a natural gift for languages, and, as we both left a prestigious girls' public school almost innumerate (though I did win batting gloves for scoring over fifty runs in a house match, Mike!), she assumed a career in medicine was not for her, but the perspicacious Principal of Somerville, Janet Vaughan, herself a doctor, encouraged her to apply to St Bartholomew's Medical School, which had a tradition of accepting mature students with previous careers. Despite scoring 10 of 100 in the maths paper—we reckon 10 for trying—she was offered a place. Here she became President of the Students Union, and, among other extracurricular activities, she was a memorable Miss Prism in a production of *The Importance of Being Ernest* . . . Margaret Rutherford she was not . . .

She played chess to a high standard, and it was a bad day if the *Times* crossword was not finished by 10.00 a.m.

As children, we drew and painted a lot, and when our first son, Jonathan, was born, she found an old copy of Walter de la Mare's "Peacock Pie", and illustrated nearly every poem in it for him.

She enjoyed doing intricate embroidery, and late in life she developed a passion and gift for calligraphy and illumination, attending annual summer schools. We have some fine examples.

She was an eclectic and omnivorous speed reader, a lover of classical music and opera, especially Mozart. And of all artists, Vermeer was her absolute favourite. It was the quiet calm stillness that appealed, she said. Perhaps the first one she saw was the lovely one in Kenwood.

And, of course, there were her worldwide trips, both professional and private, though the Trans-Siberian Railway trip left her cold in more ways than one.

I imagine most of you remember her seated in one of her professional, semi-professional, or private guises. Well, I have news for you . . . she not only loved mountains, she climbed them . . . in the 1950s and 1960s, there were several trips to the Italian Alps, the Dolomites, and Cuillin Ridge on Skye.

I end with a footnote to climbing history. Our eldest son is a professional mountain guide, the training for which, incidentally, is as long as for medicine and the law (and quite right, too). He was very close to Nina. And in May 1998, he, with seven others, went on a second expedition to Greenland. To the Sefstron Glacier, in the Stauning Alps, in S. E. Greenland. There, on 11 May, he, with three others, climbed the second highest of four unclimbed peaks, at 2395 metres, and named it, as was subsequently officially recorded, Mount Coltart . . . So look carefully next time you have access to a map of Greenland! Thank you.

(F) READERS

CHAPTER TWENTY-SEVEN

Bare attention: the love that is enough?

Gherardo Amadei and Sara Boffito

What prompted us to write about Nina Coltart is a sense of awe at her willingness to talk about herself, which makes her a unique figure in the psychoanalytic world, where therapists are over-fearful of showing themselves outside the comfortable shelter of their consulting rooms. "The writings of analytical therapists are on the whole deliberately impersonal. . . . This feature has developed almost a quality of taboo" (Coltart, 1993a, p. 97). The experience of reading Coltart is very different from that of reading traditional psychoanalytic literature, because, in all her pages, she is wholly present, *as a person*. And she was wholly present in the clinical situation as well, as she clearly implied when she wrote that her aim when "doing psychotherapy" was " 'engaging with the patient' in the fullest possible way" (p. 17).

It is fully consistent, therefore, that in the final chapter of the book she devoted to the many facets of the professional life of psychotherapists, she felt it necessary to focus on a set of problems that are usually neglected by psychoanalytic authors, for we cannot recall any other works that directly engage with *the bodily and spiritual problems of the therapist*, their being just like any other people.

And since psychoanalysts, just like any other people, have a *body*, Nina Coltart, to our surprise and wonderment, enriches her book about clinical psychoanalysis with precious suggestions on how to cope with the very real fact that clinical work "is probably the most sedentary job there is", forcing therapists "to sit still for many hours of every working day" (1993a, p. 97). We cannot help being affected by her close concern for the practical needs of the therapist, while at the same time we marvel at how little space in the now boundless field of psychoanalytic literature is given to topics such as the beneficial effects of "making the sedentary body to do some work", by which Coltart is not referring to merely "going for a walk" (p. 98). Here, at long last, we meet a psychoanalyst who feels the need to say—and write—that in order to survive as a psychotherapist one doesn't just need a good analysis or good supervisions or to attend the right conferences, one also needs a garden to tend. That is, one must seek that "primitive sort of satisfaction" the body feels when "it uses all one's muscles" (p. 98), as in swimming or playing squash. The aim is to reach an "alertness in one's very perception as well as one's muscles" (p. 98), which is part of a more general "informed responsibility for the self" p. 111).

Equally beneficial and refreshing is to read that the *spirit* too "needs stimulation" (1993a, p. 98), and that one should engage in other activities than those inherent to one's profession. You do not live off sessions, papers, and seminars alone: "the diversions that we choose will cover a wide range of enjoyable sources of psychic nourishment, my only stipulation being that they should *not* be concerned with analysis or therapy" (p. 98).

Nina Coltart has a warning for us: just as the *body*, when it is deprived of exercise, slows down, becomes numb, and is atrophied, so does the *spirit* that is deprived of nourishment wither into narrow, repetitive, and rigid views. Total identification with one's profession, no matter how involving it is, leads to a "shrinking" of the spirit: there is a risk of beginning to think that personal analysis and psychoanalytic theory have an answer to all of life's questions, and that belonging to a Psychoanalytical Society will solve all questions of identity. Both these beliefs—in a single, all-explaining theory from which to draw words that save us from all perils, and in one "church" that originates that theory and those words—are typical of religious communities, and, as Nina Coltart writes, "some of the signs of investing psychoanalysis with religious significance include devotion to the point of fanaticism; exclusive absorption; the ascribing of omnipotence of certain individuals, or techniques; and the implicit belief in the ability to possess the truth" (1993a, p. 108).

Coltart considers these widespread and mostly unconscious tendencies, which perhaps are to be found in all intellectual communities, as a symptom of "the therapist's need for a philosophy of life" (1993a, pp. 108–109); if he tries to satisfy that need with psychoanalysis, as some have done, he will run the risk of developing quasi-religious ideological traits which would be a betrayal of his founding project.

Not to benumb *body* and *spirit* alike, but to prevent their stiffening, is the lesson we draw from Coltart, whose clinical practice was founded on keeping "every sense . . . on the alert" (1993a, p. 22), thereby developing that "bare attention" which we see as the fundamental distinguishing characteristic of her approach to her work and probably also to life, since it ultimately is "a kind of loving" (1992c, p. 119).

For Nina Coltart, attention was "the constant matrix of a positive therapeutic attitude to our work" (1992b, p. 110), "the scaffolding for everything else we do" (1990, p. 181), an act of faith, and a paradoxical feature. She described it as direct, sustained, unflagging, willed, unceasing, perpetual, "both detached and involved, both scanning and focused" (1992b, p. 110); as a "highly disciplined and hard-earned skill" (1992a, p. 141); as prolonged, careful, and humane, directed to the immediate present, a "profound and self-forgetful opening of oneself to another person" (1990, p. 182); and as single-minded, close, and empathic, "as uncluttered as possible, *informed* by memory, but functionally free from it" (1993a, p. 61).

Attention is, thus, a talent, but it also requires constant development and training because nothing is easier to lose. To describe attention, Coltart needed to avail herself of another adjective, in addition to those listed earlier, which single-handedly encompassed the others and freed them from their apparent contradictions: she defined it as "bare", borrowing the term from Buddhist traditions in which "bare attention" is the distinguishing characteristic of the practice of meditation. As Coltart herself explained in a poignant interview with Anthony Molino:

> Bare attention has a sort of purity about it. It's not a cluttered concept. It's that you simply become better, as any good analyst knows, at concentrating more and more directly, more purely, on what's going on in a session. You come to concentrate more and more fully on this person who is with you, here and now, and on what it is they experience with you: to the point that many sessions become similar to meditations. [Molino, 1997, p. 205]

It is precisely in those moments in which the therapist's attention is "focused sharply with little effort", or else when he feels he knows nothing about the patient and will never understand him, that "light begins to shine through the darkness, and you have a brief phase of enlightenment about what is happening between you and your patient; and the gift of communicating an insight in *appropriate language* often suddenly occurs as part of this phenomenon" (Coltart, 1990, p. 181). Bare attention is what permits these moments of illumination (Bion (2005, p. 24) used the same word for them), ensuring that they are not simply the result of an isolated case or of the difficulty of the patient–therapist situation in a given moment, but rather that they are, even in their unpredictability, the consequence of an activity that is intentional and deliberate. Coltart certainly made no effort to hide the difficulty of holding oneself in that place of bare attention; on the contrary, she knew that what sometimes permitted treatment to go forward was a "willed and heroic attempt to maintain an island of attention in ourselves" and that "all we can hang on to is a recollection of what we know, a sort of flash of memory about the capacity to be attentive or detached" (1990, p. 186).

In place of the standard translation of *gleichschwebende Aufmerksamkeit* (as "evenly suspended attention"), Coltart preferred to use the term "evenly hovering attention":

> Only by the most continuous endeavour to focus an "evenly hovering attention" on all that is going on can we hope to maintain an equilibrium so that we can continue to *work*, to be of therapeutic value to the patient, and not to disintegrate ourselves. [1990, p. 185]

This choice of terminology, which has become rather common in recent psychoanalytic literature, allowed Coltart to use the term "focus" and gives us the opportunity to note an important distinction. The difference between "being suspended" and "hovering" is not some intellectual nuance or aesthetic quirk; rather, the difference lies precisely in the application of the will and, in a certain sense, of creativity. Any object that is light enough can remain suspended, but hovering requires an effort, a degree of intentionality, and even a certain amount of playfulness.

This type of intentionality is, like attention, a paradoxical feature, for one could justly observe that bare attention consists in precisely its opposite, that is to say, in the ability to let go, to focus on the here and now of experience by losing sight of its goal, its initiating intention, or its purpose. It is an over-seeing which obviously has nothing to do with distraction, carelessness, or inattention: any analyst striving to concentrate "more and more directly, more purely, on what's going on in a session" (Molino, 1997, p. 205) knows as well as any teacher of meditation that letting go requires intentional effort and concentration; similarly, bare attention and the analyst's tentative yielding to it while striving to keep his balance must be sustained by intention, before the former becomes "second nature".

Of all psychoanalytic authors, Wilfred Bion is the one who dealt the most directly with attention and engaged with its paradoxical qualities as bravely as Coltart. The practice of bare attention is what makes it possible to be comfortable in the state that is "the essence of our impossible profession" (Coltart, 1986, p. 2): not knowing what we are doing. We do know that, through an act of faith, our attention is capable of hovering freely and that it becomes "more total when temporarily freed from concurrent cognitive process" (p. 8)—when it is "denuded" of memory and desire, as Bion proposed. Perhaps Bion is more emphatic and less poetic in his writing style, but he is clearly in accord with such concepts when he writes, "No one who denudes himself of memory and desire, and of all those elements of sense impression ordinarily present, can have any doubt of the reality of psycho-analytical experience which remains ineffable" (1970, p. 35). The work of withdrawing from memory and desire is clearly aimed at creating the conditions necessary for the emergence of an emotion of "here-and-now" purity. In order to be like an "officer in war" who sustains his attention even when overwhelmed by the roar of battle (Bion's analogy), the analyst must become a "feeling person" (Bion, 1980, p. 77). In Bion's exhortation about attention, the emphasis is on the phrase "ordinarily present", since "sense impression" or emotions are experienced, just as in meditation, with greater purity and awareness than usual.

Coltart dedicated a significant portion of her most didactic text, *How to Survive as a Psychotherapist* (1993a), to an explanation of Bion's formulation "without memory and without desire"; she was irritated by the way in which the concept was abused and the superficiality with which it had been adopted. Even earlier, in a 1990 paper later published in *Slouching Towards Bethlehem* (1993b), Coltart had maintained that a kind of "psychic split" was both necessary and invaluable "to foster the capacity to direct single-minded attention to what is happening while at the very same time allowing the inner flow of free-associative thoughts and images" (1992c, p. 117). In *How to Survive as a Psychotherapist*, she commended this same psychic split to students so that they may become capable of attuning their

> full attention in the here and now. [So that] attention will then be as uncluttered as possible, *informed* by memory, but functionally free of it. It will also be free of "desire", by which I understand that one must try to leave aside any wishes or hopes or expectations one may otherwise have for this patient, and how he should be in the here and now and in the future. [1993a, p. 44]

Coltart's emphasis on attention allows us to interpret Bion's necessary split in the service of the ego as a source of creativity and freedom of movement, as the possibility to hover; and it also gives the analyst's mind a wider range by endowing it with qualities that are typical of other outlooks and practices, such as meditation.

As Nina Coltart's work shows, talking about attention is central to clinical practice, for not only is it at the heart of the therapeutic attitude, but it is also the path by which the analyst can attain that attitude and, thus, become a *feeling person*. But for both Coltart and Bion, attention is also a central theoretical foundation, as well as a clinical one. Both authors posited it as "the channel for the transformation of the apprehension of the ultimate reality" (Coltart, 1986, p. 4)—"O", as Bion named it. Following Bion (1970, p. 29), we could certainly say that Nina Coltart was "an analyst whose aim is O".

One of the principal functions of the application of a consistent "bare attention" during analytic work (where it should be all-pervasive to the point of becoming second nature) is to make it possible for the analyst simply to wait, to "sit out the mysterious process day by day" (Coltart, 1991, p. 174), not saturating the atmosphere with answers, but, rather, waiting for a shared creation, or, as Bion put it, the emergence of a "selected fact". What Bion called (following Keats) "negative capability" is one of the ingredients necessary for creating "the deepest atmosphere in which the analysis takes place" (Coltart, 1985, p. 174), an atmosphere that is made equally of patience, waiting, and, naturally, the continued exercise of the "second nature" of bare attention.

It is, thus, becoming clear that Coltart considered attention as first and foremost a moral quality. To explain this, in her paper devoted to attention she quotes a beautiful passage from one of Iris Murdoch's novels:

> I daresay human wickedness is sometimes the product of a sort of conscious leeringly evil intent. . . . But more usually it is the product of a semi-deliberate inattention, a sort of swooning relationship to time. . . .
>
> Body, external objects, darty memories, warm fantasies, other minds, guilt, fear, hesitation, lies, glees, doles, breathtaking pains, a thousand things which words can only fumble at, coexist, many fused together in a single unit of consciousness. . . . How can such a thing be tinkered with and improved, how can one change the quality of consciousness? Around *"will"*, it flows like water round a stone. . . . There is so much grit in the bottom of the container, almost all our natural preoccupations are low ones, and in most cases the rag-bag of consciousness is only unified by the experience of great art or of intense love [and to these I would add "single-minded attention"]. . . . [Murdoch, 1973, pp. 154–155; Coltart, 1990, p. 187; italics and bracketed text by Nina Coltart]

Here, too, that active and creative attitude, intentionality—the "will" around which consciousness so easily flows—appears to be central to this view of attention, so much so that inattention, which is the cause of human wickedness, is defined as *semi-deliberate*; the attention that the analyst gives to the here and now of his patient should, thus, be completely deliberate and aware.

Coltart did not consider following a moral or ethical system to be in contrast with psychoanalysis; indeed, she believed that the "small project" of looking for traces of such morality in all psychoanalytical papers would reveal "a strongly moral infrastructure which informs both the theory and practice of our *Impossible Profession*" (1992c, p. 111). It is not the kind of morality that is represented by the superego of the structural model, but, rather, a quality that is inherent in one's philosophy of analytical theory and practice.

Our own moral systems need to be maintained, as we have seen, by "the application of our willed attention" (Coltart, 1992c, p. 116), the lubricant that will keep our analytical cogs and wheels well-oiled and working smoothly. This particular kind of attention, which in many ways is perhaps really a gift, has in it qualities such as "patience, endurance, humour, kindness and courage", which, under close analysis, appear to be all object-related (pp. 118–119). They can all be subsumed under the name of love. "Love is a transcendental *idea*; human beings long for it, seek it, and many achieve it in all sorts of ways" (p. 119). Coltart believed that contemporary psychoanalysis has done little to clear the current "moral muddle" (p. 113) which is the confusion between the terms "loving" and "being in love".[1]

The love Coltart speaks of, together with all the other themes that are central to her thought, belongs to the realm of the ineffable: "Love is ultimately indefinable by the language of psychological theory" (1992c, p. 120). Being a free gift, love—the capacity to love, which cannot, as we have seen, be reduced to a by-product of sexual drives and their vicissitudes—is not simply a natural characteristic of human beings, to be investigated only by artists and poets: the kind of loving Coltart writes about coincides with willed attention and it is one that "can be learned".[2]

---

[1] Coltart recognizes that Martin Bergmann has been one of the few to address himself to this confusion. In his paper "Freud's three theories of love in the light of later developments" (1988), he sees three different theories corresponding to three phases in Freud's thought: the "genetic" one, beginning with *Three Essays on the Theory of Sexuality* (1905d); the "narcissistic", dealing specifically with the conditions for falling in love, which can be dated from "On narcissism" (1914c); and "the nucleus of the object-related theory", originating in a series of difficult passages in "Instincts and their vicissitudes" (1915c).

[2] Michael Balint (1952), whom Coltart quotes when talking about love, had already identified with love a series of qualities that he thought necessary to a

We are once more faced by a beneficial paradox: a capacity that at the same time can be learnt and should be a natural gift, an innate talent. Moving from such a paradox, Coltart can playfully declare that if, on the one hand, it is true that "love is not enough", yet "All You Need is Love" (1992c, p. 127). This is how she ended her paper devoted to love, to be later included in *Slouching Towards Bethlehem*. Its provocative title, "What does it mean: 'Love is not enough'?", echoes that of an early work by Bruno Bettelheim, *Love Is Not Enough* (1950), a title which Bettelheim himself later turned upside down in his paper "The love that is enough", in which, though in a very special and entirely different context, he stressed how psychotherapy should not be seen "as merely a complex intellectual task", but "also a direct emotional and personal encounter" (Bettelheim, 1975, p. 252).

This insistence on love, *real* love, might suggest the idyllic and optimistic view of a consulting room from which all negative feelings and emotions have vanished, leaving only magical harmony. Coltart was well aware of the confusion her words could engender on that point, as is shown by her explanation that love—as any good enough mother knows, we might say—"is not necessarily the prevailing affective experience in the analyst", and it is precisely in this sense that it is a true transcendence: "it is the only trustworthy container in which we may have to *feel* hatred, rage or contempt for varying periods of time. These are the occasions when the countertransference comes into its own as our most sensitive instrument" (1992c, p. 121).

True, despite their recourse to the kind of loving that can be learnt, "bare attention", apprentice therapists may still find certain situations rather thorny, but Coltart has not left them to face these difficulties alone. She left future practitioners of psychoanalytic psychotherapy two "golden rules": "When in doubt, say nothing", and "Prune where you can" (1992b, p. 102). The pruning metaphor is particularly well suited to psychoanalytical practice, because it is

---

creative technique, and which Coltart summarizes as "sensitivity, choice, generosity, the ability to be open to a certain sort of identification, and tenderness" (1992c, p. 119). He had maintained that a full capacity for loving is not archaic, like oral greed or anal possessiveness, but must be learnt, and he considered it a capacity which the child learns during its primary relationship.

a task that requires close attention: a person engaged in pruning must concentrate on dead branches—on the bathwater—and spare the buds (the baby), leaving them room to grow, confident that the goal of his or her work is the birth of something new and, to some extent, unforeseeable.

We could say that if, on the one hand, Coltart urged analysts to leave their consulting rooms and find their own gardens, on the other hand, through the quality of her attention, she brought the garden into the consulting room, or transformed the room into a garden, and saw her patients' selves as buds whose growth had to be encouraged, allowing herself to be surprised day by day by the birth of something new.

* * *

Attention seems to us to be also a personal trait, as well as the central tenet of Coltart's theoretical thought, and one of the virtues that have made of her an unforgettable and legendary figure. We began studying this author a few years after her death, in a country (Italy) where she is hardly as well-known and loved as she is in Britain. What fascinated us, besides the depth of her thought, was the extraordinary combination of decision and delicacy with which she approached themes that are often not easily definable and which shines through her vivid clinical descriptions. We believe it is a unique literary gift, the same that Christopher Bollas ascribes to her in his Foreword to *The Baby and the Bathwater* (1996), an ability to express on paper what she, quoting Betty Joseph, considered a core factor in the analyst's mental state: the ability "to keep the countertransference as 'pure' as possible" (1992b, p. 98). The image of the rough beast and its slouching is but one example of the extraordinary literary gift of this author.

When we came to single out attention as our theme, among those that are at the basis of her thought, we found ourselves thinking a lot about Nina Coltart as a human being, as well as the subtle theoretician who wrote the books we loved. Delicacy and decision, rigorousness of thought and the ability to evoke an atmosphere with just one metaphor are indeed literary qualities, and also, for analysts (and perhaps not just for them), personal qualities—we might even call them, taking our cue from Coltart herself, moral qualities. Many of them, as we went deeper into her work, appeared to be subsumed under the one word "attention"; in other words, being attentive was an aspect of Coltart's nature, and it was perhaps this deep and ubiquitous quality of such an extraordinary independent figure that attracted our *attention* most.

References

Balint, M. (1952). *Primary Love and Psycho-Analytic Technique*. London: Hogarth.
Bergmann, M. (1988). Freud's three theories of love in the light of later development. *Journal of the American Psychoanalytic Association*, 36: 653–672.
Bettelheim, B. (1950). *Love Is Not Enough: The Treatment of Emotionally Disturbed Children*. Glencoe, IL: The Free Press.
Bettelheim, B. (1975). The love that is enough. In: P. Giovacchini (Ed.), *Tactics and Techniques in Psychoanalytic Therapy. Vol.II: Countertransference* (pp. 251–278). New York: Jason Aronson.
Bion, W. R. (1970). *Attention and Interpretation*. London: Tavistock.
Bion, W. R. (1980). *Bion in New York and São Paolo*, F. Bion (Ed.). Strathtay, Perthshire: Clunie Press.
Bion, W. R. (2005). *The Tavistock Seminars*. London: Karnac.
Coltart, N. (1985). The practice of psychoanalysis and Buddhism. In: *Slouching Towards Bethlehem . . . and Further Psychoanalytic Explorations* (pp. 164–175). London: Free Association Books, 2002.
Coltart, N. (1986). Slouching towards Bethlehem . . . or thinking the unthinkable in psychoanalysis. In: *Slouching Towards Bethlehem . . . and Further Psychoanalytic Explorations* (pp. 1–14). London: Free Association Books, 1993.
Coltart, N. (1990). Attention. In: *Slouching Towards Bethlehem . . . and Further Psychoanalytic Explorations* (pp. 176–193). London: Free Association Books, 1993.
Coltart, N. (1991). The silent patient. In: *Slouching Towards Bethlehem . . . and Further Psychoanalytic Explorations* (pp. 79–94). London: Free Association Books, 2002.
Coltart, N. (1992a). Manners makyth man: true or false? In: *Slouching Towards Bethlehem . . . and Further Psychoanalytic Explorations* (pp. 128–143). London: Free Association Books, 1993.

Coltart, N. (1992b). On the tightrope: therapeutic and non-therapeutic factors in psychoanalysis. In: *Slouching Towards Bethlehem . . . and Further Psychoanalytic Explorations* (pp. 95–110). London: Free Association Books, 1993.

Coltart, N. (1992c). What does it mean, "Love is not enough"? In: *Slouching Towards Bethlehem . . . and Further Psychoanalytic Explorations* (pp. 111–127). London: Free Association Books, 1993.

Coltart, N. (1993a). *How to Survive as a Psychotherapist*. London: Sheldon Press.

Coltart, N. (1993b). *Slouching Towards Bethlehem . . . and Further Psychoanalytic Explorations*. London: Free Association Books.

Coltart, N. (1996). *The Baby and the Bathwater*. London: Karnac.

Freud, S. (1905d). *Three Essays on the Theory of Sexuality. S.E., 7*: 125–245. London: Hogarth.

Freud, S. (1914c). On narcissism: an introduction. *S.E., 14*: 67–102. London: Hogarth.

Freud, S. (1915c). Instincts and their vicissitudes. *S.E., 14*: 109–140. London: Hogarth.

Molino, A. (Ed.) (1997). *Freely Associated: Encounters in Psychoanalysis with Christopher Bollas, Joyce McDougall, Michael Eigen, Adam Phillips, Nina Coltart*. London: Free Association Books.

CHAPTER TWENTY-EIGHT

In praise of Nina Coltart

Peter L. Rudnytsky

"It is of the essence of our impossible profession that in a very singular way we do not know what we are doing".
[Coltart, "Slouching towards Bethlehem", 1986]

1

In reading the work of a psychoanalytic author, there is one question that I think we should ask ourselves above all others: would I want to be in analysis with this person? Is this someone I would trust to probe the innermost recesses of my psyche and with whom I would be likely to have a genuinely therapeutic experience?

To be sure, we also hope to profit intellectually from reading a psychoanalytic paper. But a brilliant theorist may not be the man or woman to whom one would turn for emotional healing. Even today, the figure of Freud casts by far the longest shadow over the psychoanalytic field, while both Klein and Lacan have indubitably expanded the universe of analytic discourse; but I suspect I may not be alone in feeling that I would rather have gone for treatment to

Ferenczi or Winnicott—or, indeed, to any number of lesser mortals, provided they were possessed of genuine humility and compassion.

In proposing that we assess every analytic writer by our readiness to see him or her for therapy, I am asking us to reflect on the image of the human being that we form from reading a given author's work. Indeed, with those of past generations whom we will never have the privilege of meeting in the flesh, the only way we *can* get to know them is through their texts, as well as through the memoirs of others and ancillary historical sources. (This, in turn, is how we will be remembered—if at all—by those who come after us.) Even with our contemporaries, I think we are likely to arrive at a deeper understanding of them by paying close attention to their writings than through ordinary social interactions, though the most intimate communion comes through such privileged relationships as those between teacher and student or analyst and analysand.

As with our teachers and analysts, moreover, it is not by explicit self-disclosures that we develop an inwardness with an author. Rather, it is through the experience of reading itself, the quality of pleasure and illumination it brings us—as well as our sense of the writer's tact, insight, empathy, and skill—that we come to know him or her and make up our minds about whether we would be comfortable lying on that person's couch. Out of this transferential investment in an author, however, there naturally arises a desire for closer acquaintance, a curiosity about what he or she was really like as a person . . .

2

Although she has been largely forgotten, even by mental health professionals, outside of her native England a little more than a decade after her death on 24 June 1997, and I myself regret never having met her during her lifetime, there is no one whom I would rather have had as my analyst than Nina Coltart. My purpose in this essay is to try to put into words something of the love and admiration inspired by my reading of Coltart, in hopes that others may be induced to discover—or rediscover—her work for themselves.

There are several facts about Coltart that need to be brought out immediately. The first is that, besides being a psychoanalyst, she became, for most of her adult life (after having lost the Christian faith of her youth), a Theravadin Buddhist, the practice of which centres on daily meditation; and her writing is informed by a profound synthesis between these two modalities of spiritual healing. The second is that, as far as her analytic allegiances are concerned, Coltart was a leading member of the Independent Group in the British Psychoanalytical Society; indeed, she described herself, in a magnificent late interview with Anthony Molino (1997), as "the most independent representative of the Independent Group" (p. 177). After retiring from clinical practice in December 1994, at the age of sixty-seven, and relocating from Hampstead in northwest London to a rural seat in Leighton Buzzard, moreover, Coltart formally resigned from the British Society, becoming only the third person—after Charles Rycroft and Peter Lomas—to have taken this step in the contemporary era.[1]

In the third place, no study of Coltart can fail to confront the fact that she died by her own hand, from an overdose of sleeping pills. To anticipate my subsequent argument, Coltart's suicide may be seen as either an act of freedom or an act of despair, or as both simultaneously, and how we come to terms with this painful circumstance will be inseparable from our view of Coltart's career as a whole.

Underlying everything else, there is the overwhelming trauma of Coltart's childhood: the train accident in which both of her parents were killed. Along with her sister, Gill, four years her junior, and their devoted nanny, Nina had been evacuated from London to Cornwall during the Second World War. In 1940, Gill contracted a mysterious illness, probably glandular fever; the girls' father, a respected general practitioner, was summoned by the local doctor. Father and mother boarded a night train to the southwest of England. The train jack-knifed, crushing several cars, and Nina, having

---

[1] Fifty years earlier, in 1944, Edward Glover resigned from the British Society in protest against the outcome of the Controversial Discussions. In her interview with Molino (1997, p. 170), Coltart cites the precedents of Rycroft and Lomas, both of whom I interviewed for my book *Psychoanalytic Conversations* (Rudnytsky, 2000).

gone by taxi to meet her parents at the station, was brought home four hours later, having been shielded from the news by the compassionate driver. Only on the following day, after an agonizing delay, was she informed that her parents had died.

Coltart's destiny was indelibly marked by this catastrophe of double parental loss. It largely explains the fact that she "always lived alone" and became known as "quite a recluse" (Molino, 1997, p. 180). She did, to be sure, have a gift for friendships—mainly with women—but she renounced lasting intimacy with a partner of either sex. Coltart was not an ascetic. She was an inveterate smoker, enjoyed a good meal, and, as she told Molino, she developed an "active sex life" in her late twenties, a breakthrough she correlated with having ceased to believe in God "almost overnight" (p. 200). For what it is worth, her sexual orientation appears to have been heterosexual. But it is not only in the professional domain that Coltart cultivated an extreme independence.

To the extent that Coltart's name continues to be remembered today, it is above all as the author of "Slouching towards Bethlehem", a paper she first presented at a conference of English-speaking psychoanalysts in 1982, then published in expanded form in Gregorio Kohon's 1986 volume, *The British School of Psychoanalysis: The Independent Tradition*, before reprinting it in 1993 as the lead essay in the first of her three books. Coltart did not bequeath to psychoanalysis any original theoretical concepts. But "Slouching towards Bethlehem"—the title of which comes from Yeats's poem "The Second Coming"—teaches analysts an invaluable lesson: the necessity of retaining a faith in the analytic process, the outcome of which can never be foreseen, which in turn depends on the capacity to wait without closing down by premature interpretation for the "rough beast" that is struggling to be born in the patient.[2]

As is evident from the sentence I have taken as my epigraph— the most famous that Coltart ever wrote—her stress on faith in experience (as opposed to "Faith" in a transcendental sense)[3] is

---

[2] Coltart quotes "The Second Coming" in full in her paper, and my references to Yeats's poem throughout this chapter are taken from her transcription.

[3] On the distinction between faith with a small and a capital letter, see Coltart (1993a, pp. 110, 113))

allied to a respect for mystery and the readiness to "tolerate not knowing" (1986, p. 3); and in "Slouching towards Bethlehem" Coltart pays tribute to Bion as her precursor in setting forth these principles that are far less recommendations concerning analytic technique than they are compass points for the mind and heart of the analyst. And if, as I have suggested, the true test of an analytic author is whether one would want to be in treatment with him or her, then Coltart bestowed the highest compliment imaginable when she told Molino (1997), "I've always wanted to have my second analysis with Bion" (p. 175).

Coltart left behind a comparatively small body of writing: just three books in all, the first and third of which are collections of papers, *Slouching towards Bethlehem* (1993b) and *The Baby and the Bathwater* (1996b), while only the second, *How to Survive as a Psychotherapist* (1993a), was conceived as a unified work.[4] Almost all of Coltart's writings can be divided into two categories, the first being a gallery of riveting case studies that make her the Jane Austen of psychoanalysis, and the second being her immensely valuable cogitations on practical matters, while a smaller third category comprises her essays on psychoanalysis and Buddhism (1985, 1996d), although the philosophy she spells out here, and in the final pages of *How to Survive as a Psychotherapist*, implicitly informs her exclusively psychoanalytic texts.

Paradoxically enough for a Buddhist, what Coltart has to offer her readers is nothing more or nothing less than her self. But is this not the most important quality one looks for in a healer? Coltart wrote in the same way as she practised. Having been trained first at public school and then at Oxford in the art of essay writing, she always strove "to achieve the greatest simplicity of expression" and to leave out, "as far as possible, technical language or specialized language, so that lay people can read the stuff with some enjoyment" (Molino, 1997, p. 168). What Coltart says of the Enlightened One can, with equal justice, be applied to her own prose:

> The Buddha had a memorable style, he told a lot of stories that show what an astute psychologist he was, and he also had a knack

---

[4] For an outstanding study of Coltart's life and work, see the as yet unpublished monograph by Sara Boffito (2008).

of grouping things so that they hung together; one could rapidly grasp the essentials of what he taught, and then take them away and start absorbing them. [1996d, p. 125]

In what follows, I first undertake a closer scrutiny of Coltart's life, for which the indispensable source is the interview she gave in two instalments to Molino less than a year before her death. Having retired from clinical practice and extricated herself from the trammels of institutional affiliation, secure in the knowledge that she had nothing left to write and very likely already planning to shuffle off this mortal coil, Coltart laid herself bare in this colloquy to a degree that renders my task as an expositor little more than one of recapitulation and synthesis. Besides the interview, I shall also be mining what I believe to be Coltart's most autobiographically revealing paper, "Two's company, three's a crowd" (1996f), about her experience in 1989 as a participant in a course offered by the Institute of Group Analysis.[5] Then, after having placed Coltart's life under the microscope, my endeavour will be to demonstrate how an awareness of their subjective origins enhances our appreciation of her contributions to psychoanalysis. I shall close with some brief reflections on the enigma of her suicide.

3

The inevitable starting point is the death of Coltart's parents. A curious detail, symptomatic of the upheaval resulting from such a blow, is that Coltart refers to the accident as having taken place "when I was eleven", reiterating that "you can't be in analysis for very long without realizing that it's not as if an idyllic, blissfully happy childhood of eleven years was suddenly fractured by a nasty trauma" (Molino, 1997, p. 194). But, since Coltart was born on 21 November 1927, and the train crash occurred on 4 November 1940, she was, in actuality, almost thirteen, not eleven. Psychically, Coltart must have experienced herself as still a child when the tragedy occurred. In any event, as Coltart acknowledges in *How to Survive as a Psychotherapist*, "a certain element of psychopathology, induced by a

---

[5] This paper was delivered in 1991 at a conference sponsored by the same institute, though not published until *The Baby and the Bathwater*.

fracture in my own story, contributed to the vocational sense" that led her to become a psychoanalyst (1993a, p. 101).[6]

As I have already intimated, the sudden loss of her parents is connected quite directly to what she describes in "Two's company, three's a crowd" as "an extreme degree of need of separateness", a quality that Coltart conceded might also be "called critically a sort of stand-offishness" (1996f, p. 50). Even more unwelcome to her than a romantic commitment, which always carries with it the risk of heartbreak through death or infidelity, was the prospect of having children; for, as Coltart told Molino (1997), the "neurosis" induced by her parents' death meant that she "always had an anxiety about having children, and possibly leaving them with such an affliction as being orphaned" (p. 179).

Like many abused or traumatized children, Coltart emerged from the catastrophe of her parents' death with a sense of specialness. Reverting in the interview with Molino (1997) to her metaphor of a "fracture", she expatiates, "a tragedy like that fractures your life completely, and from then on you're a different person, you lead a different life. You've got a secret life. . . . I used to feel secretly that I knew a great deal more than other people" (pp. 191–192). Even after decades as both a psychoanalyst and a Buddhist, Coltart owns up to having preserved "a sort of superiority from such a prolonged struggle with survival" (p. 192). If one were to affix a diagnostic label to Coltart's "psychopathology", it would be difficult to avoid resorting to the term "narcissism", though its outward manifestations are a secondary formation covering over her underlying insecurity and emotional fragility. With characteristic irony, Coltart relished skewering her own vanity. She writes of her "immediate reaction" to an attack unleashed by an elderly male patient that it "was almost entirely governed by my narcissism" (1991b, p. 88), and she confesses that a conversation with one of her "normal" friends outside the psychoanalytic bubble prompted her to "sigh as I realized yet again that I must inspect my narcissism and the possibility that I was idealizing, making special my new-found knowledge" (1993a, p. 57).

---

[6] Elsewhere in this book, Coltart describes herself as someone with "a long-past experience of double parental loss at a vulnerable stage in life (early adolescence)" (1993a, p. 11), which comports better with an age closer to thirteen than to eleven.

Pivotal though the death of her parents undoubtedly was, Coltart's analytically fostered recognition that her childhood had not been "blissfully happy" even before this disaster opens far-reaching vistas. As she elaborates, "I used to get very anxious and cry easily as a child", while her mother was likewise in all probability "anxious and somewhat depressed" because she was "by no means" the "favourite child" of her own mother, who "had a fearful temper and was very jealous" (Molino, 1997, p. 194).

In the trauma that was transmitted through the generations in Coltart's family, the child favoured by Coltart's grandmother was her firstborn son, the elder brother of Coltart's mother. By a tragic irony, however, this son had "fought in and survived the First World War, only to come home and be killed in a motorbike accident just up the road from where the family lived" (Molino 1997, p. 194). The bereavement of Coltart's grandmother was compounded when, "ten years later", her "relatively young husband—a handsome, dashing general practitioner—dropped dead beside her in a theatre queue" (p. 194). Finally, Coltart explains, "ten years after that, her only other child, my mother, died in a train crash" (p. 194).

Given that Coltart's parents died in 1940, and that Coltart's uncle died in the immediate aftermath of the First World War, we can date his death and that of Coltart's grandfather to 1920 and 1930, respectively. Since Coltart's mother had been predeceased by both her brother and father, Coltart infers, she must have been left with "her own increasingly difficult mother to cope with" (Molino, 1997, p. 194) in the years that she and her husband were raising their two young daughters. After their parents' death, Coltart and her sister themselves became wards of this "rather demonic old lady", a "wicked grandmother" who "didn't look after us" as a care-taker should (p. 194). Coltart's insecurity and proclivity to tears even as a young child, therefore, constituted the refracted expressions of her mother's anxiety and depression, which were in turn introjections of the emotional hole left in *her* mother, Coltart's grandmother, by the series of tragic losses that blighted that grim matriarch's life.[7]

---

[7] In a personal communication, Gill Preston has given a different picture of her and Nina's grandmother Hawke, describing her as "a highly intelligent and cultured woman, who had run a highly successful Red Cross Unit in World War I, and had been decorated for it". In later years, she adds, the girls and their

Coltart's crucial insight is that the devastating "fracture" resulting from her parents' death was superimposed on earlier experiences that were themselves cumulatively traumatic—to borrow Masud Khan's (1963) useful concept—and that her tendency as a survivor to be consumed by the massive event had the further deleterious consequence of causing her to idealize the period that had preceded it, impeding access to the grief and anger that lay buried beneath the rubble of the obvious calamity.[8] Coltart cites Winnicott's aphorism that "the dreadful has already happened",[9] which she glosses in illuminating fashion by explaining that the death of her parents "had to be preceded by what the Buddhists call 'preconditioning'", and she recognizes in hindsight that she "was in many ways an anxious child, ready for depression" (Molino, 1997, p. 194).

As I noted earlier, Coltart and her sister Gill were accompanied on their evacuation to Cornwall by their nanny, who had also been their mother's nanny in her youth, and Coltart attests that this "salt of the earth" woman was "always my primary love object" and the "saviour of both my and my sister's sanity" (Molino, 1997, p. 195). Although Coltart's nanny gave her the unstinting devotion that she sought in vain from her mother, the nanny was also a midwife who worked in Coltart's father's medical practice; this meant that, during Coltart's formative years, she would periodically vanish from the family home for weeks at a time to live with a newborn baby and its mother.[10] As Coltart recalls, "I don't think I ever quite

---

grandmother "became good friends. She had a killing sense of humour, and as we grew up, she introduced us to much, especially in literature. We all became closer, with both parties benefiting by it".

[8] In his paper on cumulative trauma, Khan attributes this phenomenon to a "partial breakdown of the protective-shield function of the mother" (1963, p. 52).

[9] Coltart's allusion to Winnicott seems to be to his paper, "Fear of breakdown", probably written in 1963, though not published until after his death. In this influential text, Winnicott elucidates the complex dynamics whereby the breakdown feared by certain patients *"has already been"*, although it is *"not yet experienced"* (1974, pp. 90–91) because it could not be assimilated by the immature ego.

[10] In a personal communication, Gill Preston has again placed things in a different light, stressing that " 'Nan' only left the family home, in Kent, on the rare occasion for a midwifery job *prior* to November 1940, i.e., when we would still be in the care of our mother", and recalling "two or three times, as a small

got the hang of her disappearances; certainly, I never knew when she was coming back, or if she was ever coming back" (Molino, 1997, p. 195). Thus, it was above all in relation to this indispensable person that Coltart became accustomed to "the comings-and-goings of someone so loved, who'd disappear and often fail to return" (p. 195); and this *fort/da* rhythm formed the "preconditioning" for the shattering trauma of her parents' death. "So in a way", Coltart concludes, "my parents never getting to Cornwall on the night they died was the culmination, an apex of sorts, of a dynamic that had always been for me a source of great anxiety" (p. 195).

Luckily, her sister recovered from her illness; had Gill also perished, Coltart had no doubt that she herself would have turned into a "lunatic" (Molino, 1997, p. 191). But the cumulative agonies of separation and loss that preceded the fatal train crash were exacerbated by the ordeals to which the girls were subjected subsequently. As John Bowlby has pointed out, in order for a child to be able to mourn the death of a parent in a healthy fashion, it is indispensable that he have "the comforting presence of his surviving parent, or if that is not possible of a known and trusted substitute, and an assurance that that relationship will continue" (1980, p. 276). But not only were the sisters given over to their "demonic" grandmother, but first Nina and then Gill were speedily dispatched by this same unreliable caretaker to Sherborne School, a prestigious boarding establishment where Nina cultivated a love of English literature but predictably became "very depressed and disturbed" (Molino, 1997, p. 191). From the standpoint of attachment theory, one could not have scripted a more devastating sequence of events, and although Nina Coltart went on to achieve great things in her life, any prospect of genuinely recovering from the tragedy of the stunningly sudden loss of both parents may well have been

---

girl, visiting her when on a 'case', and seeing the new baby", adding that Nina "obviously blocked this out". After their parents' death, however, "Nan kept her promise to our mother always to look after us and make a home for us. *Only during term time*, while we were at boarding school, did she take the very occasional midwifery job (in order to earn a little, as she had no salary from our estate)". But even when one allows for the inevitable divergences between the recollections of two siblings, since Nina Coltart's account of her nanny's disappearances pertains to the period *prior* to their parents' death, there does not appear to be any basis to question the accuracy of her version of these events.

doomed by the inability of her grandmother to provide the "comforting presence" and assurance of continuity that the barely adolescent Nina desperately needed.

Upon graduation from Sherborne, Coltart went on to read Modern Languages at Somerville College, Oxford, although she had already determined to become a doctor. Overcoming her constitutional ineptitude for mathematics and her lack of preparation in the natural sciences, Coltart won an Arts Scholarship to take a second degree in medicine at St Bartholomew's Hospital. No sooner had she achieved this goal, however, than Coltart discovered that it was not what she had wanted since (as she fathomed years later during her analysis) by becoming a doctor she had accomplished her unconscious project of identifying with her father: "I'd restored him to life" (Molino, 1997, pp. 197–198). Looking back on her journey, Coltart deprecated both her Oxford degree and her medical training as "so much bathwater" (1996c, p. 156), unavoidable detours that were not without their dividends, but not to be confused with the baby that remains when everything inessential has been jettisoned.

Coltart came to psychoanalysis through serendipity. While working for three years at a psychiatric hospital in Essex, she met a congenial woman doctor from New Zealand who was in the midst of analytic training and who encouraged Coltart to try it for herself. At the time she applied, Coltart had never read any Freud and was "absolutely, deeply ignorant" about psychoanalysis in general; she presumes that she must have been accepted by the British Society because she was "such a *tabula rasa* that they felt they could imprint me with anything" (1993a, p. 100).

Like Coltart's family history, her experience in analysis warrants detailed examination. Her analyst was Eva Rosenfeld, who was nearing seventy and induced to come out of retirement to take on Coltart as her final training case. Coltart was matched up with Rosenfeld because of the remarkable similarities between their personal histories. Just as Coltart had suffered the deaths of her parents, so also had Rosenfeld—who had the distinction of having been analysed first by Freud and then by Klein—been wounded by losses, though for Rosenfeld it was the deaths of her children that had been traumatic. Of her four children, three boys and a girl, two of the boys died of dysentery at the end of the First World War, while the girl, "whom she adored ... died as a result of a mountain climbing accident" (Molino, 1997, p. 176). Rosenfeld eventually separated from her husband and emigrated from Vienna by way of Berlin to London, where she was "left with only one son". What is more, the death of Rosenfeld's daughter finds an uncanny parallel in the fact that Melanie Klein's eldest son also died in a mountain climbing accident. In her interview with Molino, Coltart even wonders whether Rosenfeld's daughter and Klein's son might have perished in the same accident, though she quickly allows, "I may be making this up" (p. 176), and since Klein's son died in 1934, seven years after Rosenfeld's daughter, the two incidents cannot have been connected in reality.

As in her family of origin, therefore, when Coltart entered analysis with Rosenfeld she once again found herself enmeshed in an intergenerational history of trauma that had been transmitted through the female line from Melanie Klein through Eva Rosenfeld to her. The "preconditioning" for the train crash had been laid down not simply in Coltart's own childhood, but in the lives of her mother and grandmother, and this dynamic was replicated in her analytic genealogy. Like Coltart's mother, Rosenfeld "had a tragic life", which left her "depressed"; not surprisingly, Coltart came to the conclusion that Rosenfeld's sorrows "considerably influenced her countertransference to me" (Molino, 1997, p. 176).

Although Coltart acknowledges the benefits of her analysis with Rosenfeld, telling Molino (1997) that "so far as it went it helped me a lot", her emphasis falls on its limitations and her conviction that "it didn't go far enough" (p. 196). Just as Coltart says of her own anxiety, "I never got near this core in my analysis" (p. 195), so, too, she surmises of Rosenfeld, "I don't suppose Freud had got anywhere near the core of her experience" (p. 176). She rues that her analysis was "extremely classical, old Freudian stuff", and though Rosenfeld "would often say that I was angry with my parents or that I felt guilty about my parents", the words "never clicked with me. They did not become real" (p. 196). Emblematic of Coltart's frustrations is a comment in *How to Survive as a Psychotherapist* on the subject of consulting-room decor:

> I might have survived my own analysis with a little less distraction if there had *not* been an evocative picture that hung as I faced it

directly from the couch. I think a bare wall allows for freer fantasy in the patient; and I would certainly always choose to have white walls as my personal preference. [1993a, p. 30]

As always, Coltart's advice to the prospective therapist is eminently practical, but it grows out of an awareness that she had not received what she needed from her analysis with Rosenfeld. In Coltart's own terms, the "evocative picture" on her analyst's wall, like Rosenfeld's classical Freudianism, impeded the regression that would have made it possible for her to give birth to the "rough beast" that was languishing inchoately in the womb of her psyche.

Coltart is far from being the only patient to have been let down by her first experience of analysis, especially one undertaken for training purposes. It is, doubtless, the sense that Bion could have guided her into the terrain that she was unable to explore with Rosenfeld that prompted Coltart to fantasize about re-entering analysis with him. Coltart conceptualizes her psychopathology as a compound of anxiety and depression, with the anxiety brought to its "apex" by her parents' non-arrival on that night in Cornwall being "psychotic" (Molino, 1997, p. 196) in its intensity, and her mixed verdict on the analysis with Rosenfeld is that, "although it helped with my depression", it "didn't do much for my anxiety" (p. 201).

Following her renunciation of Christianity, Coltart turned to Buddhist meditation as a means of coping with the suffering that continued to afflict her even after completing her analysis. She was also able to confide in "one or two friends" (Molino, 1997, p. 195), and she continued to engage in the introspection that forms a vital undercurrent in her writings. Beyond these private and spiritual resources, however, Coltart did have one experience in a therapeutic setting that led to a breakthrough with respect to her childhood trauma. It is recorded in "Two's company, three's a crowd" (1996f), which I have identified as her most autobiographically revealing paper, even though she refrains in this context from going into specifics about the event that had taken place nearly fifty years earlier and that she found herself reliving most unexpectedly.

As a congenital outsider, Coltart regularly aligned herself with individuals and organizations from which most psychoanalysts were at pains to steer clear. She had good things to say, for instance, about both Karen Horney and R. D. Laing, and she was a long-time supporter of the Arbours Association, a residential therapeutic community in London, which currently sponsors an annual lecture in her memory. Even before resigning from the British Psychoanalytical Society, she had become disenchanted with its "authoritarianism" and resolved that she would "henceforth only take on for supervision experienced psychotherapists" with whom Coltart "thought there would be a far greater chance of an egalitarian relationship" (1996a, p. 110).

Coltart's decision in 1989 to enrol in the introductory course offered by the Institute of Group Analysis, being something that "very few, if any, practising senior psychoanalysts" had ever done (1996f, p. 43), was of a piece with her iconoclastic temperament. In addition to a weekly lecture followed by a discussion, the course consisted of "a weekly experiential group of one-and-a-half hours" (p. 41). In her paper, Coltart goes on amusingly about her efforts to conceal her identity as an analyst from the other members of the group, as well as about how she came to realize that her "running stream of inner commentary on people tended towards the critical, with intolerance at the extreme" (p. 52), leading her to give "private names" (p. 51) to her fellow participants.[11]

Beyond its grace notes, however, at the heart of "Two's company, three's a crowd" there lies Coltart's account of how, while participating in this year of group therapy, she "abreacted some buried feelings" (1996f, p. 54) about the trauma of her youth. For a considerable period, Coltart reports, she "did not detect any particular signs of transference" in herself towards the group conductor, an "attentive and containing" woman in her early forties. One day, however, Coltart "noticed that I was pleased and rather relieved for her when she said something shrewd". Coltart connected this assuaging of her anxiety about the conductor to "an ancient feeling about my younger sister, who was a worry in her teens, doing something grown-up and admirable" (p. 54).

---

[11] Nor were Coltart's patients exempt from her penchant for bestowing nicknames. As she remarks about a depressed woman whom she dubbed in the second week of her analysis the "Little Hedgehog", the "nickname thrown up by the analyst's unconscious invariably carries an apt cogency about the patient's psychopathology" (1991b, p. 84).

Initially, therefore, Coltart's transference to the group conductor was sororal, though it became maternal several months later. The decisive episode was triggered, in Gestalt fashion, "because there were some empty chairs, and quite intensive group talk about people who were absent or missing" (1996f, p. 54). Under the stress induced by these circumstances, Coltart "developed an anxiety attack" in which she "for a while felt very helpless and overcome, but also violently angry with our group conductor, wanting her to help and feeling she, too, was 'missing' this and failing me". The evocation of "people who were absent or missing" in a physical sense, symbolized by the "empty chairs", in other words, was augmented by Coltart's conviction that the group leader, though physically present, was "missing" emotionally by failing, first, to recognize Coltart's feeling of abandonment and, second, to rescue her from it. Fortunately, however, "the group, as it was capable of doing at times, rallied to what felt like a crisis and worked superbly to contain me and put me together again" (p. 54).

As a result of her breakdown, which was also a breakthrough, Coltart became aware that, beneath her "apparently rather neutral response to the group leader", she had unconsciously "been building up a primitive and strong transference to a mother, who then suddenly disappeared—or seemed to". She continues,

> After I was able to let the anxiety attack happen, then be angry, and then rescued, I gained some valuable insight into something that had never before been accessible to me, in all these years—namely, the anger towards my mother, which had been locked inside the anxiety. [1996f, p. 55]

In this unlikely setting, Coltart was able to discover the emotional reality of the transference, and, hence, of her anger towards her mother, that had remained inaccessible throughout her training analysis with Rosenfeld. This emergence of her "rough beast" from its psychic lair at least approximates the experience that she would have wanted to have with Bion, but that Coltart was wise enough to ensure she extracted from life even though she did not achieve it in the formal context of a psychoanalysis.

Pondering this anxiety attack set off by the empty chairs, Coltart stresses that what it brought to light was not a response to her parents' death, but the realization that "I had been all those years stewing away a sort of fury at my mother, from long before she died" (Molino, 1997, p. 196). She was, that is, able to get in touch with the "preconditioning" of the cumulative experiences of abandonment that had lain buried beneath the rubble of the catastrophe of the train crash. Because Coltart as a girl had been so "furious with her for letting me down, for being so absent", it was, paradoxically, only "through her death that I later discovered she'd been an absent mother in life" (p. 196). Initially, however, when Coltart's mother died, and thereby became "totally absent", any awareness that Coltart may have had "of her shortcomings first needed to go into profound repression" (p. 196). There it lay dormant for decades, until the dynamic of anxiety and anger at the failed reappearances of her loved objects could be reactivated by her transference to the group conductor and the containment afforded by the other participants when they rallied to her side at the critical moment.

Everything that I have set forth about Coltart's life is indebted to Coltart's own hard-won insights, as imparted in her valedictory interview with Anthony Molino and in "Two's company, three's a crowd". With extraordinary lucidity, Coltart has shown how her destiny was shaped not only by the "fracture" induced by the trauma of her parents' accidental death but, even more profoundly, by the "preconditioning" both of the history of losses going back three generations in her family and of the repeated disappearances of her two mothers—her biological mother and her beloved nanny—during her childhood. She likewise allows us to see how her family history was re-created when she entered analysis with Rosenfeld, and how Rosenfeld, for a combination of personal and theoretical reasons, was not able to help her very much. It is quintessentially psychoanalytic that Coltart achieved the most profound self-knowledge by re-enacting her early experiences in a transference neurosis, albeit one that she developed in the course at the Institute of Group Analysis. It remains for me now to reflect on Coltart's work in light of what we have learned about her life and then to close by touching on the delicate topic of her suicide.

4

Nina Coltart was under no illusions about her place in the history of psychoanalysis. "I don't think I should be remembered", she told

Molino (1997), "not in the way that Winnicott and Bion and others are remembered" (p. 179). As I have noted, she did not originate any theoretical concepts. It is, rather, for "Slouching towards Bethlehem", the paper that first made her reputation, that she continues to live on, however tenuously, in psychoanalytic memory. This paper struck a chord by its evocative use of Yeats's poem, with its metaphor of the "rough beast", to talk "about breakdown and the possibility of healing" (1986, p. 1), as well as by the eloquence with which Coltart propounded her radical view that "the essence of our impossible profession" (p. 2) is an acceptance of ignorance or even incompetence, since only by evincing the capacity to tolerate not knowing can the analyst aspire "to be continually open to the emergence of the unexpected" (p. 6), which is how healing takes place through the psychoanalytic process.[12]

As a Buddhist, Coltart was as reconciled as it is possible for a human being to be to impermanence, including the ephemerality of her own fame. She did admit to Molino (1997) that she was "proud" to have written her books, which "say pretty well everything I want to say. So people needn't really miss me. 'Me' is in my books" (p. 179). "Then again", she hastens to add, "everything is transient anyway!"

Although Coltart is doubtless right about transience, and even Freud's cloud-capped towers will melt into air one day, there is no need for us to hasten her passage to oblivion. On the contrary, Coltart's efflorescence of creativity during her final fifteen years is, in my estimation, one of the greatest glories in the psychoanalytic literature, and the three books in which she has distilled herself for posterity deserve to be much more widely known and cherished than they are.

When one examines Coltart's work through the lens of her life, the humpbacked shape of her career immediately solicits commentary. For after the paper she was required to present in 1967 to attain full membership in the British Psychoanalytical Society, "The man

---

[12] Coltart emphasizes that there is always a "delicate balance" between the need for faith and "our reliance on our theories and on our knowledge of human nature in many of its dimensions" (*ibid.*), but it is the mystical dimension of her respect for the unknown for which Coltart is inevitably—and justly—celebrated or castigated in "Slouching towards Bethlehem".

with two mothers" (1996e), which remained unpublished until it was included in *The Baby and the Bathwater*, Coltart wrote nothing for fifteen years until "Slouching towards Bethlehem" was delivered at the conference of English-speaking analysts in 1982. Then, firing on all cylinders, Coltart propelled herself into the orbit of her later period, which conspicuously mirrors the first half of her career in extending for fifteen years.

Even more uncanny than this temporal symmetry, however, is how Coltart's second birth as a writer in "Slouching towards Bethlehem" exemplifies the description of the treatment process that she proffers in the very paper in which she achieved her breakthrough. The theme of the 1982 conference was "Beyond Words", and Coltart writes that "profound silence itself, as well as what it conceals, can be a rough beast which is slouching along in the depths of a communicative, articulate patient and whose time may need to come round and be *endured* in the analysis" (1986, p. 9). No less pertinently, she observes that often, after a period of preliminary work, there comes a time in an analysis "when darkness begins to close in, but it is a darkness having that special quality of the unknown which is moving towards being known" (p. 7).

As her prime clinical example in "Slouching towards Bethlehem", Coltart instances an elderly male patient to whom she later devoted an entire paper (1991a), and who returns for a cameo appearance also in "The silent patient" (1991b).[13] Clearly, silence was a topic dear to Coltart's heart, and it must have possessed for her a personal as well as a theoretical significance. Coltart herself, after all, had had to endure fifteen years of silence in her analytic career in order for the darkness within her soul to move from the unknown towards beginning to be known in "Slouching towards Bethlehem".

---

[13] This example became notorious because of Coltart's revelation that she one day "simply and suddenly became furious and bawled [the patient] out for his prolonged lethal attack on me and on the analysis" (1986, p. 10). In her subsequent case history, Coltart stood by her conduct, asserting that "we can do no harm to a patient by showing authentic affect, within the limits of scrupulous self-observation" (1991a, p. 161). As Franco Borgogno has concurred, even expressions of hate and anger by the analyst can be justified if these emotions "are, in a moment of the treatment, the sentiments in play that urgently call for their recognition" (2007, p. 54).

On a still deeper level, not only does Coltart's prolonged gestation as a writer exemplify the intertwined dynamics of emotional breakdown and healing set forth in her classic paper, but her understanding of the treatment process constitutes a supremely creative response to her own most agonizing traumatic experiences. Describing the dynamic of disappearance and failed return of the caretakers in her childhood as "a wound from which one never recovers", though her ego "has had to grow various defences or skins around it", Coltart confides to Molino (1997) that "the pure anxiety of waiting for someone whom I love and depend upon to come to me is still, at times, unbearable" (pp. 195–196).

Now, the essence of Coltart's plea in "Slouching towards Bethlehem" is that the analyst should make each hour into an "act of faith" both in himself and in the analytic process, and this—following Bion—Coltart construes as "the capacity to sit it out with a patient, often for long periods, without any real precision as to where we are" (1986, p. 3). The greatest temptation, accordingly, is to try "to take possession of our patients too soon", with the forceps of intellect, but though such precipitate displays of cleverness may "appeal to quite conscious layers of the patient", they inadvertently reinforce the resistance and thereby prevent "the true unknown reality" (p. 6) that lies hidden within the womb of the psyche from being born when (in Yeats's words) its hour comes round at last.

Like those of any thinker, the value of Coltart's ideas is independent of their autobiographical roots. "Slouching towards Bethlehem" would be a sublime paper with much to teach us even if we knew nothing about its resonance on multiple levels with its author's personal experience. But, in my view, it only enhances our appreciation of Coltart's achievement when we are able to grasp that, through the metaphor of the "rough beast", she has been able to transform "the pure anxiety of waiting" that was her acutest dread in life into the source of her most generative contribution to psychoanalysis.

Similarly, when Coltart chose to call her second book *How to Survive as a Psychotherapist*, she highlighted the centrality of the theme of survival not only to her conception of psychotherapy, but also to her entire outlook. As the title of her opening chapter speci fies, by survival she means "Survival-with-Enjoyment", and not, as she puts it elsewhere, "grimly hanging on" (1996a, p. 120). Coltart frequently voiced her delight that, in becoming a psychoanalyst, she had found her true calling in life and that this serendipity allowed her to feel herself "a round peg in a round hole" (1993a, p. 8). The title of her book sums up Coltart's lesson that would-be therapists or analysts must be able to take unalloyed pleasure in their often gruelling work, including the arduous training process, and that this capacity to "survive-with-enjoyment" is an indispensable concomitant to sustaining a vocation in the field of mental health.[14]

Yet, on an existential plane, the question of survival was fraught with peril for Coltart. As we know, she diagnosed a "fracture" in her being, as well as the compensatory sense of "superiority", resulting from her "prolonged struggle with survival": after the deaths of her parents. Thus, although Coltart did find her work to be a source of fulfilment that enabled her to "survive" for decades according to the unique definition she gave to this word—while always insisting that psychoanalysis did not fill the void left by her abandonment of Christianity, and that this spiritual hunger was appeased only when she discovered Buddhism—we can see once again how this contribution to our understanding of what it means to be a psychotherapist possessed a dimension of subjective significance for Coltart. Indeed, Coltart's insight into what it means to "survive-with-enjoyment" was a further inspired transformation of her "unbearable" anxiety that someone who, at the age of twelve, had suffered an incurable wound might, beneath the surface, in fact have been "grimly hanging on" all along, and, thus, not have survived at all.

5

There can be no more painful topic for friends and family members than the suicide of a beloved person. Yet, I think it is incumbent on those of us who have come to love Nina Coltart, if only through her writings, to grasp this nettle as firmly as possible, trusting that she herself would have wanted the truth to be known and secure in our

---

[14] Coltart specifies the "five features that, together, characterize a vocation" as "giftedness, belief in the power of the unconscious (indeed, in the unconscious itself), strength of purpose, reparativeness, and curiosity" (1996g, p. 34).

conviction that the best way to pay tribute to her memory is by walking the tightrope of an infinite compassion and an unsparing honesty.

It is worth recalling in this connection that the death of Freud was a physician-assisted suicide.[15] No one, to my knowledge, feels it necessary to reproach Freud because he could no longer live with the pain of his cancer, and why should we imagine that Coltart's agony was any less excruciating or presume to deny her the same right of self-determination over her own existence?

I do not think we can do better than to try to adumbrate the mystery of Coltart's suicide by using her own most luminous metaphor. Whereas her long-delayed burst of creativity, beginning in "Slouching towards Bethlehem", represented an epiphany of the "rough beast" in the positive guise of her deepest wisdom about the meaning of analysis, fired in the crucible of a struggle with anxiety and depression stemming from her childhood traumas, when she took her own life fifteen years later this "shape with lion's body and the head of a man"—Yeats's line identifies the menacing creature with the Egyptian Sphinx—finally turned its "stare blank and pitiless" on its human antagonist and claimed her life.

When Coltart left the analytic world and ensconced herself in Leighton Buzzard—a place, as she noted to Molino (1997), that brought her life "full circle" by being "just up the road" from the birthplace of the nanny who was her "primary love object" (p. 195)—she was already in declining health and increasingly dependent on the care of others. Coltart suffered from osteoporosis, as well as heart and thyroid problems, and she underwent major abdominal surgery in the fall of 1996. Thus, just as she had been forced as a child to hang on, as it were, for what seemed an eternity before being informed of the deaths of her parents, a cataclysmic blow that seared her forever with "the pure anxiety of waiting for someone whom I love and depend upon to come to me", to which she had already been subjected repeatedly during her prior years of "preconditioning", so, once again, at the end of her life Coltart unconsciously recreated the situation that she found most

---

[15] For an authoritative review of the actual circumstances and often untrustworthy narratives concerning Freud's death, see Lacoursiere (2008).

"unbearable"—one that she had symbolically re-enacted in the transference when she felt abandoned by the group conductor during the "empty chair" episode—in which she would have to wait for a mother or sister who might or might not show up when Coltart needed her most.

But, like an anamorphic image, Coltart's suicide, which seen from one perspective is an act of despair, is from another vantage point also an act of existential freedom. Coltart was for four decades a member of the Voluntary Euthanasia Society, and, in addition to notes addressed to her family and doctor, she left in her kitchen an article about suicide from the newsletter of the Society under which she had written, "I agree with this" (*Hampstead and Highgate*, 1997). With characteristic pungency and practicality, she posted a note on her front door, "Please do not disturb—having an extra lie-in".

The shadow of Coltart's impending death looms over her encounter with Molino. Praising his perspicacity in questioning her about this theme in her writing, she observes that "quite a lot of my patients die", including two by suicide and several others "relatively young" (Molino, 1997, p. 192), such as the subject of "The man with two mothers".[16] It was, she says at the very close of the interview, "to keep the memory of a patient alive" that she wrote the chapter, "Paradoxes", in *How to Survive as a Psychotherapist*, and she describes this woman who, in a fit of rage, had swept the objects off Coltart's mantlepiece and had even brought a knife to one of her sessions as "a great, great character" (Molino, 1997, p. 208). In "Paradoxes", Coltart remarks with tragic poignancy that "one cannot escape the stark knowledge that suicide stands for failure" (1993a, p. 45); and it is impossible to read her account of this patient's suicide without being reminded of Coltart's own.

---

[16] There are many striking parallels between this sexually perverse patient and Coltart. Each of the following statements about him could also be taken autobiographically: (a) "he has known about the strangeness of his inner world for years, and often had a conscious dread of breakdown" (1996e, p. 9); (b) "if he chooses one mother, he is guilty of having betrayed the other" (p. 1); (c) "he abandoned his belief in God, though, I suppose inevitably, he sometimes looked back to it regretfully" (p. 12); and (d), in the patient's own words: "'I was just feeling so good last week, and as if you were a real good person I could rely on. Now you're not even bad, don't flatter yourself—you've *gone*, don't you see?'" (p. 15).

Although Coltart had mailed her a postcard after a Friday session, expecting it to arrive on Saturday, it was not delivered until Monday, after the patient had killed herself. In a last letter to Coltart, written on her deathbed, the patient had said she knew the card would come on Monday, but, in Coltart's words, "its non-arrival had been all (all?) that was needed to tip her over the edge" (p. 54). Can it be a coincidence that, just as her life had come "full circle" by returning to the birthplace of her nanny, Coltart's thoughts should have returned, in her final public testament, to this forlorn yet indomitable woman who was likewise undone by "the pure agony of waiting"?

Of her other patient who committed suicide—a voluble and intellectually gifted man who chose to end it all on the anniversary of the day he had terminated his analysis, and whose case is recounted in "A philosopher and his mind"—Coltart pays tribute to his reticence in not leaving a note: "I admired the dignity and forbearance of his silent departure" (1995, p. 90).

References

Boffito, S. (2008). La piu indipendente degli indipendenti: La psicoanalisi e la vita di Nina Coltart. Tesi di Laurea. Università Cattolica del Sacro Cuore, Milan. Unpublished manuscript.

Bowlby, J. (1980). *Loss: Sadness and Depression.* Vol. 3 of *Attachment and Loss.* New York: Basic Books.

Borgogno, F. (2007). *The Vancouver Interview: Frammenti di vita e opere d'una vocazione psicoanalitica.* Rome: Borla.

Coltart, N. (1985). The practice of psychoanalysis and Buddhism. In: *Slouching towards Bethlehem ... and Further Psychoanalytic Explorations* (pp. 164–175). London: Free Association Books, 2002.

Coltart, N. (1986). Slouching towards Bethlehem ... or thinking the unthinkable in psychoanalysis. In: *Slouching towards Bethlehem ... and Further Psychoanalytic Explorations* (pp. 1–14). London: Free Association Books, 2002.

Coltart, N. (1991a). The analysis of an elderly patient. In: *Slouching towards Bethlehem ... and Further Psychoanalytic Explorations* (pp. 144–163). London: Free Association Books, 2002.

Coltart, N. (1991b). The silent patient. In: *Slouching towards Bethlehem ... and Further Psychoanalytic Explorations* (pp. 79–94). London: Free Association Books, 2002.

Coltart, N. (1993a). *How to Survive as a Psychotherapist*. London: Sheldon Press.
Coltart, N. (1993b). *Slouching towards Bethlehem . . . and Further Psychoanalytic Explorations*. London: Free Association Books, 2002.
Coltart, N. (1995). A philosopher and his mind. In: *The Baby and the Bathwater* (pp. 75–90). London: Karnac.
Coltart, N. (1996a). "And now for something completely different . . ." In: *The Baby and the Bathwater* (pp. 109–124). London: Karnac.
Coltart, N. (1996b). *The Baby and the Bathwater*. London: Karnac.
Coltart, N. (1996c). The baby and the bathwater. In: *The Baby and the Bathwater* (pp. 155–166). London: Karnac.
Coltart, N. (1996d). Buddhism and psychoanalysis revisited. In: *The Baby and the Bathwater* (125–139). London: Karnac.
Coltart, N. (1996e). The man with two mothers. In: *The Baby and the Bathwater* (pp. 1–22). London: Karnac.
Coltart, N. (1996f). Two's company, three's a crowd. In: *The Baby and the Bathwater* (41–56). London: Karnac.
Coltart, N. (1996g). Why am I here? In: *The Baby and the Bathwater* (pp. 23–40). London: Karnac.
Hampstead and Highgate (1997). Coltart suicide was clear decision. 1 August.
Khan, M. M. R. (1963). The concept of cumulative trauma. In: *The Privacy of the Self: Papers on Psychoanalytic Theory and Technique* (pp. 42–58). London: Hogarth Press, 1986.
Kohon, G. (Ed.) (1986). *The British School of Psychoanalysis: The Independent Tradition*. London: Free Association Books.
Lacoursiere, R. B. (2008). Freud's death: historical truth and biographical fictions. *American Imago*, 65: 107–128.
Molino, A. (Ed.) (1997). *Freely Associated: Encounters in Psychoanalysis with Christopher Bollas, Joyce McDougall, Michael Eigen, Adam Phillips, Nina Coltart*. London: Free Association Books.
Rudnytsky, P. L. (2000). *Psychoanalytic Conversations: Interviews with Clinicians, Commentators, and Critics*. Hillsdale, NJ: Analytic Press.
Winnicott, D. W. (1974). Fear of breakdown. In: C. Winnicott, R. Shepherd, & M. Davis (Eds.), *Psycho-Analytic Explorations* (pp. 87–95). Cambridge, MA: Harvard University Press, 1989.

CHAPTER TWENTY-NINE

For Nina Coltart: in memoriam, or calling the thing by its name

Anthony Molino

In a note dated 3 July 1997 and appended to the introduction of my *Freely Associated: Encounters in Psychoanalysis with Christopher Bollas, Joyce McDougall, Michael Eigen, Adam Phillips, and Nina Coltart* (1997), I cited my withdrawal from the manuscript of the original "sketch" of my encounter with Dr Coltart written prior to her death by suicide on Tuesday, 24 June 1997. In the aftermath of that sudden and sad event, "reflections of a different sort", I noted, "now seem in order". If my memory serves me well, only three people had read that sketch submitted for publication with the rest of the manuscript. One of them was Nina Coltart herself who, in a handwritten letter to me dated 28 January 1997, gave her unequivocal stamp of approval both to the final version of our interview as well as to my highly idiosyncratic and potentially shocking impressions of our time together. Convinced, as I remain, that Nina had intended our interview to serve and survive her as a final testament of sorts, and entrusted, as I was, with the dissemination of its contents, the invitation to contribute to this commemorative volume occasions that I herewith make public, for the first time, those paragraphs originally penned for *Freely Associated*.

* * *

This book closes with my conversations with Nina Coltart. For several reasons. First off, these conversations were the last to take place in the compilation process. Second, as the senior member of the group represented in this collection, Dr Coltart has been a privileged witness to, and participant in, some of the most fertile and controversial decades of the first century of psychoanalysis. In this light, it is only fitting to have her reflections provide the coda for this volume. Third, as Dr Coltart emphasizes in *The Baby and the Bathwater*—her most recent and final book—she is now officially "retired". The significance of this "status", if you will, is not to be overlooked. My impression is that, for Nina Coltart, to be retired is not only a signpost along the way of a lifetime weathered and enriched in its dedication to psychoanalysis; rather, I get the sense that retirement is also something of an existential achievement, of a new inner plateau, removed from the fray, from which the grand horizons of Freud's legacy can be seen to blend with the discreet and gentler contours of the vegetable patches and flowerbeds to which she now, serenely, awakens every day. . . .

In spite of my awkward attempt to convey something of Dr Coltart's Buddhist sensibilities, I do believe that it was those very sensibilities that allowed our time together to alchemize quickly into a golden trust. Not that there was anything syrupy, mind you, about our two afternoons together. Both times my impression was of an eminently sensible, no-nonsense woman who proved charmingly affable in her own sweatsuit brand of disarming domesticity. In a room papered with old photographs and postcards from every corner of the earth, suffused with the rippling smoke of endless cigarettes and warmed by a potbellied stove (which in all likelihood my imagination is now contriving, to counter the bleak, dreary chill of an early winter dusk) . . . in that room not only did memories come alive, but also the precious experience of somehow being granted permission, by Dr Coltart, to visit death and the dead with her. . . .

Already the town where she resides, Leighton Buzzard, Bedfordshire, had for me an ominous and eerie ring to it. Echoes of blackness, of Van Gogh's *Cornfield with Crows*. But more pressingly, after reading *The Baby and the Bathwater* I was left with the distinct sense that the book had been written as a final testament of sorts. Even the black-and-white photograph of the author, which opens the book, registered with me as the kind that might accompany an obituary. Intimations of death whispered to me from the book's pages, and the fact that they only whispered left me even more ill-at-ease, suggesting that the topic was not one open, or altogether ripe, for discussion. How does one ever discuss such thoughts, let alone in the course of interviewing a person never met before? And yet, somehow, the trust and safety inspired by Dr Coltart and her environs made the experience not only possible, but ultimately rather . . . ordinary. Reflecting, I would suggest, the genuine reaches of her own Buddhist practice, and the authentic wisdom of a life well-lived. Well-lived and, quietly, still thriving.

* * *

My interview with Nina Coltart took place over the course of two days, 12 September and 7 December 1996, in her home outside of London. The first day was a momentous one for both of us. In order to interview her, I was making a pit stop in London after having just left the USA the night before, en route to a new life in small-town central Italy, where my wife and I had chosen to settle. My own frame of mind, of course, upon setting out via taxi from Heathrow to Leighton Buzzard, was anything but settled, as I was staring at a new and altogether uncharted beginning from the transitional spaces of this brief but long-planned British interlude. After being most graciously welcomed by Dr Coltart—whom I had never met previously—and given a tour of her treasured vegetable garden, we proceeded with the interview, had lunch, and ended up spending close to five hours together. The plan, if I remember correctly, was to meet again in a day or two to wrap things up. Instead, later that evening, I learned from Paul Williams—whom I had met through Nina and had previously interviewed for another project—that just minutes after driving me to the local railway station and seeing me off, she was rushed to the hospital.

There is a neat expression in Italian, *deformazione professionale*, a phrase awash in healthy self-irony, that alludes to the process whereby the demands of a given profession will likely bend a person out of shape, to the point of somehow *de-forming* the subject in a way that accords with the specific nature of one's professional pressures. As analysts, we are prone, often enough, to overvalue the effects of words, whether those of our patients or our own. That evening, when word reached me via Paul of Nina's urgent hospitalization (for what only later we learned was a perforated ulcer), I remember him asking quite naturally if anything had been said during our encounter that may have so distressed her as to warrant this kind of aftermath. I remember being overcome by an ambivalent feeling, as I knew well that we'd talked at length about death, about the tragedy of her parents' death and of my own sinister impressions regarding her latest book. There was then, analytically speaking, reason to feel guilty for having somehow, unconsciously, instigated the ambulance ride to the nearest operating table. But at the same time I simply could not believe that the affable, easy frankness with which Nina had opened her mind, heart, and past to me could be concealing a soul so ravaged that it might bleed, literally, to death at what I considered to be at worst my respectful and tactful prodding. It was only the next day, I believe, that a medical report ascertained that the bleeding episode was caused by an antiinflammatory drug that Nina had been taking to manage a severely crippling form of osteoporosis.

* * *

An Israeli colleague and friend of mine, Gershon Molad, has written much about the peculiar, often awkward form of dialogue that takes place between analysts, stressing—as he emphasizes in a paper titled "From interpretation to interpellation" (2003)—"the difficulties we have to talk about ourselves, for fear of being 'out-of-line'. How we fear delegitimization, being destroyed, dead". Recalling Ferenczi's complex relationship with Freud and his ability to let himself be known to and felt by his patients, Molad goes on to reflect upon the damage resulting from "that which did not happen, that which is hidden in the background and difficult to recognize and attain". Since learning of Nina's death, I have long cultivated the conviction that she had planned her suicide. Retrospectively, I have also come to believe that, unless circumstances otherwise warranted, she knew she would wait to approve the interview before carrying out those intentions. It is clear to anyone who reads the interview that she had some bones to pick, and a few scores to settle, with the world of British psychoanalysis in which she had lived, thrived, and battled. In fact, throughout our two afternoons together, I came to feel like a favourite grandson of sorts, who was being told a precious story and made its privileged depositary. A grandson entrusted with the serene but charged reminiscences of a fading but unquestioned matriarch, who wanted to make absolutely sure that what she had said had been properly recorded and would reach its intended audience.

Indeed, as our interview reveals, Nina was remarkably comfortable discussing death at length and in depth: that of her parents, of patients, of friends, and her own. When I wrote the sketch that opens the present reflections, months before her passing, at a time when no one could imagine what was to transpire, two people close to Nina thought it highly inappropriate that I would make public what seemed to be such patently offensive impressions. Nina, to the contrary, in the cited letter of 28 January 1997, clearly appreciated the "little introduction, or whatever *we* are to call it" (my italics). "I like it", she wrote, "and think you have done an unusual and good job". Objecting only to my portrait of her as a somewhat inveterate chain-smoker—she had told me on the sly that friends and family were under the impression that she had quit, and she didn't want to disappoint them!—she thus concludes her letter: ". . . otherwise I'm quite *happy* with it, and think you are stylish and quite an original. *Thanks very much!*" (again, my italics). No Dylan Thomas here, no raging whatsoever against the dying light. Or against the black backdrop I myself might have been painting and insinuating. Uh-uh. To use Molad's words, something clicked between Nina and me that allowed "that which is hidden in the background and difficult to recognize and attain" to emerge. Something not unlike an unconscious connection, which several reviewers of *Freely Associated* have also perceived and highlighted.[1]

* * *

In a recent review of Jennifer Michael Hecht's book *The Happiness Myth* (2007), the Italian philosopher Remo Bodei discusses our

---

[1] See Laurie Jo Wright's review in *The Psychotherapy Review* (1999), where she writes: "I am sure that each reader will bring their own unconscious into their reading of this evocative and final interview. This certainly seems to have

contemporary knack, as consumers, for feeding off of fabricated myths, especially those concerned with physical fitness, sex, and the infinite extension of biological life. Invoking the lives and the lessons of Montaigne, Luther, and Marcus Aurelius, Bodei writes,

> To think continually about death is not fashionable nowadays. It is elsewhere, hidden, so much so that we have come to believe that the butchered meat in our supermarkets is actually born there, all rosy pink and innocent. Even Christians today do not bother much with life after death . . . [My translation of an excerpt of Bodei's review that appeared on 16 March 2008 in the cultural pages of the daily *Il Sole 24 Ore*]

It has come to my attention that many people close to Nina, friends and colleagues alike, have turned down invitations to revisit publicly their relationship with her. They will not have contributed to this volume, and many have similarly declined requests to talk about Nina with the Israeli editors of the forthcoming Hebrew edition of *Freely Associated*. While such choices are deeply personal and deserving of the greatest respect, the frequency with which they continue to occur and be repeated moves me to some final considerations.

Why, first off, so thick a wall of silence around so powerful and engaging a figure as Nina, who was known to have touched the lives of so many people? Has her suicide come to be experienced by those close to her as a personal betrayal? And has it perhaps branded itself like a stigma on to the flesh, and into the collective memory, of the professional community she had, in part, iconoclas-

---

been the case for Molino. . . . When talking to Coltart about her last book, his comments are ominously poignant" (pp. 34–35). Consider also what Pina Antinucci has to say in her review in *The International Forum of Psychoanalysis* (1999):

> I found Coltart's openness to Molino's probing questions really touching, particularly with regards to the themes of death and dying. It is almost the story of a death foretold and perhaps contained as a potential psychic event with the tragedy that marked her life so profoundly: the loss of both her parents in a train accident when she was only 11 years old. [p. 277]

tically renounced? Is silence—and its correlatives of repression and denial—the antidote of choice to pervasive, painful, and shared feelings of outrage, disbelief, and, again, betrayal at her loss? I can only wonder.

But in my experience, and as any psychoanalyst knows, to avoid calling "the thing" by its name is to court, at best, an uneasy and restless compromise. Where Nina is concerned it is, in a way, to diminish what her dear friend Nina Farhi once called "the hugeness of spirit that she inhabited". For me, ultimately, to mince words would mean to collude with forces that want or need to forget, in an unwitting pursuit of oblivion. I can attest, for example, that yet again, as I set out to write this piece, perplexity surfaced at the idea that I might evoke Nina's death—let alone be explicit about her suicide. But as I wrote to the editors of this collection, I am convinced that Nina would have had it no other way.

True to her Buddhist spirit, death to her was not the ominous, dastardly menace that most of us envision. It was neither grim nor persecutory, but just one more transformation—the final one, perhaps—among the countless rotations of the spinning wheel of life. Had she been a Franciscan, Nina Coltart might well have invoked it as "Sister Death". And who knows, from the depths of her own unfathomable pain and suffering, maybe, just maybe, she did.

References

Antinucci, P. (1999). Review of *Freely Associated: Encounters in Psychoanalysis with Christopher Bollas, Joyce McDougall, Michael Eigen, Adam Phillips, Nina Coltart*, A. Molino (Ed.), *The International Forum of Psychoanalysis*, 8: 276–277.
Hecht, J. (2007). *The Happiness Myth: Why We Think Right Is Wrong*. New York: HarperCollins.
Molad, G. (2003). From interpretation to interpellation. Paper presented to the 14th annual Conference of the International Federation of Psychoanalytic Education, "The Transformational Conversation". Pasadena, California, November 7–9. Unpublished manuscript.
Molino, A. (Ed.) (1997). *Freely Associated: Encounters in Psychoanalysis with Christopher Bollas, Joyce McDougall, Michael Eigen, Adam Phillips, Nina Coltart*. London: Free Association Books.

Wright, L. (1999). Review of *Freely Associated: Encounters in Psychoanalysis with Christopher Bollas, Joyce McDougall, Michael Eigen, Adam Phillips, Nina Coltart*, A. Molino (Ed.), *The Psychotherapy Review*, 1: 34–35.

PART II
UNCOLLECTED WRITINGS
(A) TRAVELS

CHAPTER THIRTY

The Grand Tour of New England

"Pay here by American Express—'That'll do nicely'—he actually said it. Can't remember now how or why I got an A.E. Card, but it's certainly useful abroad."

8.46 pm Sat Nov 15. FABULOUS! Loving every minute of it!! Jan [Webster] came right to Concorde Lounge, and *in it*, and we had a real little party—champagne, delicious little sandwiches, very elegant. Concorde waiting quietly outside on its own place. Flights called, and off Jan went, and in I went. Seat 22A, by window, 22B empty so just put my legs and coat there. The pop group Duran Duran—3 strange but q. nice, but noisy, young men were just in front of me. I think one was high on cocaine—he threw himself about and shrieked with laughter—at one point he threw himself so hard against his seat back that he upset my orange juice—not on me! I poked his shoulder hard, and said WILL YOU STOP DOING

November 1986. Handwritten on stationery of the Warwick hotel, 54th St. on the Avenue of the Americas, New York, N.Y. 10019. Each entry is in the form of a single paragraph, and many "ands" appear as ampersands.

THAT? He was very apologetic—but as Concord was ½ empty I moved back 2 rows to peace and quiet. Had another orange juice, and 3 darling canapés—a thick lush chunk of paté de foie w. a big truffle in it, on a tiny round of toast, a midget pastry boat with 4 tiny shrimps and mayonnaise on it, and a little whorled round sandwich of smoked salmon. Then elegant white cloth, tray and DINNER—by now, incidentally we are going at Mach 1.5 and soon at Mach 2, = twice the speed of sound, at 59,000 ft. We had a delicate, delicious serving of lobster, surrounded by (a) a few prawns, (b) some chopped onion, (c) some whipped mayonnaise in a scooped out half tomato, and (d) about a dessert spoonful of beluga caviare in half a hard boiled egg, yolk scooped out and chopped beside. !! With a beautifully tossed, dressed, small salad of lettuce, peppers, celery, walnuts and pineapple. Then steak or partridge, so I had partridge, 3 delicate breast slices rolled in bacon with crispy bacon bits stirred in with crispy hot cabbage, broccoli, carrots, and courgettes. I had 2 glasses of a nice chablis with all this. Then a fruit jelly with grapes, fresh orange, and fresh pineapple, then cheese and bics, coffee, and a tiny *box* of chocolates which I've saved. Liqueurs and champers flowing like water, and Duran Duran getting noisier, but I didn't have any—had some more orange juice and coffee. I read the Times and the Spectator and started my K. Amis book—but only just. The flight took 3 hrs and 25 mins! We landed at JFK at 5.35, their time, and I had the Concorde Limousine Service downtown. And boy, do I mean Limousine! About 15 feet long—a whole *room* in the back, with a cocktail cabinet! and *black glass*. I hoped everyone thought it was the Queen at least.

My hotel is a good old fashioned European type—I asked for a quiet room, and it's absolutely quiet, at the back, as well as enormous. A huge double bed, 5 big table lamps, two bedside tables, huge dressing table and chest of drawers, 3 walk in cupboards, writing table, and several easy chairs! Kit [Bollas] has rung me up to welcome me—nearly died when the phone went!—I've been for a walk along some of 6th Avenue as far as Radio City, and along 54th and 55th Streets to look at signs and shops, and buy some Coke and a map—pitch dark since arrival, and temp 46°C—not bad, and no snow. Now because I've only had one tiny meal today, I've ordered a chicken sandwich and a large fresh orange juice from Room Service, and it's just come, looking like a meal for 4! Orange juice standing in cracked ice, glass of water, linen napkin, silver knife and fork, 2 *enormous* sandwiches with 4 layers of meat in them, *jug* of mayonnaise, lettuce, tomatoes, and pickled cucumbers. Lucky I was *11 stone* exactly this morning. By my dear little new clock it is now 9.15 N.Y. time, so by my inner clock it's about 3 a.m., which just suits me nicely . . .

Nov. 16 Sunday Slept like a log for 10 hours—10.15 p.m. U.S. time to 8.15 a.m. when alarm went off. Sprang up, and went down for breakfast—this is a very cosmopolitan hotel, a lot of European staff. I couldn't resist having griddle cakes with maple syrup and bacon and sausages = 3 enormous hot drop scones, on which you put butter *and* maple syrup—the waiter said "It's decadent, but it's delicious". So it was. Soon deep in conversation with the couple at the next table, whose cousin runs the Stag at Leighton Buzzard! So we had various chats stemming from that, including a study of the Great Train Robbery. It's a heavenly coldish sunny day, and I went out walking quite soon, thanking God for Indocid, which makes walking so painless and easy again. I went into St. Thomas church on 5th Avenue, huge, neo-gothic, *very* nice, with beautiful glass with a lot of Chartres blue in it. There was a choir practice 10.30–11 which I sat for and enjoyed, and meanwhile church filled up— *packed*—for matins at 11 a.m. at which point I left and went to MOMA—Museum of Modern Art on 53rd Street. I only did one floor and the gardens, and that took 2 hours and I was whacked, but I must try and come back next week, and do the next floor up. This one was about 1880–1920, and full of goodies, if you like that sort of thing, which I do. Particularly the Brancusi and Giacommetti sculptures, and the Max Ernst paintings of which they have a large number. I think he was very *funny* a lot of the time, and meant to be. It seems odd to stand and laugh at a painting, and could be misinterpreted, so I did it quietly. A lot of Picasso, which I'm simply sick of, and a lot of Mondrian—OK—and Matisse and Klee. And one whole room with 3 whole walls for Monet's Water lilies. Then I had a beef sandwich on rye—about six slices of delicious beef, lettuce and tomato—looking out on the sculpture gardens, and good coffee. So far very good coffee. Why can't we do that? Still a lovely sunny cold day. Now I'm going to hump my belongings like a camel, and walk down 5th Avenue, then 43rd St., then Madison

Avenue—to Grand Central Station and look at things on the way. I just have time and much nicer than a cab.

Mon evening 9.30 p.m. Knackered! And I've only done a day here—but in a good sort of way, not like after a Monday at home with Board and Council at the end of it. Also some mild jet lag and coming down a bit from a 48-hour high, the longest I've had in ages. I walked to Grand Central Station, as above where I left off, it was twelve blocks, and by the time I got there my baggage was pretty heavy—plus I had Brandy and fags in a duty free bag [next line indistinct, so deleted] and lots of odd Sunday artists selling things on pavements—*sidewalks*, sorry. Quite nice pictures, a lot of them. Grand Central *is* grand—dirty, but grand—huge vaulted arches, a bit like the old Euston and St. Pancras. I was *boiled* by the time I got there, tho' thank goodness I had removed my thermal vest, and stuffed it in Duty Free bag, or I think I'd have fallen down from heat, the weather suddenly got warmer.

I got my train—Amtrak to Schenectady—Hudson being en route, 2½ hrs—I had a lovely comfortable Pullman type seat—all the same price, and as we left at 3.30 and it wasn't pitch dark till 5.15, had a glorious view of the Hudson River with the sunset slowly developing over it. We were *right by* the river *all* the way—very wide and still and quiet, very little traffic on it—little islands and small boats, and hills the far side. Very comfortable nice ride, and nice conductor who shouted each station clearly 5 minutes before you got there, and which side to get out. We stopped at Croton Harmon, Poughkeepsie (Pokipsy), Rhinebeck and Hudson—by P'k it was quite thick snow lying everywhere, and from then on.

Kit met me and took me straight to his house, and we had a glass of wine and delicious chicken and mushroom stew, and vanilla ice cream with roasted almonds. His wife Suzanne is *lovely* and *very nice*, sweet and kind with it. She has 2 children, Danny 18, and Nisha, 14, by a former marriage, and Kit and she have a smashing little boy of 8 called Sasha, whom I fell for instantly. He was enormously excited about "the lady from England" coming, and very friendly and funny, and I won his heart by giving him one of these pens, fortunately I had 3 with me. Then Kit took me to my "apartment" which is in a house about 10 minutes walk from the main A[usten] R[iggs] building.

My flat looks out on the main Stockbridge street, but as it is a tiny, peaceful country town, it is absolutely quiet and peaceful, and I am so THANKFUL for it, I realise to the full today. It is enormous—a huge "living room" with 3 sofas in it and that's just a start—of course I shan't use it at all, I should feel odd and lonely in there, so I use my bedroom, also quite large, with a lovely double bed, 2 massive cupboards, 2 chests of drawers, a table, 2 bedside tables, a huge easy chair and 2 ordinary chairs, and a TV, which I probably shan't watch, as I have so much to read, write, and *do*. The bathroom is across a passage, by the *spare* room! and the kitchen down a little passage from the hallway. *Enormous* fridge, new electric cooker, etc, and everything I need, except I do my own shopping which is *lovely*, and last night there were eggs, butter, jam, milk, bread, tea, coffee and a carton of orange juice there. I had a bath and drank the orange juice and was asleep by 10.30.

By 8.15 am I was over at AR, and have been on the go most of the day—I am the first analyst who's been asked here for a week (instead of just to give a paper) and I am very honoured and flattered, I realise, as by gum, it is a *very* high powered place, and I have a punishing schedule, all drawn up for me. Today I attended the morning conference at 8.30 when the weekend and overnight nursing staff gave their reports—the whole staff were there—there are 10 senior staff, open-ended (timewise) jobs, mostly senior and about my age, or a bit less or a bit more: about 8 less senior, including Kit, who is nevertheless also Director of Education and senior administrator as well as having patients. And about 10 4-year doctors there are Fellows all in training as analysts, either with people *here*—seniors—(very odd in my view) or with the New England Soc. at New Haven, Conn, or at Boston, to which they have to commute, as well as having patients here. The patients live in a separate, *very* nice large building called The Inn, or another one for patients soon to be discharged, or working locally, called The Elms. More later, as I haven't met them yet.

After the morning conf., I met the Activities Staff, who run a mass of things like art, drama, horticulture, weaving, carpentry, electronics etc. And it's not just your old fashioned OT., either. Stockbridge is a famous area for artists, etc, and they come in and teach here, plus a New York theatre director comes up twice a week, and they do proper plays as a sort of rep. in the local theatre. He is coming all this weekend, and is very keen for me to be there as much as possible, not only on general lines, but because he is producing Hay Fever and wants me to act as their 'dialect coach'! That was 9.30–10.30, a.m. Then I did 2 supervisions till 12.30, then lunch, then at 1.00 I read my Bethlehem paper—very well received indeed, and a good way of sort of introducing ME to the whole staff at once, instead of them getting to know me piecemeal. Then thank God I had a hour alone in my flat—well, 40 minutes, what with walking here and back through the snow. Then I met all the nursing staff for an hour and a half—16 who were there, some off duty—a very super and powerful bunch, powerful in that (a) they do *so* much of the real work with the patients and (b) their backgrounds—degrees in psychology, philosophy, sociology, agriculture, you name it—and mostly with a 'post-graduate Master's' in psychiatric nursing! Then I rushed out in the snowy dark along to the village, and did my shopping, at one of the 2 market stores—stocked up on juice, milk, bread etc. Then back and read for 10 minutes, and Kit picked me up and took me for a drink at a famous old coaching inn (1770)—The Red Lion; and we had a good chat, then back to his place for nice din and chat there, and home by 9, bath and here I am! Soon to settle down after a bit more delicious Kingsley Amis, and reading a paper of the Medical Director's—whom I am to supervise tomorrow! amongst others—phew!

Wed 1:15 p.m. Yesterday, Tuesday, was just as enjoyable as so far, quite a lot of work of varying kinds, in the a.m. 3 hours running of supervision, all interesting and good, and I was able to see things about the material, including of the last presentation, which was by the Senior Med. Director, Dan Schwarz—a very nice man, human and funny and thoughtful, of about 62. His 'office' is a lovely large room with a coal fire burning—super, tho' quite unnecessary as the C[entral] H[eating] is just right. Then I had an hour to myself when I wandered round Stockbridge in the sun, and then at 3.30 was taken on a tour of all the patients' quarters, workshops etc, by a nice woman patient of about 40, called Christy who comes from Cal. and has been here 3½ years! Many stay 4+ years, and the longest, being presented in a long Review conference on Friday a.m., for 9! The insurance systems make it possible—Christy told a great number of interesting things about 'their' end of it all, and I have been invited to an informal patients' group on Friday afternoon, which is small, no staff members of any sort go to, so I am pleased and flattered. Anyway, one of the things she told me is that it costs 106,000 dollars a year for a patient to be here! They only have 50 patients and they live in great comfort. Her room was lovely. About ⅓ of the patients are psychotic and there is very intensive one-to-one nurse attendance over 24 hours at The Inn, but less at the Elms, which is a transitional on-the-way-out house. The patients seem to manage each other very well, and I shall see more on Friday—Sexual relationships are Against The Rules of the hospital, though they must happen. Otherwise there are not a lot of rules, and the whole place seems (a) amazingly free (b) *amazingly* well-organised and disciplined.

At 6 I went to a party at the house of one of the Fellows—a fascinating young man called Jonathan Aronoff, who is married to a stunningly pretty and very nice woman called Valerie. Jonathan was born in Stockbridge, and went to kindergarten in the house he now lives in! The Fellows are *not* the top-rankers, as the name would suggest—they come for a 4-year stint, and are the Registrars' equivalent, and they wanted me to themselves for a bit, and so did I. There are 8 of them, and very bright, funny, friendly and learning their skills. They are all in analysis as part (free) of being here, some actually with senior staff, some with analysts 50–70 miles away. We had a wonderful free-flowing chat, and then Jonathan and Valerie and I went on to dinner with Kit and Suzanne, and at 10.30 I said 'I'm old enough to be the mother of all of you, and you must take Mummy home to bed'. I was knackered. I sleep very well here. A snowstorm was on by the time we drove home—all cars have snow tyres, the roads are ready salted, the snowploughs come out, and nothing grinds to a halt.

Got up at 7 a.m. and thick snow everywhere, looking fabulous, and sun coming out. I enjoyed my 10 minute walk to the main building. This morning 2 supervisions—one with the head of nursing staff, who has a Master's in Psychology and is doing a doctorate in Theology! and was extraordinarily interesting. We had a terrific conversation. Then a Clinical Review, with 25 staff present, of a patient who wants to be discharged. It was very intelligent, thoughtful and informed, very high-level, not a word *wasted*, I felt, unlike such a lot of that sort of thing where so much hot air goes up. Now Kit and I are setting out for Boston, where we are to be given dinner by the B. Psychoanal. Soc. and I will give a paper. It takes 2½ hours East by car and should be fabulous in the snow and sun.

Fri Nov. 21st We did have a *lovely* trip—2½ hours—out to Boston. We had another 'limousine', supplied by Austen Riggs, driven by a cheery old fellow called Al—and fortunately the car had normal glass, not dark. The country ride—through the Berkshire Hills, pronounced *as spelt*, over the Connecticut River, and the motorway—or Turnpike—across nice wooded country with some old colonial towns, beautiful old distinguished looking wooden houses: we stopped at a Howard Johnsons at my request and had an ice cream—I had double vanilla and chocolate chip, absolutely *delicious*—they do make wonderful ice cream here as a matter of course.

We got to Boston just as it was getting dark, and went round Cambridge and saw Harvard and Radcliffe, all covered in snow, with lovely trees in their big courtyards and quadrangles, mostly the buildings again colonial style, which is late eighteenth and early nineteenth century. Then we went to the Ritz-Carlton hotel, which is the same age as me exactly! and I was given a room which had a special term attached to it, can't remember it, but what it meant was it's usually 450 dollars a night, and they let me have it for (only!) 200! It was 2 rooms—a most elegant little sitting room, with old colonial furniture, a sofa, desk, easy chairs, upright chairs, and huge cupboard thing containing (a) a TV and (b) a *packed* fridge, for which they do *not* charge for the contents, unlike any other hotel with a stocked fridge I've ever seen. I *wished* I was a drinker—tho' I'm not—heaps of miniatures of everything, and a small bottle of champagne, red wine, white wine, six different beers, 4 different fruit juices, peanuts and chocolate. There was also a beautiful chandelier in the room, and heavy blue silk curtains. I was on the 8th floor and could see the sun just setting and sparkling on snowy Boston. My bedroom and bathroom equally grand, and thank goodness with a radio, as there is a very good day-long classical music programme, and I miss it here. There's a TV in my flat, which I don't watch, and I did tentatively ask for a radio, but nothing happened, and I'm being so totally spoilt anyway, so I left it. I hastily switched on this programme, and heard some Handel, Bach, Mozart while I sat with my feet up on my sofa sipping orange juice mixed with Perrier water, which I very much like. I changed into my new dress and decent shoes and stockings, having thanked God 2 million times for my boots, and Concorde Sox which I wear inside them (they are dull and plain and not marked Concorde any more—I suppose too many people snitched extras—but they are wool and come half-way up my legs which is just right in this weather). Then I met Kit in the hall and 5 members of the Psycho-An Soc. met us and took us to dinner there in the hotel.

Apparently the BPs. Soc is the most prestigious and largest in the country—I had no idea! These fellows were all very nice and welcoming and chatty and friendly and delighted and *honoured* to have me, isn't it all a lark, I can hardly believe, (well, *not* believe,) I am, apparently, *really* seen as an extremely distinguished individual. It all seems so extraordinary after years of humdrum slog. I keep slightly wondering if they know what (who!) they're talking about, but they *all do* it. It's largely to do with my Bethlehem paper—Little did I know when I wrote it that it was going to be so remarkable and bring me so much fame and perks and plaudits. The dinner was beautifully served and rather dull. I wasn't very hungry—I am not nervous *at all* when I do things at any point, but I sometimes notice I am just not very hungry, that's all—perhaps partly because, unlike my usual way of life, I eat a large lunch—just salad and eggs and ice cream but still, I eat it. I had chicken and veg. all of which was undercooked *too* far. I've heard of nouvelle cuisine but this was out of the ground practically.

Then we walked through 2 snowy streets to their Soc. H.Q. Rather large and imposing and not totally unlike ours. There were only about 45–50 people there, which they said, and I do believe, was largely due to the weather, which up there *was* v. snowy and had only come that day. I gave my Transvestite paper, and there was quite a lot of reasonably good discussion afterwards—though of course it is *not* as good or sort of magical (apparently) as Bethlehem and anyway I wrote it a long time ago, though I've tidied it up since. Then usual chats with lots of people—('oh, *thank you*' 'oh, how very nice of you' 'Goodness, how kind, what a lovely thing to say'. 'And it's a real pleasure to *be* here, too' 'Yes, I'm loving meeting you, too'. 'It's an enormous treat you're all giving *me*' 'No, it doesn't snow like this in November in England' 'Yes, I think New England is perfectly *lovely*' ETC).

Kit and I slipped and slithered back to the Ritz, and I listened to more music and had a nice comfy night in my enormous bed, and breakfast on a trolley in my room, and we set off at 8.30 a.m. Al had stayed overnite with his daughter. Arrived in time for a Clinical Conference at 11.30, then I did some supervisions, and at 4.0 Kit and I left for Amherst where the Univ. of Massachusetts is. It was snowing heavily by the time we left, and the journey, which should take about 1¼ hours, took 2½—nevertheless, I feel quite safe and untroubled. The speed limit on all main roads is 55 and a very good thing too, and people keep to it. And most cars have (a) front wheel drives and (b) all-weather or snow tyres; and (c) the ploughs and gritters and sanders get out early and there are *heaps* of them. Nevertheless there were long queues of traffic most of the way, partly because rush hour from one town to another, and partly because it only needs one or 2 minor accidents, and there are tailbacks. There *were* 3 'accidents' but nothing nasty, only cars skidded into others or off the road, but of course it's the police rather than the cars themselves who hold everything up.

We had dinner from 6.30–7.45 with a *very* nice bunch of people, the Prof. of English who's a very well-known critic in a psychoanalytical style [Murray Schwartz, Dean of Humanities and Fine Arts], and his wife, and nice daughter of 16, and a jolly woman who is Professor of Film [Cathy Portuges]. A much better dinner than the Ritz—I had shrimp salad—the shrimps are fresh, and about 2" long—and a 'Yankee Mixed Grill' because unlike the night before, I was *starving*. It was 2 tiny steak fillets, a big pork chop, and some marinated roast chicken with cranberry sauce, and roast potatoes and broccoli. Then we drove to the old library building where the Prof. of English has his huge and yet cosy study, and we had a long and extremely interesting discussion *on* my Bethlehem paper, which they'd all read. Kit does the leading, or opening, of that sort of thing, very well, but they all had plenty of intelligent, good things to say, and it was far and away the best discussion I've ever had on that paper, and not an analyst among them, thank God just a real and lively interest in the subject. There were only 12 people there—again the weather—they had a lot of apologies, and usually have about 40–50, which was a shame in a way, but in another way, we had such an excellent chat with the smaller group that I didn't mind at all. They were so intelligent and perceptive about what I meant, and I was absolutely on top form, thinking out things as I went along, and stimulated to clarity and also making several good jokes, as I went along. I am sort of *amazed* at this ability in myself, really only discovered late in life—it's extremely gratifying and great fun. I really do feel in excellent form, and I can hear that I am interesting and unusual and enjoyable to listen to, and converse with. Kit told me later they are paying me 500 dollars just for that, and I nearly fainted.

We had a much better ride home, as it had warmed up and was raining, and there was hardly any traffic. Kit is an excellent companion, and we *chat* the whole time, and obviously both enjoy it. I feel one of the bonuses of the whole thing is that I've actually made 2 new friends—him and his wife—and they are coming back to England for good in 2 years time. It all goes to show you never know what you are setting in train by your actions—(apart from the stunning and to me, totally unexpected, continued success of Bethlehem), I got Kit to come on the Clinic Directorate in 1977 by asking him personally, and also I sent him 3 patients when he qualified and also *once* gave him a supervision session when he asked for it, and didn't charge him: he remembers all that, but he also remembers how happy and harmonious and hard-working we all were on the Directorate when I was there, and—along with 12 other people who also remember—how it all fell apart when I left. Well, amazing! Cast your bread upon the waters . . .

I was in my flat by midnight = my birthday! so I just read a summary of a case which was to be presented for review next morning, and went to sleep. Thicker snow again this morning. I enjoyed my a.m. trudge through it. 2 supervisions, and then 2 hours Case Conference, most interesting, they are very very good at all that here. Then lunch, then another Case review; now almost as a birthday treat but quite by accident—I have 2 whole lovely hours before I am taken to a grand dinner in the Red Lion, the old (1770) coaching inn here, then give my Transvestite paper to what they expect will be a big audience, as apparently the A.R. Friday night meetings are famous all over, *and then* a 'cocktail party' at the home of Ess White, a nice and amusing older man, of about 70, the Senior staff member here. Phew!

—**later, Fri:** I forgot to say I did 2 things yesterday after returning from Boston besides supervision, which I liked: one was I sat in on a Community meeting, of most of the patients, and a handful of staff. A psychotic huge Fat Boy from Texas blathered on about getting Jewish books for the library—some of the ♀ pts got fed up with him, as did I, and they in quite a nice direct way told him to belt up. Then I did another seminar with the nursing staff, which they'd asked me to come back for—*very* good. We talked about liking and disliking patients, *hating* patients, loving patients, letting them go, and variations on those themes. Very lively and thoughtful and fun. I am *not* after all invited to go to the completely informal, i.e. private meeting, of patients today—they on the whole voted against it. 2 or 3 very nicely came up to me and apologised and explained why—constricting to their freedom, they don't really know me, etc. Gosh, I quite understood all that, and said so. Besides it gives me an extra birthday hour alone in my flat, which I'm so enjoying—just had a bath and dolled up for tonight's dinner, paper and party in my nice dress which I'm 100% pleased with!

Sun morning, Nov. 23rd It hasn't snowed in 2 days, but is still lying thickly, and as this is such a quiet country town, it hasn't turned to filthy slush. The sun is shining and it is another lovely day as it has been most of the time I've been here. The Friday night dinner and paper etc went very well. Thank goodness it *wasn't* a large dinner party: there was Dan Schwartz, the medical Director, whom I like a lot, and to whom I have given 2 supervisions on a patient of his! (Thank goodness I thought of something interesting but not too intrusive or showing off about his patient); and Dan's wife a nice woman with 4 grown up children; they know Rafael [Moses] very well, so we had lots of chat about Israel, Agi [Bene], Rena etc. Also Kit and Suzanne were there, and Kate, the head nurse, the one who is already a psychologist, doing a degree in Theology and got a small private practice of her own as well, whom I also like, and in various ways have got to know quite well. And Jim Sachstedter, a bachelor of a very sophisticated amusing type, whom I also like, and is one of the Senior Staff members, has been here 7 years. He travels a great deal, and I sat next to him and we had lots of chat about Places. I had a delicious salad, and a thing called Chicken

Almondine, chicken in breadcrumbs and almonds, and a dish of braised cabbage and another of carrots went round the table.

Then we went over to AR. and Jim introduced me to the audience, which, sure enough, was a good big one, with about 70 people from all around the countryside there. We had a good discussion on dear old R— (the Transvestite) and lots of people came up after and said how much they appreciated my 'openness' and lack of defensiveness about things that had been difficult or had gone wrong, and my humour, and my willingness to listen and discuss—blah, blah. Also several people said it was the best Friday evening they'd ever been to at AR, ho ho, what a super joke it all is. Then someone drove me to Ess White's elegant house up in the hills, and he gave me a lovely party, and after I'd been there about 10 minutes, suddenly they all gathered round—about 40 of them—and sang Happy Birthday to You, and produced a wonderful cake—chocolate and cream, with 'Nina—Happy Birthday—No. 60!' written on it in cream icing. I was quite overcome, but managed to make a tiny little speech saying how terrific they all were, etc—which they are. I had a nice chat with Ess, who is distinguished and tall and lean, about 72–73, very humorous, very drawly—from the South. We came home about 10.30—I am always *exhausted* by late evening, and they are very good about getting me home.

On Saturday morning I slept in, thank God, then did what lots of people had said was a MUST, and walked along and had breakfast in the Red Lion and read while I was eating bacon and eggs and rye bread toast—lovely. Then I wandered about Stockbridge, and went to the Norman Rockwell museum—I knew his work already from way back, much to peoples' surprise and pleasure—sheer luck, it was because long ago I used to read the Saturday Evening Post for awhile, after coming to America the first time, and he used to do the covers. He died in 1979 aged 86, and he lived here. There was a conducted tour of the little gallery, with about 8 rooms with his original draft in, and I enjoyed it. Homely, very clever, detailed paintings of American Home life. Then I did a bit of shopping and came back to the flat and did a supervision from 1–2—with the head nurse again, Kate, quite interesting—on a Problematic Staff Member, whom I'd already spotted as such in my group: also I had diagnosed that she might have been a nun, and she had!

Then I did a perfectly fascinating, and—I later discovered—exhausting thing for the next 5 hours, which was attend a rehearsal of the play which is being put on on Dec 5, 6, 7, 8 and over New Year. The director is a hypomanic enthusiastic character, called Ike something, who's apparently quite well known in New York, but—presumably as his Charity work, or out of interest, or something—does 2 productions a year in Stockbridge, which is *mostly* patients, and some local people. This one is Hay Fever, and I had been nabbed earlier in the week as 'dialect coach'. There is a nice little theatre over the place where all their art rooms, workshops—pottery, weaving etc—and their shop, are. The theatre holds about 100, but at present there's a lot of rubble, props, cigarette ends, coffee mugs, coats, etc, and Ike and me and the cast. Considering all *sorts* of things, like 3 weeks still to go, amateurs, most of them patients etc, it was already *very good* and by The Night I think will be terrific—which is the reputation Ike has here. They used me a *lot*, and I enjoyed it, and it really made me *think* about the way I speak. Also I tried very hard to be a good and supportive and boosting audience, since it obviously must make a difference to have an audience at all, and especially one that laughs at some of the right places. Fortunately they are good enough, though still reading lines a lot, to make that not too hard—to my relief—and also I find Noel Coward very funny anyway, which was a help.

It is a cast of nine, and they were all on some of the time—5 women and 4 men: only one of the women, the big dramatic lead, an (in the play) ex-actress called Judith, was not a patient, and she's had a lot of experience in local rep, and has an excellent voice and is a natural comedian, and was just *very* good—carrying it really, so far. The other 4 are patients, and 2 of them were very good—the maid and the next dramatic lead—no, 3 of them were good—and one isn't but has to play a shy little ingenue which is always tough, anyway. The one playing Myra Arundel—who is a patient because she's an ex drug addict and made a suicide attempt—is also an experienced actress, and is good, and moreover not at all a bad English accent. They certainly do find it hard to speak English the way I do! Apparently very simple things are the hardest of all—ironing out the 'rs' in words, for example, and saying *aw*fully and *daugh*ter instead of ahfully and dahter. The daughter of Judith, called Sorrel in the play, is a patient for I'm not sure what, but she was a good little actress, with a creditable and sustained attempt at an English accent—the only problem *about* her was that they had decided it was pronounced Sorr*ell*, and I *had* to change that—some things I just left—and as they've already been rehearsing for 3 weeks, it was quite hard—someone would say, 'oh, Sorr*ell*, come here' and a great chorus was going up by the end of the afternoon from all the others—'*Sorr*el'—; the maid, who has quite an important, funny little part, is meant to be a Cockney, and in a way she was ghastly—not as an actress—and her accent, tho' certainly not American, sounded like pretty near nothing on earth to me, but I worked at simple things like dropping her aitches—which people just don't do over here, even the working class—and toothike, for toothache. The two older men are town people, and weren't bad, tho' not good, and the two younger men were patients—one an ex-psychotic—he was the weakest link in the chain, though he had a boring part—but by the end of the afternoon he was way behind the others in his English accent, and stuck out like a sore thumb. They would stop every half hour or so for me to do coaching and I'd make notes in between—this one would listen to me without looking at me, and then go right on talking just as he had before! The other was a bright young man whom I'd heard a Case Conference on, he is being discharged at Xmas having been here 3 years and done well—he's a good actor, and he worked the hardest at changing his accent through the afternoon, you could really hear him at it. The last 45 minutes they ran right through Act I and I nearly fell off my chair in my efforts to laugh when I could, and make appreciative noises, and clap loudly at the end, and it really wasn't at all bad.

Then Kate picked me up and drove me out to dinner at Kit's place, and we stopped off en route to have a drink with her mate, who is at present being a cook in a rather nasty little restaurant in Great Barrington. As I suspected, she is a woman and a tough, rather intimidating lesbian, whom I rather liked, and we had a good chat about the subject of her Ph.D. thesis, for which she got an A, almost unheard of, and which was on Catholicism and Theravada Buddhism so weirdly enough we had a big subject of interest in common which we rallied about in a somewhat surrealistic manner in this hot little kitchen with two Austen Riggs patients who are employed there cooking onions and hamburgers right alongside us. She and Kate have a tiny studio flat in N.Y. and to my horror are going to be there on Tuesday and suggested I should go and see them. Thank God I thought quickly and decided honesty was the best policy (which I think is part of the secret of my whole success as an analyst out here, I must say!) and said I would rather have my remaining very short time in N.Y. to myself and I had various things I had already planned to do—which I have. Then we went on to Kit's and Suzanne's and had our usual nice evening there, lovely swordfish steaks and rice and salad—but I was suddenly *so tired*, I could hardly speak, and Kit and Suzanne are both very noticing and solicitous of me, so they got Kate to bring me home about 9.30, and I was thankful to return to my peaceful flat.

I don't still go to sleep till about midnight, but I *long* to stop chatting and being On Show, and I love sitting up in bed and reading. My books have lasted me *just right*, and been lovely. I had a lovely bath and long sleep, got up about 9 a.m., and did up nice little presents for Kit and Sue and Sacha. I'm giving Kit the Kingsley Amis novel I brought out and have finished, and which I thought was an inspiration to do—and Sue, I brought out a B[ritish]M [useum] 1987 calendar and tea towel for her, and bought an expensive box of delicious cookies in the village for her, and Sacha a large chocolate bear, and another pen, and a card of Concorde, because he was fascinated by me being on it. As is everyone I tell, but I haven't told many.

Kit called for me about 11.30 and we've had a perfectly marvellous day going for a long, long drive up through Northern Massachusetts, into Vermont and back by another route taking in New York State. Sue was coming, but her father in England is rather suddenly dying of leukaemia, it seems, and she had a phone call early this morning and is flying to England tomorrow, so had to stay home and do things. Anyhow Kit and I get on *extremely* well, and probably *chat* as well as I ever have with anyone, and especially about psychoanalysis which is not so easy if someone else is there. We talked almost non-stop from 11 a.m. to 5 p.m.! So I'm tired *again*! We saw some wonderful views—went up part of the Appalachian trail, and high over the Green Mountains, leading to the Catskills, and saw hunters, and skiers, and skaters and highest of all, huge trees on which the ice and snow had frozen on everything as pure ice, which glittered in the sun and against the blue sky like a magical forest of diamonds. We saw Bennington College, v. smart woman's college, very isolated and more like a convent, and we hated that, and then later Williams College, where Anne Earle's daughter has just finished, and that was *very* nice, in a bustling little lively college town, a bit like a tiny Cambridge. We wanted Real American food for our day out, so for lunch we had a huge and delicious hamburger with lettuce and tomato and french fries, and for 'tea' in Williamstown at 4 o'clock a chocolate hot fudge sundae! Got in here by 5 pm and Kit dropped me off, so I'm having a nice quiet couple of hours to myself, and he and Sue will pick me up for dinner later. I told him how specially grateful I had been to be driven about everywhere, as I had not relished driving myself— tho' as it turns out the roads are quiet, wide and empty most of the time. But I've preferred it this way.

Mon Nov. 24 Back at the Ritz Carlton Hotel in Boston! Kit and Suzanne took me out to dinner last night at the Federal House, an elegant restaurant in an old house, with only about 5 tables in each room—I keep trying to *pay* for things for them, but K. just signs bills on Austen Riggs, who must have spent 100s of dollars on me, including my limousine up to Boston again today. Sue has just had a phone call from her mother about her father and is going to fly home on Tuesday with her daughter aged 14, a rather sulky-looking girl called Nisha, who didn't take my fancy nearly as much as her elder brother, Danny, or Sacha. We had a nice quiet dinner, I had chicken as I usually do, done in different ways—this was 2 thick slices in pancake, with potatoes and broccoli, and I had watercress soup first. It's a wonder to me *all* Americans aren't 18 stone, though quite a few are that I see around, because *all* the helpings of everything are gigantic. We had a white Californian wine with it extremely nice, in fact one of the nicest white wines I've ever had—a Chardonnay. It's full bodied and medium dry/sweet, but really much more fruity and sort of *there* than even my favourite Niersteiner. But it's odd how I've basically sort of gone off drinking. I've hardly drunk anything but fruit juice while I've been here.

I had a good sleep as usual and put my alarm for 6.45 a.m. to make *sure* of getting to the morning Conference at 8.30 because (a) it's interesting on a Monday and (b) I thought it would be the best time to say goodbye to people and it was. Thank goodness I did, too, because at the end Ess White asked Dr. C. for her general impressions etc of Riggs, so I made a graceful little speech saying how much I had enjoyed it, and how wonderful and friendly they had all been, and how impressed I was by the level of work and discipline and attention to the task in hand, whatever it might be. All true. I *also* managed to work in that I was 'very puzzled' (= deeply critical) of the fact that patients not only seemed to change therapists if it got tough going in their treatment but were also allowed to choose their own therapists. I said I didn't see really how the negative transference ever got worked out, and furthermore I didn't know on what criteria patients shopped around; then I hastened to finish off with more nice things, and lots of people said nice things back etc., and came and shook hands with me, and that was that. I went and did some shopping in the village, bought some soap for Betty Homage, Kit's secretary, who's done a lot for me one way or another, and a bottle of Chardonnay (16 dollars!) for Dan, and then came back and delivered them, and collected some things from my office, and went back to my flat to pack, which didn't take long. I've got things in pretty easily. Perhaps even giving Kit one book helped. The only things I absolutely haven't used are my swimsuit and my thermal vest and pants. The former was worth bringing, just in case, and the latter was *not*, and is a salutary lesson in Not Listening to Other People, but sticking to my own ideas. It was Cecil, of *all* people, who said you must take them—I must be mad. She's crazy about things like that, and lives in the coldest flat in England anyway, and I just didn't stick to my instinct and my own *knowledge* which is that America has good central heating and warm cars, and even if it snowed, which it has, I should *not* need them.

Then at 12 Kit took me out to lunch at the Red Lion, as usual on A.R—I had a roast beef sandwich on rye, and he had an *enormous* salad. Mine was 4 slices of (nice) beef, masses of potato crisps, a whole dill pickle, and a side salad of coleslaw! I ate the beef and the dill pickle and one slice of bread. Then I bade a fond farewell of Kit, after we had had a very intense chat about this hopeless defect at AR of people changing therapists if they get upset or angry, and saying it was a *real* drawback and very anti-analytic, and a real blind spot there. He *hopes* to change it gradually, but has no real support—so I'm very glad I said even what I did. He says, interestingly, he thinks it's like a great American flaw right there in the hospital—that you've *got* to be Nice, and things can't be tolerated if they go a bit wrong—they can't be worked through, or used, but have to be changed, and you have to look for something 'nicer' and easier—cf. marriages, etc. I couldn't stick that at AR—I'd soon be fighting over it, and that lovely Dr. Coltart wouldn't be so amiable after all. I must remember to tell Rafael, who I think understands the analytic thing about working with negative feelings, and who is going to AR for a year in 88–89 as the Erikson fellow. Can't think how his own patients manage the way he gads around. Al drove me up to Boston again, and I had a comfortable snoozy ride. The snow has all gone. Now I shall have a bath and await someone to collect me—I'm not sure when they are going to, but that's their problem . . . !

Tues Nov. 25 7.30 p.m. in the *War* – wick Hotel, 54th Street and 6th, N.Y., after a packed and lovely day on my own, Thank God. // No-one collected me till 7.45 p.m! at the Ritz in Boston. I had a bath and changed and was quite happy reading and listening to the classical music programme, but didn't like to go out and walk around in case anyone came to pick me up at 5.45, 6.0, 6.15, 6.30—etc. They are a bit dozy at the Boston Psychoanalytic and that's a fact. I forgot to say, and it was *very* funny—Kit and I giggled about it on and off all that evening, and the next day—that *after* my meeting there on Wednesday, just as I was leaving, I said to Andy Morrison, who's their Chairman—no, he *can't* be—he does the lecture arrangements—'Where shall I come to on Monday afternoon?'—and he gazed at me, speechless, and his mouth *literally* dropped open—I don't think I've ever actually seen that happen before. I said—'You know-Monday—24th Nov.—I'm coming back here again . . .' — 'Yes', he said eagerly. 'To do the workshop in the evening', I said. 'Yes, yes', he said, faint but pursuing. 'I've got to stay somewhere', I said. (I didn't like to say—'Shall I go straight to the Ritz?', as it's so expensive, and for all I knew someone was putting me up—obviously not Andy Morrison, however, who probably lives under a library table somewhere.) Fortunately Howard Levine, who is marginally more with us, joined us at that point, and he said come to the Ritz, and we'll collect you. . . . So I did.

Anyway, I don't get hungry in the evenings, not the way I do at lunchtime, and I always have lunch here. Howard and a nice woman called Enid Caldwell, whom I vaguely remembered from having met her in England sometime, came to get me, and we walked to the Society, and were joined by only 6 others. I was slightly horrified, not because I *at all* mind a small group, in fact I like it, but because I knew by then from what Kit had told me that they were paying me an enormous sum of money for these two evenings. We had a good group, once it got going. I missed Kit, and it was a bit stickier without him. But we got it under way. Interestingly, this was *not* as good, or at least as sympathetic, or in tune with, my ideas in the Bethlehem paper—which they'd all got with them—as the very nice group at U. of Mass.—(not analysts). 2 of these were very 'old-fashioned'—which a lot of American analysts are—and both of them brought up things which are simply miles off anything I was talking about.

One of them, an oldish man called Sam, who I actually thought was sweet, made a long rambling comment about 'drives' which is an ancient Freudian concept which no-one talks about in England for the last 25 years or so. I really had to wrench my head about to come up with some sort of cordial rejoinder. Then another, rather attractive Jew of about 55 called Martin Something got going on me 'shouting at a patient', which I'd already said had been the main subject of discussion and controversy at the original English Conference, and I was sick of it—ha ha—it's amazing how some people just *can't* keep off it, it hypnotises them. He made a comment about it which was so absolutely *not* what I thought about it, and God knows I've been forced to think about it almost more than anything I've ever done, that I just had to argue, but that was OK and quite lively, and the others were dying to get at that anyway, but had been too polite, I think.

Then dear old bumbling Andy—he's only about 45—gave a long report of a couple of sessions of someone he's working with which he finished up lamely by saying 'I thought that was sort of relevant to your paper—I'm not sure why now'. I couldn't make head nor tail of it, except that what was made very obvious is just *how* Freudian and old-fashioned and simply *years* behind my paper their sort of analytic style is, if that's a sample, and the others all discussed it quite animatedly as if it *is*—so I guess it is. He was making a *very mild* interpretation of the female patient's fantasies about him, and this is in the *sixth year* of her analysis, and I gather it was meant to relate to my paper because it was a sort of great new insight. I did fish up a few very simple and gentle things to say, and they were quite suitable as it turned out. Anyway it all went OK, and at the end, a rather snooty-looking man called Julius Silberger, whom actually I'd talked to at the dinner on Wed. and found it quite easy, as he is attractive to me, gave me a copy of his *book*, about Mary Baker Eddy—which naturally I'd quite genuinely expressed an interest in—all nicely signed, etc, *and* a paper of his, ditto, and was quite coy about it. Then Andy, with somewhat of a flourish, gave me an envelope in which I knew was this colossal cheque (for 750 dollars!), and I blushed a bit and said I simply didn't think I was worthy, which is quite true, but a bit hammy, because of course then they all had to do a sort of 'Oh yes, you are' thing. Then they took me back to my hotel—10.30—and I was on my own with all the work of my American trip over, so of course I was both relieved and a bit flat, so I had a bottle of beer!

I got up at 7 and had a delicious bacon and egg breakfast at 7.30 on a trolley, with Dvorak's cello concerto, and then I got a taxi to Logan Airport—only 5 miles, to catch the 10 a.m. shuttle. Log. Airport sticks right out into Boston Harbour so had a wonderful view of it as we took off, and I looked out the window the whole trip—only 50 minutes, as we flew across Massachusetts and into New York, and landed at La Guardia airport, which is in Queens. As I am so stinking rich, I had a limousine into Manhattan, and got matey with the driver, who is going to pick me up at the Frick Museum tomorrow morning and take me to JFK airport. I got to the Warwick Hotel at about 11.30, and checked in, and put my wallet containing my passport, ticket, and most of my money into the hotel safe, as yet again Michael [the driver]—I mean, yet another one—had warned me about pickpocketing etc. in N.Y.—especially from now to New Year, now being Thanksgiving—at least, Thursday is, I think. Actually, I think it's largely common sense—I twist my handbag strap several times round my wrist, and carry it, with the fastener inwards, and although I walk a lot, I'm sure I don't *look* easy prey. Michael said one should always walk as if one owned the place anyway, and he commented that I'd walked out of La Guardia like that anyway! (I had booked a limousine ahead from Logan Airport, and I was the only one *on* that Shuttle so he was looking for someone.)

I am on the 23rd floor here, and so it is nice and quiet, though I have the window open, as it has been sunny and warm today—55°. I walked up some of 6th Avenue, and outside Rumpelmayer's, a very grand hotel, I thought I'd get a cab. There was a line of them, moving slowly up to the hotel, so I went to the first one, who refused me, and I said 'Why?' and he said 'Because I'm going to take a hotel passenger', and I looked round rather vaguely, really just looking for another cab, when the most enormous Commissionaire from the Hotel bore down on us, and said 'What's da madder, lady?' and I said 'I just want a cab' and that gigantic man immediately lost his temper with the cabdriver, a rather small Puerto-Rican, and really bawled him out—'Whaddy a think you're playing at, you stupid little bastard? You refusin' to take a lady?—Who d'ya think y'are? Whaddy a waitin' for? Come on, now, take the lady—get *in*, lady'—I was very embarrassed and annoyed, there was a whole queue of people, presumably *from* the hotel, gazing at us with their mouths open. Anyway, I got in, and as we inched off in the ghastly N.Y. traffic, I said 'Sorry, sorry, I didn't mean to get you into all that'—but this little man was FURIOUS, and gabbled away, partly to himself and partly *at* me—for almost 10 minutes, half under his breath—'Shit, shit, what the fuck—I bin waitin' there an *hour* (I don't believe that) to get a decent fare, I'll get out of New York as soon as I can I'm not staying here, shit, shit, fuck, what am I doing here, if I had the money I'd get out tomorrow' etc etc. I was going to the Guggenheim Museum, about 25 blocks, so I don't know what he'd wanted, quite. Anyway, the fare only came to 5.20, so as I was sorry for him I gave him 20 dollars, and he didn't sort of believe it, and was fumbling for change. So I said 'That's for *you*, say thank you!' And he did, very nicely.

Anyway, Kit had said what to do in the Guggenheim, and that I *must* go. It's the most extraordinary building, circular, like a great layered cake, and was designed by Frank Lloyd Wright. You take a lift to the top—seven floors, but high ones, and then walk down a long, huge, spiral ramp—the building is domed inside, and all the way down the ramp you can look right up to the top, and right down to the ground floor, and sort of *at* all the spiral as it is. The two main exhibitions in the spiral were modern French, and Richard Long—an amazing Englishman that I know a lot about, and have always wanted to see his stuff—such as you can, because it's mostly huge photographs of his art, for which he uses nature. He's not the man who wraps up bridges, he's the one who makes marks with stones and goes for long walks on Dartmoor, and makes trails in snow, in the Himalayas—it's almost impossible to describe. It's all meant to be absorbed back into nature, or most of it. There were two 'things' of his there—about 30 yards of slate tiles, making a path down part of the ramp—and a big circle of flints. It sounds ridiculous, but it isn't at all. I did that in about ½ hour, quite swiftly—then walked 6 blocks to the Met. Museum of Art, and just went in and spent ½ hour there, fantastic collection, and a new Van Gogh Exhibition, starting today. But I wasn't going to get exhausted there, and I can see Van Gogh in Holland, and have, and anyway there was a queue for that—so I came out again into the brilliant sun, and then walked about 10 blocks, just gazing at New York and the shops, and was still only in the 70s, so I took another cab to the Museum of Modern Art, which is in the 50s, and which I was determined to finish off. I had some lunch there—orange juice and a hamburger and coffee, as by then it was 2.30, and then did the upper floor. All very modern, right up to early '80s, and I was interested, though most of it is beyond me.

I eavesdropped on a *fascinating* Event. A very distinguished looking man who had bad polio legs and walked slowly with a stick, and was, I think, probably The Director, was standing with a sycophantic retinue of about 7 people planning when and where they are going to hang a new Matisse. By pretending I was gazing at 3 they already have, I backed right up and almost into their group, and listened to the whole thing—he was just *exactly* what I imagine an immensely powerful, rich New York businessman or Director to be. He had all his retinue nodding and becking and being obeisant, and trying to be very Bright and lick his Arse at the same time—he's going to Europe next week, and it's got to be Up and In Place by the time he gets back. Then they scattered and he hobbled off with his Secretary or P.A.—a pale, beautiful, languid girl all in black who seemed more up to him. I trailed them all the way down to the ground floor, as I had finished by then.

Then I thought for Auld Lang Sync and Something Completely Different, I'd go to Radio City Music Hall. I went there in 1950. It's in the Rockefeller Centre, and I walked, only 5 blocks. They have their Xmas Show newly opened, 'several shows a day'—with the 36 Rockettes, whose predecessors I saw there—36 years ago. My luck ran out, as my 'What's On' had not mentioned there were no shows on Tuesdays. So I went for a long amble round the amazing enclosed shopping precinct on several floors there, and bought lots of cards. The Observatory Roof on the 60th floor or so is closed for repairs, and I wouldn't have been tempted by that again anyway. By this time it was 5.45 pm, and I was exhausted. I decided I felt like a DRINK—just like a normal person. In my 60th year I seem to have become rather suddenly a normal drinker. So I walked back to my hotel which has what turned out to be a very popular, nearly dark, bar on the ground floor. By 6.30 it was *packed*, mostly with men. I began to feel like 'I came here tonight to be Insulted, and I'm not going home until I am', sitting at my little table. I suddenly remembered a mixed Vermouth, and thought I wanted that more than anything. So I had it, with a bottle of soda on the side—of course the drink itself was full of ice: and it was a brilliant idea, I *so* enjoyed it, it *was* exactly what I wanted. Then I had one more, and after that I absolutely didn't want any more, and it had done for me what I suppose Having a Drink does for normal people. Then I went and bought a carton of orange juice, and came up to my room at 7.30, and was thankful to be here, and take my clothes and boots off, and put my feet up, after a lovely day. Now I will have a bath and maybe even go to sleep early, because of course tomorrow the clocks go forward 5 hours, so I leave here in Concord at 1.45, and don't get in till 10.30 p.m, when by my clock it will only be 5.30 p.m., so my sleep will be knocked sideways for a bit. I plan to go to the Frick Museum tomorrow morning as soon as it opens—10 a.m.—taking my bag and briefcase, and Michael will meet me there and take me to JFK. So I won't write anymore in USA, but may put in a closing note on Concorde—after dinner!

On Concorde I am *so glad* I went to the Frick Collection for an hour *this* morning. It is absolutely stunning and I wouldn't have missed it for anything. It is just an old house on 72nd St., I think, not one you wd. notice—with several large and elegant rooms, with this *amazing* collection of mostly Old Masters, obviously put together privately by an immensely rich family earlier this century. Treasures include 3 Rembrandts—one youthful self portrait and one old age one; 3 *Vermeers*—I didn't know there were any I hadn't seen!—some Turners, 3 Constables, a Fra [Fi]Lippo Lippi, a Gerhardt David Deposition from the Cross—I *love* him and have only ever seen a few, in Bruges, I think; a Memling; some Van Dycks, and Van Eycks; 3 El Grecos; a Bellini; 2 Velazquez, 4 Goyas, a Bronzino, a Titian, 2 Cuyps, a Ruysdael, 3 Piero della Francesas, a Fra Angelico, about 5–6 Franz Hals, an Ingres, some that escape me for the moment, and a Degas, a Matisse, and 4 Whistler portraits. It was *pouring* with rain today and I was so pleased about how sunny and lovely yesterday had been.

Michael collected me in my limousine at 11 a.m, and we had a slow, trafficky journey to JFK airport. The Concorde lounge was luxurious but not as good as the British one. We took off exactly on time and immediately put our watches forward 5 hours, so it became 6.45 p.m., and we had dinner instead of lunch. The plane was nearly empty—only 8 people in 100 seats in my section. We had 3 little canapés, one cheese, one caviare, and one disgusting thing which was called 'quail and kumquat' and tasted like the smell of a lavatory which is also in a French restaurant. Then salad and crab and smoked salmon, then delicious lamb and baby courgettes and mashed carrot and turnip, and a squidgy sweet biscuity thing with cream and raspberries, and cheese, and coffee. I had one glass of champagne, which I don't really like, and otherwise orange juice. We arrived at 10 p.m. = 25 minutes early! having taken 3½ hours. Jan was there to meet me which was lovely and a nice end to my superb time, instead of a flat nothingness.

HERE ENDETH THE
SAGA OF MY GRAND
TOUR OF NEW ENGLAND
14–27 Nov. 1986.

CHAPTER THIRTY-ONE

The Trans-Siberian Railway*

8th April   Fly to Moscow
10th to 18th April   Trans-Siberian Railway
18th and 19th April   Beijing
20th April   Fly to London

We packed a suitcase each and an overnight bag—my black Samsonite, as you know, is very capacious. Because we'd read two books on the Trans-Siberian Express, one by Eric Newby when he'd gone on it in 1977, which actually, as it turned out, wasn't all that out of date, and one by someone who'd gone on it in 1991, which brought us up to date and they had advised about (a) presents for people who looked after us on the train, and on the hotel floors, etc., and (b) food for ourselves, because it's so sparse and unspeakable on the train (and it was), a

---

*Extract from a typewritten personal letter dated 3 May 1993. This journey was taken with Nina Coltart's friend and neighbour in Leighton Buzzard, Dr Vicky Plumb.

223

lot of our luggage consisted of that and got lighter and lighter as we went along.

I'll jump ahead, and say that there were three conductresses who worked in shifts, on the train, and they were tough sourfaced old cows who gradually softened towards us as the week went by, because from the beginning we made a habit of being Fairy Godmothers every evening about 6 p.m., and took them presies, and they really were touched and thrilled. We used cigarettes, soap, tights, coffee, chocolate and glossy magazines. Things are just *not* obtainable in Russia. There was one lump of soap in the washroom at the beginning of the journey, ugly, lardy brown stuff, which had been stolen within a few hours and was never replaced. And what the Russians do (many of them were using the train as a conveyance between stations in the ordinary way—we stopped at about 20 places all told) is to get out at the stations, and peasants would be crowded on the platform selling things—eggs, cooked chickens, fish (by Lake Baikal), vegetables, cooked potatoes, coleslaw, and of course, vodka and beer, and then a lot of bartering and buying would go on. We were the oldest people on the train *by far*—we hadn't realised we'd be rather a focus of interest because of it—and the young 'British contingent'—about 15 backpackers doing world travel before going up to University—all soon got together, *and* discovered us, and, again, were rather fascinated by our age and us, and would drift along the corridor and chat to us, leaning up against the door of our carriage. Well, *they* hadn't thought to bring any food, or probably hadn't got room, so firstly, they went to the restaurant car at every meal time and jolly well ate what there was, and secondly, they would leap out and buy bread and salami and potatoes, etc., so they were glad of it—as were the Russians.

There was no one, but no one, on the train who could speak English—or Russian from our end—so a lot of signing and nods and becks and wreathèd smiles went on. The Russians really do drink tons and tons of vodka—it seemed to be mostly men, travelling, and they would start their *breakfast* in the dining car, with bottles of vodka! Ugh!

Where had I got to? Oh, yes, well, off we set for Heathrow—we had a taxi from Leighton Buzzard. And we flew Aeroflot—there *were* others, but we thought we might as well do it properly. If I'd read then what I've read since getting home about Aeroflot, I might not have been so keen. Ghastly safety record. We went economy, as it was only 4 hours—and really it wasn't so bad. And the food that way had been prepared in London.

Moscow Airport was pretty grim—very poor and dirty, but fortunately we found the Intourist desk where there was a girl who spoke some English, and our taxi had been booked for us as part of that package (Heathrow to Moscow hotel) so we just went with the taxi driver who appeared out of the gloom. I forgot to say it was dark by the time we got there, and *anywhere* we experienced in Russia in darkness was *very* poorly lit. Thank God my suitcase has wheels and a little doggie lead—it was bad enough *walking any* distance with it *and* my Samsonite (following a virus infection immediately beforehand), but it would have been worse if I'd had to carry it.

The hotel is one of the best in Moscow, and it was like a youth hostel, I kid you not. Our room was sparsely furnished, with poor light and *very* hard beds, and one thin pillow, and a washroom without (we'd been warned and had a squash ball and a plug with us, the former used all the time on the train too) plugs for the tiny grimy bath or basin. We had the next day in Moscow, and for me, it was the worst day of the whole thing. We (the 'British gang' were all in the same hotel) had a very nice guide called Igor, who spoke good English, and he took us on two tours in an old rickety bus, one morning and one afternoon. It was a filthy, freezing day, with icy rain spitting down, and we were meant to do a lot of walking and that really did it for me. After the Kremlin, we walked to Red Square. Fortunately the bus was parked there, with the driver still in it, so I went and he let me in, and the others walked for about another three-quarters of an hour—thank heaven for the bus! Of course that singled me out as 'not so good' from the beginning, but everyone was very nice—because I hardly ever went to the restaurant car on the train, whereas V. kept up a valiant effort except for supper, which we had ourselves in the carriage.

We had to wait till 11:30 p.m. that day to leave for the station, and really, if we hadn't had Igor, I can't think how we'd have found the *train*—Moscow station at midnight was The Nightmare of all time. It was still raining and icy, and the station was very dimly lit and *filthy*—mud and puddles and uneven ground, and thousands of people and what looked like hundreds of trains. But we had to stick with Igor because, little darling, he carried my suitcase—I'd never have got it up stairs and over the bumps, and he found our 'de luxe first class two-berth compartment' for us. There are only 10 on the whole train, and they are practically indescribable, except to say they are like old B[ritish] R[ail] 3rd-class carriages—one long hard bench down either side (mildly upholstered)—one small fixed table between us, one hook each, a mirror, and two bedside lights and one overhead light. No racks, nowhere to put anything! It was actually huge fun, and a real test of ingenuity, living in this thing for a week—we got it to a fine art pretty soon. The bootfaced conductress delivered one tea-towel (= towel), two half tablecloths (sheets) and a pillow case and, mercifully, one good thick, *clean* rug each, and we made up our own beds every night. The windows were smeary but seeable through.

At the end of the corridors, each one, there was a vast, ancient, complicated samovar, which they kept going well, and was a constant source of boiling water, so we made lots of tea, coffee and packet soup, which latter was a great boon. We'd taken 2½ pints of long life milk each and that just about lasted us. The package soups were a great standby on the train—chicken and vegetable, chicken and mushroom, and tomato and vegetable—delicious.

Well, anyway, it was a great journey, and I wouldn't have missed it for anything, and the fact is, I think (a) we might never have got round to fixing it all again, and (b) they won't take—or rather, won't insure—anyone of 70 or over. So I'm jolly glad I was so determined—and I *had* thought well, sitting on a train must be fairly restful—and it was.

The lights in the train were very dim, so much so that when darkness fell, one really just had to chat or make up the beds and go to sleep—*until OMSK*. You know, where the nuclear explosion was, that They said mysteriously little about on the news etc., the week before our journey? Well, after—just after—we'd been through Omsk—which was about 8 p.m., so pitch dark, we had our miserable carriage lights on still—they all SUDDENLY got very BRIGHT!! And *stayed* that way until we got to Beijing. I don't mean they stayed on all day—but when they came on at night, which was only *as* darkness fell, even the ones we were able to switch on and off ourselves, our bedside lights—they were still bright; I think *actually* the train generator must have picked up oomph as we travelled. But it seemed at the time both hilarious and sinister, as if a sudden burst of nuclear radiation had hit them (and not only them, one assumes, but us. I wonder when I shall grow another head?).

A lot of what we looked at out of the windows was pretty samey, of course, once you've done a bit of gazing at rocky tundra or 20,000,000 trees, you've got the general hang of that, and it's not exactly a thrill a minute. There was tons of snow, still, and no greenery, no signs of spring until we got a long, long way on, quite near China—no wolves or tigers, I was very disappointed. Lots of little settlements with very mean, poor wooden huts and houses—no electricity anywhere—but every now and then, a richer-looking one, or a really industrial town, with brick houses, and roads, and a few cars. But not many. The best bit was going alongside and round the bottom of and up part of the other side of Lake Baikal: the largest freshwater lake in the world, 400 miles long (London to Penzance or Edinburgh!), with species of fish in it that exist nowhere else. It was brilliant sunshine all day, and the lake was still thickly frozen; I think one of the most dramatic things we saw anywhere was waves frozen in the act of breaking—I suppose really they had built up and frozen gradually, but they *looked* as if they'd been caught breaking and frozen instantaneously. Every now and then we saw little huts far out on the ice with people moving about near them, and chopping holes in the ice and fishing through them; and men sledging out on the ice or walking on snowshoes or skis. It was just amazing, there was something hypnotic about standing in the corridor (it was that side) and gazing at this immense lake, which of course looked like the sea.

We had the worst hitch at the Russian–Chinese border. They made us fill in forms—all in Russian, fortunately one British girl could read them—and then took them, *and our passports*, and shoved us all out of the train on to a huge station with a huge waiting room, and Customs offices and banks and shops—of a sort; and they said, the border guards or Customs men, whatever they were—'Not allowed to take more than $50 out of Russia—go to Customs office and give over all other money'. Of course this came as an absolutely hideous blinding and, at first, terrifying shock. The British gang soon got together amidst all the crowds in this vast waiting room, and discussed it at length and In Depth—we'd none of us heard anything about this or like it *ever*, from anyone, beginning with our travel agents. We simply decided that we Were Not Going to Do It. We went to the Customs office, a smallish room with 15 officials in it, one of whom spoke English; and when we said "what are we meant to do with our other money?" she said "spend it—or put it in bank—get receipt for it, and collect it again on way back". "But we aren't coming back!" we yelled in chorus. She shrugged. "Any time in next three years!" Of course if we hadn't been so alarmed—because the newly ex-Soviet officials aren't used to *not* being Soviet bullies yet, and they had said it all very rudely and fiercely—we'd have seen the hole in that one, which we eventually did, because if we came back next week and collected it, we were still going to take it out of the country, as likely as not, when we get to where we're going. Anyway, we went to the bank out of interest; and if we had gone to pay all our sterling and dollars into accounts, we would have had to *change it all into roubles*, which are grossly inflated, it would have been thousands and thousands and you can't take *them* out of the country either! Nobody wants them, in my view.

One of our gang actually managed to telephone the British Embassy in Moscow—('sorry—everyone's gone to lunch'! Plus ça change . . .) and then the American Embassy, and the minion he got hold of there said what we'd already decided—he'd never heard of it (even the Russians were saying 'it a New Rule') and not to do it. So after that—we still weren't allowed on the train, so we fortunately found two benches in the waiting room, and sat it out there—we just kept saying 'no' or variations of it 'niet'—'piss off'—'don't you *want* Westerners to get a good impression of your New, Improved Country?'—'this will provoke an International Incident, you know'—'if you try to take it by search and force, we shall immediately contact the British Embassy, *now*', etc. etc. The only things that worried us were (1) that we had all trustingly filled in on our forms, because that was just *before* we started on this lark, exactly how much we had, and it was quite a *lot*, worth having. The youngsters had all been working like Trojans at whatever odd jobs they could pick up, to finance their world trips; (2) They still had our passports. I still in one bit of my mind thought they *might* mean it, so, as I'd been meaning to buy a fur hat anyway and did *not* like the cheaper raggedy ones that the beggars (heaps of them in Moscow) were offering for $5 or $10 in Red Square, I went to the Luxury Shop, for foreigners only (and it was *packed* with Western foreign goodies—scent, make up, silk etc. etc.) and bought a decent one. The very first one I picked out miraculously fitted me, which a lot of the others didn't, and I came back to it. It's squirrel and exquisitely made, lined with silk, and with wonderful earflaps and back neck flap which can either pull down and tie beneath your chin or tie back up across the top of the hat. It was $85!

[sketch of four views of a fur hat with earflaps, with handwritten annotations]

Anyway, we all sat there, idly discussing Life, and the current problem, quite interesting bunch of kids, thank goodness, and got steadily colder and hungrier and thirstier and the ones who smoked more gasping for a fag, because most of us had left *everything*, really, in the train, which had not only been locked after us, but had for a long while disappeared altogether! *Eventually* there was one of those mass crowd movements when no one has actually said anything but everyone knows it's time to move, and we clambered back (it is quite a clamber, up 6 steep mobile steps which are retractable), and, thank heaven, the train was still warm and the samovar boiling—ee, it was joost like 'ome—and we all made soup or tea or coffee—*and* They came round in a Body, handed back our passports, and one, the head bully, clicked his heels, bowed, *smiled*, said ''ave good journey', and the train pulled out of the station!! Talk about anticlimax! We could only think it was all a colossal try-on—but what a *nerve*; and supposing we *had* put all our money in their bank, or just *handed it over*, as I did see some Scandinavians doing??? Anyway, we *did* write to the Russian Ambassador here, and the British Ambassador in Moscow, when we got back, so it will be very interesting to see if and what they answer.

The change in the landscape the minute we got into China was amazing. I know they've been a terrible bloodstained dictatorship, and I don't want to say anything with the faintest ideological meaning, but I just *liked* China, everything about it I saw, *so* much more than Russia and the Russians, it's no comparison. The Spring had been gradually caught up with, and by now it was warm and sunny, and the landscape was green, but the noticeable thing was that people were working the land—everywhere—and there hadn't been a *sign* of that in Russia. Everything about Russia just seemed so grim and poor and hopeless and sullen. I *loathed* Moscow, and the countryside, our book told us, is packed with coal, and tin, and goldmines, and God knows what, and no one was doing anything. They have *not* got the idea of distribution right, is what it seems to me. My goodness, there's a lot for old Yeltsin to do. And nobody *smiled*, ever—or hardly ever. In China, people stood up in the fields, where they were working, and waved to the train and smiled and called out, and the little houses were painted and fresh, and it was just so much nicer all along. And the same went for Beijing—it may be ghastly under the surface but they sure have got the surface right for tourists. Our 'luxury hotel' really was—it was a marvellous treat, thank goodness it came at the end and not Moscow. We had a huge splendid room, with a balcony looking on to a courtyard with a pond and fountain and flowering trees, and two huge double beds, and a lovely bathroom and a fridge and a bar, and lots of lights. We ate in the restaurant and had Chinese food, of course, delicious. We only had one day there, too, so we chose to go to the Great Wall, on our own, in a taxi just for us, not a tour or a coach. It's a two-hour drive out of Beijing, and one sees that Beijing is surrounded by a great ring of mountains, and to the West is built (*was* built—in 2000 bc no less!) the Great Wall. We didn't actually climb up to it, but our nice driver stopped us at what was obviously a popular place as there was dancing, and bands, and acrobats, and jugglers, and little shops, etc. And we stopped in a fascinating market on the way back, which was good.

We had to get up at 4 a.m. (room service available) to catch our Air China plane, and for some complex reason, were hiked up from Club Class to First Class, so that was an extremely good way to end. A 17-hour flight, but with time changes we got in at 5 p.m., and J. met us and we drove to Leighton Buzzard—lovely.

CHAPTER THIRTY-TWO

A Tuscan holiday*

Friday, 15 Nov. [1991] Betty [Tamblen] collected me in her car 6 a.m. Parked in Long Stay Car Park of H'row. Caught 9 a.m. (50 mins. delayed) Alitalia flight to Pisa. Airport train to Florence, ugly countryside veiled in mist and rain. Arrive Fl. ca. 2 p.m., taxi to Hotel Berchielli, extremely nice—old fashioned posh, we *each* had a double room right over the R. Arno, which is running fast with debris, and rising, and people are *worried*. Walked in rain to Sta. Maria Novella, great empty church with Ghirlandaio frescoes around the high altar (p[ost]c[ard]s)—very enthralling and lifelike = 14c. Also a half-gone Masaccio fresco of Trinity, and a ?Donatello Rondel of m. and child. [*In margin:* 2 or 3 annunciations, 2 v. nice, one by Botticelli = Earthly life begins with a tiny picture of Christ rising from the tomb, underneath it – Heavenly life.] Walked home. Dinner in little trattoria just along Lungarno—I had pork chops and 'tiramisu', a delicious creamy, almondy, chocolatey trifle, and white

---

* Handwritten on stationery of the Hotel Berchielli (four stars), Lungarno Acciauoli 14, Piazza del Limbo, 6r, 50123 Firenze. Each entry is in the form of a single paragraph, and many "ands" appear as ampersands.

house wine. Betty had *tripe*—roasted, or baked which she said was lovely!! Walked home, still pouring. Meal *cheap*—around £15 each: (2,000 lira to the £).

Sat. 16 Nov. Breakfast in elegant hotel breakfast room, fresh carnations, coffee, ham, rolls, etc. Walked to the Uffizi (£5 entry) and up 127!! stairs to main galleries. Saw Duccios, Masaccios (tho' he died at 28), Botticelli Primavera and Birth of Venus, both recently cleaned and brilliant, and other good things (p.cs). Did half of it. Walked to Piazza Signoria, raining ++, lovely big empty piazzas, statues of Michelangelo's David and Neptune. Lunch in nice trattoria, veal escalope, spinach and chips, white house wine. Visited a grand chocolate shop. Walked to Piazza Santa Croce; Church shut—at 1 p.m. (Sat.) Walked to Baptistry and Cathedral. Bapt. has magnificent high relief gold doors of Bible scenes; Cathedral has a great dome by Brunelleschi, built in 15c. *without scaffolding*. Ghirlandaio fresco. Ghastly modern crib scene with dreadful china baby Jesus with soppy expression. Walked home—still raining but not cold. Arno about 3 feet risen, very fast and swirling. Read on bed for 1½ hours, while B. out walking again! Walked over Trinita bridge, along other side of Arno, and home over Ponte Vecchio, crammed with gold, silver and jewelry shops. There and in Lungarno did lots of bits of present-and-Xmas shopping, exclaiming constantly at the relative *cheapness* of everything, including food. Drink in the bar, change, walk to 'I Latini' for Tuscan food—already packed, so walked to Il Corsini, rather large and grand, and slightly more expensive and practically empty. I not hungry, slowly ate tough nasty Chicken a la Pisa, cheese and tomatoes, and green salad. B. had huge plateful of Tortellini, roast duck and spinach, and creme caramel, which she much enjoyed. 1 bott. White house wine. Walked home ca. 10.30, raining. Bath, bed, KNACKERED—and feet—ouch!

Sun. 17 Nov. Met B. in breakfast room at 9.15, she already having been walking and taking photos for over an hour, her being a lark to my owl which was the main reason I decided in Sept. to ask for separate rooms—tho' our rooms are each huge, double and with lovely long baths. Bright day, rain stopped, Arno already dropped about 2–3 feet, having risen 4–5 feet (actually 3m = 9 feet!). A woman in a silver and bric-à-brac shop on the Ponte Vecchio showed us the floodmark of 1966, about *8 feet* above the *floor* of her shop which is *already on the bridge* which is about *40 or 50 feet* above the water. Terrifying. All her goods—and everybody's on the bridge and shops etc. alongside, were simply *washed away*, and no-one was insured as they can't against flood. 'I lost *every*thing', she said. 'We all did'. 'My God,—what did you do?' we said. 'Started again . . .' After breakfast we walked to Piazza Santo Spirito on the other side of the river, where of course sung mass and then a sermon were going on, so couldn't go in. Walked to Piazza Carmine, ditto, of the Chiesa Carmine.

A beggar woman with a dirty little girl of about 5, and a baby in her arms and all wrapped up in a huge, dirty, plaid rug, including her arms and hands, and pregnant plus, had her hand *in* my handbag (shut, and over my shoulder, but behind me) when B. saw her, and I whipped around. They went on begging right up close to us: the little girl dancing about in front of us and jumping up and down, and while I got out some money and was carefully unzipping my small purse to give it to *her*, the *mother's hand*, under the loose rug, had stealthily slipped back and *right into* my bag again, now hanging right in front of me; I looked down from giving the money to the *child*, who's thus the decoy, and slapped the mother's hand away just as it was closing round the kitty-purse—gave me quite a turn. Some able bodied young men were begging, too, in various places, whom I ignored, tho' I gave money yesterday to a nice, dirty, shaky old man at Santa Signoria.

We could not get into the Brancacci Chapel till 1 p.m., adjoining the Carmine Church, so altogether we had a pointless sort of morning, with a lot of walking, tho' apart from hips and feet, which I try to ignore, I like it, as Florence is smallish and comprehensible and *everywhere* is old, and there are stunning views and aperçus up little side streets, and beautifully decorated (in black and white geometrical patterns) churches, and overhanging balconies, and flagged streets, and cobblestones, and every now and then a glimpse through the old buildings of the Tuscan hills all round with pines and poplars = Florentine Renaissance landscapes in fact. So we went and had lunch at 12 in a tiny trattoria, Agostino, with otherwise Italian *men* in (where are the women?) and a nice family with a beautiful and sweet daughter doing the work. I had Tortellini with bolognese, which would have been better cooked another 5 minutes and was just *too* al dente. B. had Penne, ditto sauce, but not undercooked. I left ½ mine because I will no longer eat to please people—can't, in fact. Then I had a v. *nice* piece of plain roast chicken with crispy salty skin—a whole leg, and some Salata in Stagione (seasonal)—OK. B. had Tuscan sausages, v. coarse and spicy. And Tiramisu for pudding and white wine: simple place, beautiful yellow linen tablecloth and napkins and heavy silver!

Walked to the Pitti Palace, the Medici posh place, by the Boboli gardens which have an amphitheatre. Up another 80 stairs, and then many ornate rooms crammed with Titians, Rubens, Veroneses, Agnolos, one Ghirlandaio et al. 2 or 3 v. stunning and ornate ceilings. (p.cs) A lovely Murillo Madonna, and Raphael Madonna. Also extraordinary ornate inlaid marble tables with stunning colours, esp. blues and yellows—one with flowers—polyanthus, tulips, and one I didn't know. Walked back to the Carmine, church now shut (at 1 p.m.) but Brancacci Chapel adjoining open—and the best so far. Small, with about 8 scenes from life of St. Peter (Carmine monks were devoted to the Pope)—really full of life and incident (pcs). And an old, old Madonna and Child painted on wood, dark but brilliant reds and blues, and nothing to tell us who it was by—but I think *not* Masaccio or Masolino who did the frescos—and like Masaccio died in mid 15c. Walked to Santo Spirito—shut completely. So we missed it both ends.

Walked back to hotel, I read and wrote this from 3.30–6. B., who has boundless energy—and obviously painless feet—went off again with her camera, today being bright without sun and rain has stopped, and river quietened down. We intend to go to 'I Latini' for dinner tonight, planning to get there earlier to get in: → *later* met in the bar, and had a drink; there are 2 American alcoholics here who prop up the bar most of the day—one was left tonight, talking very loudly and *de*finitely, and farting gently a lot of the time. We walked round to 'I Latini', and queued, near the beginning, for nearly ½ hour, by which time about 60 or 70 there behind us; we sort of got friendly with a smart Italian woman and a plump, nice American-Italian woman, and in the event sat with them. Place at once packed—the hugely efficient staff of about 12 men were a real Show in themselves. The other two women had 3 sorts soup, twice! then artichokes. B. had bread and tomato and garlic soup, lamb and rabbit and broccoli and I had roast lamb and broccoli—simply delicious, tender and juicy and wonderful veg. Chianti all round. Then sweet wine w. almond biscuits to dunk in. GHASTLY din, noise, I mean. Got out at 9.30.

Mon. Nov. 18 We arranged that Betty should take my key last night and come down and knock me up and come *in* and make sure I *got* up, as I am not reliable these days, and tend to shut off the alarm and go straight back to sleep—and she gets up at 6 a.m. anyway. I did get up just before she came so that was OK—breakfast and left here just after 8 to walk to the Piazza della Repubblica, as the coach for Siena and San Gimignano left from there, supposedly at 8.20 a.m.—actually about 8.35. A nice trilingual woman, Daniella, was our 'hostess'—It., Eng., and German; there were only 4 Germans, but of course they had to have it all, all over again in their reprehensible Language—which later, in Siena, with the guide, was a BORE. About 20 English and Americans, and fortunately a lovely sunny day, though colder than before.

Arr. Siena about 10, and were handed over to a plump woman with a beautiful complexion called Anna, also trilingual and very enthusiastic and Betty thought her excellent and I thought her a bit of a bore, as well as all the German stuff. First just a quickie round the huge church of San Domenico where there is also an active Dominican monastery and various white-robed figures about. The head of St. Catherine—who, along with the wolf who suckled Romulus and Remus, dominates Siena, is in a glass case in a side chapel—or it is said it is, it looked a bit shrunken. They were restoring another chapel, and the 3 Restorers' names were up, the first being Paola Mariotti! Must tell my Paola M. (21.11.91 sent her a p.c.). Then what I found most boring and tiresome began—Anna moved very slowly—or rather fast from A to B—but A and B were simply *on* bits of street, looking at old palaces and bits of architecture and history and we all had to stand around *interminably* meant to be listening, and then on a bit, then *another* stop, etc. Siena is perfectly *beautiful*, crowded, narrow streets, *no cars* only vans if nec, and built up and down, up and down, higgledy piggledy on 3 hills, with these wonderful soft reds and browns in all the bricks and tiles, all old, all lovely—but *very* cold, and I got cold and fretful and kept wandering off—bought a fresh doughnut and ate it, and a cocky American lad said severely 'You'll spoil your appetite for lunch' so I gazed blandly at him, and said 'Yes, Nannie'. I didn't know how much he was joking and he definitely wasn't sure about me either.

Spent ages in a vast wonderful square—the Piazza del Campo, so big that they do hold the Pallio (bareback horse racing) round the grey circle of flagstones round the edge of it every July, putting down earth on the flags first. There were buildings *all* round, and this was when Betty got really hooked on Anna, and I went right off her, and went for a long walk all round: a huge Renaissance palace, a church, a town hall, archways, heaps of shops, and all round this great circle nearly 1000 yards across. Eventually we clambered up to the Catedrale, and Duomo, where there are some not-special frescos, and chapels etc. I left again, and went and watched things outside, including an active little hospital about 500 years old. Caught up with them again as they went to a special little museum and crypt where there were lovely frescos by Duccio and Cimabue, particularly a Madonna and Child, and lots of little ones telling Bible stories (pcs). Frozen, so got warmer in there and at last—an *hour* late, we met Daniella again and were taken to a little trattoria and lunch was served very efficiently. I had fresh crisped hot salty toast with fresh olive oil on, and a hunk of roast pork and spinach.

Betty and I have been hypnotised all day by a ghastly woman, English I'm sorry to say, whom we instantly, and as one, christened 'La Hysterica' early on—she had a terrible garment, v. expensive, made of black leather and mink, rather down-at-heel comf. shoes, a long black skirt, an intermittently-worn white floppy cricket hat (honestly dark glasses), 4 chiffon scarves—white, blue, red and flowery—and thin, dirty, greasy dark grey hair with two little slides. She had a wet husband; *all* the time in Siena—when she wasn't talking in a mimsy voice—she held one or another of her chiffon scarves across her mouth and nose; 'oh, she's seriously mad', said Betty at one point, when she dropped her scarf for a moment to repair her powder and lipstick for the *fourth* time.

After lunch, back to the coach, and drove to a hill town of many towers, *San Gimignano*. I think this was the BEST of everything for me, even better than the Brancacci Chapel. We clambered up and walked through the city wall into the Piazza della Cisterna, a big old iron well in the middle, and then into La Catedrale—which is *covered*, absolutely alive and bursting with Ghirlandaio frescos every *inch* of the way. Masses and masses of wonderful pictures, like a huge Biblical comic book. From God making Adam and Eve right through the Crucifixion and Deposition. It was perfectly stunning. Fortunately we had enough coins to keep the clever light-meters going, and spent nearly all our precious hour there. Then walked down the steep narrow, reddish Siena stone streets, having stopped only to get a whopping great gelato each as we determined to have one some time, and this was it. Betty had fruity ones, I had stracciatella (choc. chip), caramella, and crema. Glug! Couldn't quite finish mine, too cold and full. Dusk falling by now. I forgot to say that La Hysterica plunged into the Cathedral, raced up to the altar, gave it a cursory glance, turned round and hurried out, glancing neither right nor left nor up—she must have been in there all of 50 seconds.

A drive, as dark fell, back into Florence, where they let us out v. near our hotel; we had a drink in the bar after a much needed pee and then read and bathed from 6 till 8, when B came to my room for a drink as we'd stocked up on Martinis on Friday evening. Walked to the restaurant just along Lungarno where we went on the first night and I 'discovered' Tiramisu. Nearly empty = peaceful after last night. I had tomato and cucumber salad, B. tomato and mozzarella; then she had Ossobucco, and I made a Big Mistake and had 'Fried Chicken and Zucchini' which I fondly imagined as slices of fried chicken (browned) with chopped zucchini. Not a bit of it. I was presented with a large oval platter containing an Enormous Pile of things which looked just like twiglets in batter—except it was tiny bits of chicken (and bone) and zucchini in batter—rather thick and getting colder by the minute, and more like suede jackets than batter. I ate *approx.* a quarter and then gave up, telling the nice concerned waiter it was All my Fault. Never mind, I thought, I'll make up on Tiramisu. B. finished her O.B., and we asked for 'sweet'—I asked for Tiramisu—confidently. 'All gone', he said. 'Lunch time—big one—all go. Monday night—well—you *see* here—empty, so no worth making new one.' Howls of frustration from me. 'Tomorrow,' he said eagerly, 'tomorrow tiramisu!' 'No good', I said—'Too late!' 'You go?' 'Tomorrow morning we (fell asleep here! 11.45 p.m.) go to England . . .' 'Ah well—next time'.

Yes, maybe. I certainly like it well enough—understatement—to try to persuade V[icky Plumb]. Betty said would you and me and Vicky go as a three if we could all come again? And I think we might well.

Tuesday 19 Nov. Raining again. A quick trot down to the Uffizi to do the other half, which—apart from 3 Rembrandts and generally good Dutch section (but no Vermeers)—wasn't nearly as good as the first. Shopping. Crowded little trattoria for lunch, a real joker doing the serving and singing opera. I had Minestrone. Train to Pisa, aeroplane 6.30, *home by 9.30.* V. GOOD.

CHAPTER THIRTY-THREE

Hotel drama in New York*

Setting

The main Reception Area of the Warwick Hotel, West 54th Street, New York.

Time

7.30 p.m., on a hot and humid Saturday night.

Dramatis personae

An elderly and weary LADY DOCTOR.
MATTHEW: An insolent young man, at Reception.
RALPH: An ever-smiling bellman, probably both cunning and thick. He may be Austrian.

---

* Undated typescript. Presumably later than the 1986 "Grand Tour of New England".

MUHAMMED: Another receptionist.
A VOICE.

Scene one

(LADY DOCTOR has worked all week in Washington in a temperature of 90°, then been in Boston for 35 hours, where she has done a small seminar, a long evening lecture and a whole-day Workshop of 80 people—that very day. She had then flown into New York and been driven by a sullen lunatic from La Guardia to mid-town Manhattan. She heaves her heavy overnight bag to the long counter in the empty hall, and waits.

MATTHEW appears. He is a fierce-looking young man, with a fuzz of black hair, though he is white, with brilliant light blue eyes. He goes to the far end of the counter without looking at LADY DOCTOR, and starts flicking importantly at his computer, holding a sheaf of card-index notes.

There is a short Pause.)

LADY DOCTOR
(Neutrally but clearly)
Good evening. I've come to check in. (Pause)

MATTHEW
(Without looking up)
Move down.

(LADY DOCTOR looks around, wondering whom he is addressing.)

MATTHEW
Move *down*, I said.

(LADY DOCTOR stifles various retorts, and shuffles self down the counter—about 4 yards.)

MATTHEW
(Not looking up)
Yes?

LADY DOCTOR
I've come to check in. Coltart's the name.

MATTHEW
Ya got a reservation?

LADY DOCTOR
Yes, Dr Corrigan made it in January. I confirmed it before I checked out last Saturday.

MATTHEW
(Does things with the computer for some 3 to 4 minutes)
We've got no room right now.

LADY DOCTOR
But the room was reserved—Dr Nina Coltart—and it *is* a quarter to eight.

MATTHEW
Quarter *of* eight. (Pause) We're very busy, we haven't got any rooms ready.

LADY DOCTOR
But what do you suggest? It's nearly eight o'clock, and I'm tired, and I've been working all—

MATTHEW
What *company* ya with?

LADY DOCTOR
I beg your pardon?

MATTHEW
(Irritably)
What *company* ya with, I said.

LADY DOCTOR
I don't know what you mean. I'm a private doctor, and I have been asked to work for the—

MATTHEW
(Interrupting with a savage sneer)
Yes, yes, I know all about that sort of thing, my *mother's* a private physician.

(The impression given by this brief speech is that LADY DOCTOR had suddenly started, quite gratuitously, boasting and telling some appalling immodest story about herself.)

LADY DOCTOR
(After a pause)
Could you tell me how long it will be before there is a room, please?

MATTHEW
Go and sit over there, I'll tell you when there's a room.

> (LADY DOCTOR seats herself on one of the large, overstuffed, Viennese-type sofas. After about 10 minutes, MATTHEW shouts across the hall that there is a room now—rather as if a miracle has been made to happen, to meet the importune pleadings of this egregious LADY DOCTOR. RALPH appears, and retrieves LADY DOCTOR's suitcase from a storage room, and takes her up to Room 2223: this is on the 22nd floor, of course. He throws open the door with a welcoming flourish, as he is a kind old man. The room is not made up; it is, in fact, in chaos; it has obviously not long been vacated by two hot and untidy people.)

RALPH
Oh dear, ze room is not ready.

LADY DOCTOR
So I see.

RALPH
I vill ring ze Housekeeper; she will come at once and do it.

> (He does so, turns on the television, moves the armchair in front of it, and benevolently ushers the lady doctor into it.)

RALPH
You sit down, lady, make yourself comfortable. Soon ze housekeeper come and make up. *Lovely* room. You vill be happy here.

> (LADY DOCTOR gives RALPH a dollar, as currently it is either that or $20, and she is not yet that desperate for paternal care. She is, however, temporarily speechless, or rather, unable to think her way through this new hideous blockage. It is extremely hot, stuffy and unattractive in this room; she has been up since 6.00 am, and working and travelling ever since. She is weary and fed up and getting angry. RALPH backs out, bowing and smiling.

LADY DOCTOR fairly rapidly regains her wits and rings the
front desk: it is answered by a brusque, male voice.)

MATTHEW
(For it is he)
Yeah, wadja want? Front desk.

LADY DOCTOR
It's Dr Coltart, Room 2223 here. This room is not made up. It is now
half past eight. A room was reserved for me in—

MATTHEW
Look, I got eight people to be checked in. I'm very busy. The *hotel*
is very busy.

LADY DOCTOR
If there are eight people there, what do you plan to do with them?
Don't tell me—I want a room, ready made-up, *now*, please.

MATTHEW
I'll call you back. (Rings off)

(LADY DOCTOR lights a cigarette, and gladly, almost ecstatically
for about 30 seconds, remembers the ¼ bottle of wine
which she put in her bag off her snack tray in the aeroplane.
Opens it and drinks it slowly. Nothing else happens.
After about 5 minutes, she rings Housekeeper, and
urges her case. After about 10 minutes, she rings
Front Desk.)

A NEW VOICE
Hello, Front Desk. May I help you?

LADY DOCTOR
Well, it would be very nice. How are you getting on down there?

VOICE
We-ell, that's a very interesting question. What had you in mind,
actually?

LADY DOCTOR
(Realising this is not MATTHEW)
Oh, it's a *room*, a room I have in mind, a made-up room ... (Tells
her story briefly)

VOICE
That's terrible—I'm *sure* you want a made-up room, Ma'am. The only thing is, we're just terribly busy right now, and—

LADY DOCTOR
(Becoming very mildly hysterical)
But I was there at half-past *seven*, why can't you be busy with *me*? My room was reserved 4 months ago, and it's now nine o'clock and ... (this illogical sequence, and the sound of her own shrill voice, stops her)

VOICE
(Noticeably *less* kind and calm)
Yes, well, I'll see what I can do, Ma'am, I'll ring you right back.

LADY DOCTOR
That's what the other fellow said, the one I dealt with, *he* said that about 40 minutes ago, and—

> (The phone is sharply put down. At almost the same moment, as if to save her sanity in the nick of time, there is a sharp knock on LADY DOCTOR's door, and the housekeeper— or one of her minions—arrives. She is quite quick, and willing, and pleasant, and only speaks Spanish. A small pantomime ensues, as LADY DOCTOR's rusty Spanish deserts her completely. In 15 minutes, the room and the bathroom are transformed. LADY DOCTOR has a bath and sinks into the rather hard bed. The telephone has not rung.)

Scene two

> (The LADY DOCTOR's room. 7.00 a.m. the next morning. LADY DOCTOR realises that she can see no sky, and no ground, from the windows of Room 2223. There are only the soaring, dirty, brick walls of other buildings. The room would make a fairly creditable prison. In the dim filtered daylight, she examines the carpet and curtains, which are all old, and not very clean. She leaves for New York University, where she works until noon.)

Scene three

(4.00 p.m. the same day. LADY DOCTOR has decided to leave, and over the telephone has booked herself into the Park Central Hotel, 57th Street and 7th Avenue. She is in the Hall again, having brought her luggage down herself. Behind the counter are MUHAMMED, who wears a name-badge, and MATTHEW, who does not. In fact, the stage directions have preceded events for the sake of dramatic economy. LADY DOCTOR does not, actually, yet know MATTHEW's name.)

LADY DOCTOR
(Settling her account with MUHAMMED)
And could you give me the name and address of the manager of this hotel, please?

(MUHAMMED goes into the back office, and comes back with a piece of paper with Mr. *Tom Travers'* name on it, and another Warwick Hotel address.)

LADY DOCTOR
I see you have a name-badge, Muhammed. But that gentleman (glancing at MATTHEW, who has already arrived beside MUHAMMED—from the moment he heard the manager's name) does not.

MATTHEW
Is anything wrong, Ma'am?

LADY DOCTOR
I was wondering what your name is, since you don't have a name-badge. (Silence.)

LADY DOCTOR
(Pointedly, looking straight at MATTHEW)
What is it?

MATTHEW
(Uneasily and reluctantly)
I'm Matthew, Ma'am. Is anything wrong?

LADY DOCTOR
Yes, Matthew. Quite a lot. Maybe you don't remember last evening. I do. As far as I'm concerned, I'm still waiting for you to ring me back, to give me a made-up room.

MATTHEW
Oh, but . . .

LADY DOCTOR
Thank you, Muhammed. Goodbye.

(Crosses to the door with her luggage and leaves the hotel.)

Curtain

(B) ESSAYS

CHAPTER THIRTY-FOUR

Diagnosis and assessment of suitability for psychoanalytic psychotherapy*

In day-to-day work, one draws on principal conscious skills, knowledge, and intuition. But the situation in which you need to be consciously in touch with a whole range of ideas and concepts is the diagnostic interview. Here I would stress *diagnostic* in conjunction with assessment for analytic psychotherapy; we have to be getting at some sort of diagnostic picture, in order to think about the patient coherently and, if necessary, to be able to discuss him with colleagues to whom we may be referring. This picture has to include, of course, what the patient is not.

My main qualification for writing this paper is the amount of consultation I do in private practice. The diagnostic interviews at the London Clinic of Psycho-Analysis are pretty specialized and it is in private practice, where for many years I have done an average of three consultations a week, that my experience of diagnosis and assessment for analysis and psychotherapy mainly lies. Of these

---

* Published in 1987 in *Contemporary Psychoanalysis*, 22 (1986), 560–569. All rights reserved. Revised version in the *British Journal of Psychotherapy*, 4(2): 127–134.

249

consultations, only about 10% turn out to be "therapeutic consultations" in their own right, i.e., do not require referral for therapy, and only about 5% are subsequently placed in full five-times-a-week psychoanalysis.

First, we must consider the "real" role of the psychoanalytic diagnostician in contrast to a mythical role which often exists somewhere around the edge of many people's half-conscious fantasy. I am of the opinion that a good solid block of experience in general psychiatry early along the line of one's own development is a real help; this is principally linked to the fact that I myself had that and, therefore, my view immediately underlines another factor, which is that we cannot expect or even desire that subjectivity be absent from our work in this field. I do not want to imply that one simply does a sort of extended psychiatric interview, or that one operates exactly as one used to do in the acute admission wards. This would be to imply that people without psychiatric experience cannot assess a patient with a view to deciding about analytical therapy, which is not true. But I think it will be found that those who have had it are the people who do much of the day-to-day assessment work within the body of those who practise as analysts and therapists in London, and are the main sources of referral within that body. Also, it is a help if one has a full practice and is, therefore, usually not assessing with oneself as therapist in mind; one is facilitated by a somewhat increased mobility of objectivity if one is not personally looking for a patient. The "real" assessor relies to a certain extent on intuition. He has his own theoretical, philosophical, and experiential framework, both personal and clinical. He may hold quite strong opinions—reasonably well thought out, we would hope—on some things such as "The widening scope of psycho-analysis" (Stone, 1954) or, alternatively, "The need to limit the scope of psycho-analysis" (Kuiper, 1968); or the effects of certain specific traumata; or the possibility of working with a transference psychosis. He must have a working knowledge of alternative therapies and avenues of placement for people who are not suitable for full analysis (Baker, 1980), so that there is no pressure at all to opt for analysis as a sort of last ditch and only solution. This is often a despairing view held by non-analysts rather than analysts. Finally, he should have well-thought-out ideas, again grounded in experience, of how and why the odd process of analysis works, and why it may be desirable and appropriate for some people. It has been only too truly said that an expert is someone who knows everything about a subject except what it is for.

The mythical assessor, who does not exist, has an omniscient knowledge of all possible criteria of analysability, a peculiar capacity to predict the full course of treatment, a clairvoyant power to read the whole personal history and potential, both conscious and unconscious, of someone whom he is meeting once in a life-time for two hours, and a God's eye view of the details of this person's therapeutic relationship for the next five years. This may sound ludicrous when spelled out, but if you examine your own half-conscious expectations, I think you will find that this creature exists somewhere on the fringe of them.

It is important to remember what a momentous thing you are saying to a patient when you seriously and thoughtfully advise analytic psychotherapy as the treatment of choice. You are

> involving the patient in an adventure which is not comparable with any other medical treatment (and yet which curiously falls somewhere in the outer boundaries of that category): and furthermore the way in which such advice is presented shows clearly that it is no ordinary prescription. [Diatkine, 1968, p. 266]

You try to help the patient to see and feel some psychodynamic aspects of his problems. You convey to him your own considered beliefs on how and why analytical therapy might help him, you tell him something of the basic rules, you give no guarantee either of cure or of length of treatment and you leave the ultimate choice and responsibility to him; as a referral source, however, you will probably be instrumental in "matching" him with his therapist. I would stress here that matching is not twinning. It is not necessarily advisable to place, say, the obsessional patient with an obsessional colleague; the turmoils of divorce are not necessarily best handled by the therapist who is also going through this. These examples need not be multiplied; the implication is that a good referrer needs a good working knowledge of his colleagues' capabilities.

Now to criteria: perhaps we should start with certain features which are not exactly controversial, but which in an odd way tend to get left out of discussion, and out of the literature. It is almost as though it is thought not quite nice to acknowledge them. It may be that in ignoring them we underline our own high-mindedness and nobility of purpose; here, as so often, we find that Freud is an exception. I refer specifically to the features of intelligence, moral character, and money. However ethically utopian or politically idealistic our views, it is no good pretending that these things do not matter, because they do. A case may be argued for the widening scope of psychoanalysis, but we must not ignore the voice of experience and the dictates of our culture. Shortly after the war, before the London Clinic of Psycho-Analysis became organized and structured as it now is, the waiting list there was more than 400; this was due to a shortage of experienced consultants, a lack of selection technique, and perhaps to a kind of naïve enthusiasm about the potential of psychoanalysis. All that it led to was hopeless confusion among students taking on cases, endless disappointments among people languishing on the waiting list for years, and interminable analyses for many of those chosen. In 1895, Freud wrote that there was no point embarking on the treatment of "low minded and repellent characters who are not capable of arousing human sympathy" (Breuer & Freud, 1895, p. 265). Ten years later he wrote that the prerequisites for psychoanalysis include "a reasonable degree of education and fairly reliable character", adding, rather mysteriously but evocatively, "We should not forget that there are healthy people as well as unhealthy ones who are good for nothing in life" (1905a, p. 263). A philosophy of treatment is embedded here!

Neither intelligence nor ethical development is easy to define or measure. The fact remains that a good measure of both is a necessary ingredient for the prescription of a workable analytical therapy. Intelligence of the sort I mean is fairly easy to assess in a diagnostic interview; it does not necessarily equate with intellectual brilliance, which can be a formidable defence and a nuisance. The intelligence has to be fairly quick and fairly verbal (but not excessively so—slow thinkers often make good patients) and, above all, it has to be linked to two other features which I will come to in a moment. Ethical reliability is not so easy to assess accurately, although experience helps to develop a feeling for it. Thirdly, money. It may be a sad state of affairs, but generally speaking a certain amount of money is needed to undertake analytic therapy at present. I believe that the most that therapists can do about this is not to be too rigid about set fees, but to work on a sliding scale that correlates with patients' capacity to pay. I should add that I am of the opinion that it is psychologically much more effective and beneficial to treatment for a patient to pay what he possibly can; I do not propose to explore this statement at length, but I am confident that it is one with which most experienced practitioners would agree.

To return to the two criteria that I linked with intelligence, and for which one listens and searches in an assessment. One is the "will to be analysed". Namnum (1968) refers this vital feature to what he calls the "autonomous ego" and it will be seen on a moment's reflection that this must join up with the important concept of the possibility of a treatment alliance being formed, and put alongside the need to assess the possibility of the creation of a transference neurosis. The will to be analysed is not by any means the same thing as the more random, changeable, and drive-motivated "wish for recovery", although in initial interviews they may appear to be the same thing. One should listen with the third ear in an initial interview to search for this potential function of the autonomous ego, because this is what ultimately keeps the therapeutic alliance alive, and keeps the analytic therapy an open and going concern. The will to be analysed in the therapeutic alliance will be of vital importance when the transference neurosis becomes active and resistant, and opposes treatment, and when the early wish for recovery is forgotten in the day-to-day work of the therapy. A brief way of assessing this potential function in an initial interview is by temporarily going against the flow of the patient's thought and feeling for you at some well-judged dynamic moment, often late in the interview.

The other criterion that I link with intelligence is what has been called psychological-mindedness. This feature is very much easier to pick up in a diagnostic interview than is the true will to be analysed. There are various ingredients of psychological-mindedness, which can be roughly defined and located; with this aim one can usefully hold the following queries in one's own mind while doing an assessment interview:

1. Is there the capacity in the patient to take a distance from his own emotional experience? This must be nicely judged, as

obviously it should not be such a distance that one senses there is a great chasm, as in very severe denial, splitting, or repression.
2. If one listens beyond the full-stops in a narrative, can the patient go on, and begin to reflect on himself, perhaps in a new way as a result of being listened to in this particularly attentive way? If there are no signs of elaboration or extension by the patient on trains of thought, there may be severe inhibitions and/or anxieties, or extreme passive dependency, and a valuable capacity for free association may never develop.
3. Are various memories brought forward with different charges of affect? And are the affects, so far as one can tell, more or less appropriate? If not, a flat and uninflected history may bode ill for analytic therapy and indicate severe affective splitting and blunting. In other words, a lot of memories with no feeling are suspect.
4. Is there a capacity to perceive relationships between sections of history, and between details that are recounted, and the patient's prevailing sense of discomfort? If the patient starts by complaining of one or more symptoms or states of mind, but shows no sense of related significance when he goes into his history, then again there should be a warning signal in the assessor's mind.
5. Is there some capacity to recognize and tolerate internal reality, with its wishes and conflicts, and to distinguish it from external reality? You will see that this connects up directly with the continuing judgement in the interviewer's mind about the possibilities of maintaining a therapeutic alliance in conjunction with a transference neurosis. Does the patient show some facility in interview to move between the two, that is, internal and external reality, in a way that shows a certain cathexis for the value, and the enjoyment of interpretation and the taking of psychic responsibility for the self?
6. Does the patient show a lively curiosity and a genuine concern about this internal reality, if he has already shown that he got a good glimpse of it? This is a crucial point. Psychoanalytic therapy has nothing to offer a patient who only wishes to be relieved of his suffering. If he can make even a tenuous link with the idea of relief from psychic pain, with an increase in

self-knowledge, and if he then shows some real pleasure in finding out some tiny thing about himself in the initial interview, this is one of the best criteria for the analytic approach. This kind of drive and interest about the sources of pain in oneself is the greatest possible help in therapy, and is a sustaining tributary to the therapeutic alliance. It can help to counteract even very severe, including acting-out, pathology.

7. Is there some capacity for the use of the imagination? Fantasies may be presented in a diagnostic interview, but even small signs, such as a striking use of metaphor, or the voluntary reporting of a dream, are positive indicators.

8. Are there signs of a capacity to recognize the existence of an unconscious mental life? Is there some acknowledgment that in some ways the patient is in a state of involuntary self-deception? Are there some signs of a willingness to undo this state of affairs?

9. Does the patient show signs of success or achievement in some, even if limited, areas of his life and some degree of proper self-esteem in relation to this? It is an important truism that he who fails at everything will fail at analysis. Here I would emphasize the areas of study, or work, and one or more important relationship.

So much for some of the vital questions that are part of one's active inner processes during a diagnostic interview. Now we must consider briefly some of the more or less labelled categories which, by a sort of long-term consensus of experience, seem to be either more suitable for dynamic psychotherapy, or less suitable. Here again we are up against the fact that much of this labelling derives from psychiatry. This need not be unhelpful or constricting so long as we ourselves do not feel too wedded to our labels or categorizations. It should be remembered that we are using every method at our disposal to marshal information on all sorts of levels in one single interview. I propose to make two quotations, in order that they may be reflected upon in this context. The first is by Glover, writing in 1955, when he referred to what he called "signs of analysability" and, in decreasing order of appropriateness, they are "hysteria, compulsion neurosis, pregenital conversion states, neurotic disturbance, character disturbance, perversions, addictions, impulsiveness, and psychosis". There is room for discussion of many of these categories and Glover's placing of them in the hierarchy of treatability. For example, the phrase "neurotic disturbance" is almost too vague to be useful. Personal choices also play a part. Some therapists would far rather treat a character disturbance or a perversion than a compulsion neurosis.

There is a most valuable and readable paper written as part of a symposium on criteria for analysability; this is Elizabeth Zetzel's (1968) paper "The so-called good hysteric". Zetzel's four categories of diagnosable hysteria and their potential for response to analysis are most helpful for a diagnostician. If, at the end of an interview, you feel that more or less accurately you can say, "This patient is something like a Zetzel Group 1 or a Zetzel Group 2", then most of the questions outlined earlier will have been answered in the affirmative and you can go ahead with the analytic prescription. An experienced practitioner would also willingly take on a Zetzel Group 3 patient. Sooner or later, usually by mistake, one finds oneself referring or treating a Zetzel Group 4 patient and this is a difficult, often disastrous, good learning experience!

I would like to refer momentarily back to Glover's list, with special reference to "character disorder". Since 1954, when the paper was written, extensive and helpful advances both in the theory and technique of understanding and treating severe narcissism have been made. These advances bring a whole category of character disorders into a more accessible treatment arena. Severe narcissistic character disorders are, however, extraordinarily difficult to treat and, furthermore, they are sometimes difficult to locate in diagnostic assessment. Severe depression allied with a kind of affective flatness, allied again with subtle projective mechanisms, should make one suspicious of the concealed narcissistic disorder.

The other quotation containing compressed information comes from a paper by Knapp, Levin, McCarter, Wermer, and Zetzel (1960), which is called "Suitability for psychoanalysis: a review of one hundred supervised cases". Knapp and colleagues consider the following categories to be very difficult or unsuitable for psychoanalysis: "psychosomatic states, delinquents, psychotic signs or behaviour trends, adverse life situations, schizoid borderline psychotics, too long periods of previous treatment, very high levels of anxiety and tension, and some patients older than the analyst".

This list should also be reflected upon and reconsidered by each individual diagnostician and therapist. Some therapists like working with psychosomatic states, and recently analysts such as Murray Jackson have extended our knowledge of them. They often get better, and even if they do not, the whole cathexis of the somatic symptoms may change. "A high level of anxiety and tension" may be tackled and contained if the two-pronged therapeutic alliance and transference neurosis can be established rapidly. Many dynamic psychotherapists in recent years are exploring the treatment of patients older than themselves.

To close, a brief consideration of the style in which one conducts this particular and specialized form of interview—the diagnostic assessment. I would like to quote from a paper by Limentani:

> The accurate forecast of the patient's behaviour before therapy has begun is a challenge to the diagnostician who nevertheless has the means of eliciting evidence of the analysand's capacity to move freely within his own psyche. But he will do this only if he is prepared to move freely within the interview situation, so that he can induce fluid responses in the interviewee. The silent and inactive evaluator who clings faithfully to the psychoanalytic model of behaviour will obtain only a partial if not distorted picture of what he is meant to be observing. [1972, p. 358]

I would like to stress the important point being made here. Interviewers should not behave, in my opinion, like a caricature of an analyst. Such an interviewer does not help to start the patient off, does not ask any questions, does not comment, may write notes during the interview, makes no intervention or summing up, and at the end may mysteriously advise long-term treatment with someone who will be presumed to be like the very cartoon model he has presented. I cannot emphasize enough how counter-productive and, to some extent, actively sadistic I think this is. In an assessment interview one has to work. All the attitudes listed just now may be appropriate to a session when a patient is settled in treatment—all except taking notes, that is, which in my opinion should never happen in a patient's presence. The consultant diagnostician must draw on all his skills and use his whole personality with confidence and concern to meet the patient's personality at every possible point in the short time available to him. It seems to me deeply narcissistic to sit and do nothing. It more often happens in younger assessors and is, of course, at a charitable estimate, a defence against anxiety. But it is not good enough, and not helpful to the patient, for whom this may be one of the momentous days of his life, and whose anxiety level can be guaranteed at the very least to be higher than that of the interviewer. On the other hand, one is not required to make the patient particularly comfortable, nor to seduce the patient into liking or appreciating you, either in a diagnostic interview or in treatment. You need to establish a certain rapport and keep it going, and within that framework, think about and learn to deploy all the skills you have to find out about this stranger's inner world. This may involve a considerable amount of questioning, some interpretation, some link-making comments, sympathy expressed in your whole attitude of extremely attentive listening, and some concise summarizing of your own views towards the end of the interview.

It should always be remembered that if you are prescribing psychotherapy on a long-term basis, you are making a powerful statement, and your respect for the patient should entail that you give him your own insight into his needs and his character, and your reasons for making the prescription.

References

Baker, R. (1980). The finding "Not Suitable" in the selection of supervised cases. *International Review of Psychoanalysis, 7*: 353–364.
Breuer, J., & Freud, S. (1895). *Studies on Hysteria. S.E., 2.*
Diatkine, R. (1968). Indications and contraindications for psychoanalytical treatment. *International Journal of Psychoanalysis, 49*: 266–270.
Freud, S. (1905a). On psychotherapy. *S.E., 7*: 257–268. London: Hogarth.
Glover, E. (1955). *Technique of Psychoanalysis.* New York: International Universities Press.
Knapp, P. H., Levin, S., McCarter, R. H., Wermer, H., & Zetzel, E. (1960). Suitability for psychoanalysis: a review of one hundred supervised cases. *Psychoanalytic Quarterly, 29*: 459–477.
Kuiper, P. R. (1968). Indecisions and contradictions for psychoanalytic treatment. *International Journal of Psychoanalysis, 49*: 261–264.

Limentani, A. (1972). The assessment of analysability: a major hazard in selection for psychoanalysis. *International Journal of Psychoanalysis,* 53: 357–361.
Namnum, A. (1968). The problem of analyzability and the autonomous ego. *International Journal of Psychoanalysis,* 49: 271–275.
Stone, L. (1954). The widening scope of indications for psychoanalysis. *Journal of the American Psychoanalytic Association,* 2: 567–594.
Zetzel, E. (1968). The so-called good hysteric. *International Journal of Psychoanalysis,* 49: 256–260. Reprinted in: *The Capacity for Emotional Growth.* London: Hogarth, 1970.

CHAPTER THIRTY-FIVE

The assessment of psychological-mindedness in the psychiatric interview*

In the last paragraph of his paper "A defect in training", Yorke (1988) has a sentence which serves as an excellent link to the opening of this paper : "For all their importance, empathy and awareness of patients' anxieties do not in themselves amount to psychological understanding" (p. 160). In his paper, he had made a plea for more psychoanalytical psychology to be included in a general postgraduate psychiatric training, and I am in complete agreement with his cogently argued case.

However, I want to concentrate on a particular aspect of this point. When an experienced psychoanalyst is carrying out a diagnostic consultation with a view to assessing a patient's suitability for analysis or analytical psychotherapy, he is exercising his own skill and psychological-mindedness in this intensive exploration The prospects of a successful treatment will be greatly enhanced if he finds the patient is "psychologically-minded"—whatever the presenting complaints, or however unpromising the superficial

---

* Published in 1988 in the *British Journal of Psychiatry, 153,* 819–820. Some of the material in this paper overlaps with the preceding chapter.

impression. Therefore, I would like to detail some of the qualities of this feature, with a view to offering some guidelines to colleagues who are still learning their technique. Because of the value of brief lists for the purpose of consigning to accessible memory, I shall lay out these points in an approximate order of discovery, rather than of importance, under two main headings. Nevertheless, it should be remembered that the whole may be larger than the sum of its parts.

The history

The diagnostician should look for:

1. *The capacity to give a history which deepens, acquires more coherence, and becomes texturally more substantial, as it goes on.* This may happen in a rambling, and not necessarily consecutive way. Indeed, a very tidy, chronologically exact history without diversions, or patches of apparent inconsequence, may suggest a constricted, over-anxious or very heavily-defended mind.
2. *The capacity to give such a history without needing too much prompting, and a history which gives the listener an increasing awareness that the patient feels it is currently related to himself, to his own story;* he sees himself properly—if unhappily—as the product of the connective aetiology of his life's circumstances. A history which has to be coaxed, dragged, or frequently prompted by the assessor does not show much potential for the development of further free associative ease, and also suggests severe inhibition, anxieties, or cast-iron resistances. Here, there is a strong implication that the assessor himself can effectively use a disciplined, well-judged capacity to maintain quite a lot of silence—often for longer than the patient either feels that he might want, or is socially accustomed to. However, I am not referring to a stultifying, unhelpful silence which may be experienced by the patient as frustrating to the point of sadism, and which, in inexperienced assessors who are aping an ill-digested model, may actually be so.
3. *The capacity to bring up memories with appropriate affects,* and some sense of how both of these, although perhaps not easy for the patient, may relate to his present state of suffering.

Developments in the interview arising from the history

4. *Some awareness in the patient that he has an unconscious mental life.* There are people who cannot tolerate, and stoutly deny, that they have an unconscious—especially if it may contain "outdated" material which is powerfully influencing their current feelings, behaviour, and thought-processes. Such people are unsuitable candidates for the analytical approach. It is extremely important, therefore, to assess the capacity both to allow for the existence of these as-yet unknown powerful influences, and to hope that with skilled assistance from another, they may become known, accepted, and transformed.

5. *Some capacity to step back, if only momentarily, from self-experience, and to observe it reflectively*—either spontaneously or with the help of a simple interpretation from the assessor, who should make opportunity for this sort of intervention. In the presence of psychological-mindedness, the use of such an intervention should lead to a more mobile recognition by the patient that he may be able to tolerate, even welcome, and use, a new light on the darker, more hidden side of his internal reality, with its wishes and conflicts. The intervention, in other words, is a subtle directive towards the unconscious, and contrasts with interventions on other levels and with other aims, which come under the heading of advice, counselling, or guidance to behavioural change. These belong more to the realms of the already conscious ego, and of external reality: cognitive therapy is more of this nature.

6. *A capacity, or more strongly a wish, to accept and handle increased responsibility for the self*—the whole realm of the unconscious, its affects and effects, and the "maturational" processes (Winnicott, 1965). This is also a crucial factor; psychoanalysis has little to offer to the patient who only desires to be rid of his own irrational suffering through the work of another person. A passage in an assessment interview arising from some tiny interpretation or enlightening, new-angle comment from the assessor, in which the patient experiences a tiny insight, some relief, a movement; or in which a link, however tenuous, is made between a slight easing of psychic pain and a fractional increase in self knowledge—these are reliable pointers to the existence

of psychological-mindedness. Moreover, they are promising signs for the development of true dynamic work in treatment, and the establishment of the therapeutic alliance.

7. *Imagination*. A totally unimaginative person may find it hard to dream, to use or understand metaphor, to elaborate—or even to have—a fantasy.

8. *Some capacity for achievement, and some realistic self-esteem;* he who fails at everything fails at analysis. The sort of achievement I refer to here does not necessarily include anything very great; areas in which to look are those of work, and/or an important good relationship somewhere along the line.

9. *Overall impression*. This has to be the last ingredient. The presence of several, and preferably all, of the foregoing criteria tells the assessor that he is with someone who is psychologically-minded. Absence of them will add up to an overall impression of a character who may be socially and intellectually sophisticated, and a competent personality (although probably with some alien-seeming symptoms), who nevertheless does not show, and is not likely to develop, psychological-mindedness. There is something deeply recognizable, but ultimately not fully definable, about the assessor's experience of a thorough, intense, working consultation with a psychologically-minded person.

Pitfalls

Our own trained capacity for creative silence needs to be kept in context:

> The accurate forecast of the patient's behaviour before therapy has begun is a challenge to the diagnostician who nevertheless has the means of eliciting evidence of the patient's capacity to move freely within his own psyche. But he will do this only if he is prepared to move freely within the interview situation, so that he can induce fluid responses in the interviewee. The silent and inactive evaluator who clings faithfully to the psychoanalytic model of behaviour (i.e. behaviour during the course of a long psychoanalysis) will obtain only a partial, if not distorted, picture of what he is meant to be observing. [Limentani, 1972]

An interviewer should not behave like a caricature of an analyst. This "model" hardly speaks, does not make interventions, makes no clarifying comments or statements toward the end, may deliver himself only of a weighty interpretation directed at a deeper unconscious, which mystifies the already frustrated and probably frightened patient, and never varies this "technique", whoever he is with. One of the excuses for this type of behaviour is that it "brings out the patient's anxieties". Of course it does. This "goal" is wheeled out as if it were some Aristotelian cathartic ideal in its own right, but it is nothing of the sort. Aristotle was referring to the art of dramatic tragedy, enshrined in a whole play. There is no drama if the consultant does not speak or work; the only tragedy will be a traumatised patient (I see several in subsequent consultations every year) whose last state is worse than his first. The work required of the interviewer entails drawing on all his own skills and talents, in fact his whole personality, insofar as he trusts in its unselfconscious value to serve his professional aims in a creative, flexible way. He does not have to make the patient too comfortable, dispel all his anxieties, or offer solace or exaggerated hopes; these are the dangers when the interviewer only has 'empathy and awareness' at his service (Yorke, 1988). It is his job to create and consolidate an ever-deepening rapport, and keep it going. In other words, to deploy as extensively as he can the structure he has created on the foundations of his own psychological-mindedness.

References

Limentani, A. (1972). The assessment of analysability: a major hazard in selection for psychoanalysis. *International Journal of Psychoanalysis*, 53: 351–361.
Winnicott, D. (1965). *The Maturational Processes and the Facilitating Environment*. London: Hogarth and Institute of Psychoanalysis.
Yorke, C. (1988). A defect in training. *British Journal of Psychiatry*, 151: 159–160.

CHAPTER THIRTY-SIX

To go or not to go*

I used to be clearer in my views on this controversial subject than I am today. A combination of growing older and Buddhist practice has made it harder to hold a line. Early bereavement, and, later, becoming a doctor made me begin to reflect on death much earlier than most people, and this has deepened as death becomes a more real event for me instead of a remote possibility.

I joined the Voluntary Euthanasia Society, founded in 1935, about thirty years ago, simply to acquaint myself with the thinking and aims of the people who also belong to it, many of them Christians, and all serious and morally sensitive.

There is a tendency in the public to react strongly to the very word euthanasia. It is an interesting example of the power of conditioning, which so often leads to mindless prejudice. Like child-rearing and psychoanalysis, euthanasia is one of a small group of subjects upon which almost everyone confidently holds an opinion,

---

* Published in the Winter 1989–1990 issue of *Raft*, the journal of the Buddhist Hospice Trust, of which Nina Coltart was a member. The paragraph in brackets has been added from a manuscript.

usually characterized by profound ignorance, and vehemently expressed, particularly if negative, whenever the right button is pushed.

[I am, for example, frequently amazed, in any social gathering of otherwise reasonably intelligent, tolerant people, at the intense conviction with which a complete stranger will tell me precisely why psychoanalysis is (a) old-fashioned, (b) newfangled, (c) all about sex, (d) pernicious, (e) the scourge of the century, (f) only for intellectuals, Jews, and rich women with not enough to do ... "In no time, people will be bumping off their old relatives" and "What about Nazi Germany?" are only two of the emotional comments I have encountered from people who, in most respects, display normally civilized behaviour, and who, furthermore, expect the same from me, i.e., who do not see me personally as a granny-basher or a fascist murderer.]

Being a doctor, in respect of this particular subject, is to be in a unique position, since we are usually, to put it crudely, the answer to the "Who pulls the trigger?" question. I think it is therefore demanded of us that we reflect on the problem with great care, and in so far as an opinion is required, formulate one with precision. It is a matter of some concern to me, therefore, that I have become less clear about my views as time has passed.

For many years, I was of the opinion that, provided necessary safeguards had been observed, I would have no hesitation in complying with the wish of an individual to be released through death from certain stated (written down and witnessed) conditions. However, several things have happened over a period of about twenty years for me: age, Buddhist practice, and direct knowledge both of how much other people change their views, and also of just how difficult it can be, technically, to extinguish life in some people. These factors raise queries in the mind that are not easily banished.

A person who, in health with alert consciousness and full intention, has properly prepared a Living Will may rationally want to stand by it, especially if overtaken by immobilizing, intractably painful or, worst of all, dementing illness. However, it is well known to doctors and nurses that quite extraordinary reserves may be called upon in an individual when challenged by breakdown in his systems: furthermore, these reserves—of patience, humour, courage and endurance—may, in their own right, bring experience of increased self-esteem, of "proper pride", even of pleasure, as the person realizes more fully what he is capable of in the later part of his life. This phenomenon is not predictable and one can by no means rely on it, but in the most unlikely people, perhaps characterized hitherto by superficiality, querulousness, and immaturity, one may be almost awestruck at the exemplary wisdom of some late developments. Sometimes one feels that stress in older age, perhaps the first real challenge in an easy life, evokes capacities long dormant in a person that it would have been sad to miss.

Even the most dreaded of all events, dementia (where, by definition the decision to terminate life has to rest on a previously prepared request, since the rational person is "lost") may present certain features which speak of continuing development of the spirit.

My own view is that provided I am still capable of reflection in this framework I am conditioned to accept as "me", I would like to "know" death. I would have no hesitation in turning off life-support machines, and would try to persuade relatives to my point of view, for an indubitably brain-dead patient. This seems to me hardly to come under the heading euthanasia. But to make the decision, or to carry out the act of terminating life, either for myself or another—even in the presence of an authentic long-standing request form—in any state where reflective consciousness was still present, would, I think, be very much harder for me than it might have been ten years ago.

CHAPTER THIRTY-SEVEN

Psychoanalysis and Buddhism: does the ego exist?*

Within the confines of our small space, it is well to define and clarify the overall title straightaway. *Collins' Dictionary* has this to say of religion: "Belief in, worship of or obedience to a supernatural power or powers considered to be divine and/or to have control of human destiny . . ." *Chambers'* and the *OED* reveal almost identical definitions. So the answer to the question which forms the title to this book is obviously No. Then why does it get asked? Because there are people, in analysis, pro-analysis, and—these must not be forgotten—strongly anti-analysis, who behave *as if it is* a religion. I shall consider why and how.

Freud himself, alert to the possibilities, maintained throughout his life that he was not intending to create a *Weltanschauung*, a "philosophy of life", nor a moral system. Psychoanalysis was and is a method of mind-investigation, which Freud, a scientist,

---

* Published in 1993 in *Is Psychoanalysis Another Religion? Contemporary Essays on Spirit, Faith and Morality in Psychoanalysis*, I. Ward (Ed.), London: Freud Museum Publications. Reprinted in the Spring 1995 issue of *Interbeing*, the journal of the Leeds Network of Engaged Buddhists.

invented. He then observed that this particular method had a therapeutic effect on those under investigation. Most of us practising analysts are mainly interested in this effect. It is in our own practices, as well as by reflecting upon what some people say about it in society, that we notice that there are those who treat psychoanalysis as if it is a religion.

Certainly it can be argued that to work for improvement in the well-being of our fellow humans is a moral pursuit. I intend to speak of the moral philosophy of Buddhism a little later, which is why I add now that the Buddhist equivalent of "Amen" is: "May all beings be well and happy". The Buddha knew that if one is really happy, one is not ill or morally bad; therefore, the apparent simplicity of the phrase contains the complexity of a whole spiritual discipline, productive of goodness, though not necessarily aimed at it.

In *Brazzaville Beach*, by William Boyd (1990), an unnamed person is quoted: "There are three questions that every human being everywhere at any time . . . wants the answers to: What can I know? What ought I to do? What may I hope for?" (p. 2). We find ourselves in this mysterious thing called Life, and we try to make sense of it, give it meaning, with its only given fact—that we shall die. Religions intend to help us answer the three questions, and for many they succeed. Philosophically speaking, psychoanalysis does not intend to answer them, though sometimes it lends itself to the enquiring process. Because it does not intend to, some analysts and some patients feel the need of something else, a workable philosophy of life—perhaps even, for certain temperaments, a religion. They seek a disciplined practice, which, among other benefits, informs their professional lives.

By accepting consciously that a certain amount of splitting and projection can be part of normal psychological adjustment to life, some patients (but very few analysts) manage to sustain Faith in a theistic religion in tandem with psychoanalysis. But the dictionary definition of religion clashes strongly with the theory and practice of psychoanalysis, which is essentially about taking full responsibility for oneself. There is a definition of Faith in the Epistle to the Hebrews: "Faith is the substance of things hoped for, the evidence of things not seen" (2:1). The reference is to Faith in the religious context; it does not mix well with the pragmatic quality of psychoanalysis. One certainly needs faith to wait creatively through the dark, silent areas of a long psychoanalysis; but this is faith in oneself and in the process, and, as you can see, I distinguish between the two by means of the first letter.

But where do we turn? Many people half-consciously cobble together some "humanist" notions, which are really only applied common-sense; but the religiously-minded seeker, who desires a theory of the sacred, and a practice marked by reverence and devotion, is, for a while, and maybe forever, at a loss. A fortunate seeker, determinedly ploughing on, may realize that a-theistic Buddhism provides an answer. It has transcendent aims, which need not concern us further, except to say that Faith is at no point required; all the aims are realizable by the human mind in the here and now; but the path of the practice, for a considerable distance, is in uncomplicated harmony with the theory and technique of psychoanalysis.

Buddhism is founded on the Four Noble Truths. These state (1) that suffering exists, (2) that all suffering has a human cause, (3) that the suffering is remediable through our own efforts, and (4) that these efforts will be maximized if we try to follow the Eightfold Noble Path. Their connecting links, which need to be ever more deeply understood, are called the Law of Dependent Origination, which we might more easily call "cause and effect". The Path is not esoteric; it is simply a series of signposts to qualities of being to be aimed for, in the context of good teaching and the daily practice of skilfully taught meditation. Its ingredients are attitudes, thought, speech, action, ways of earning money, effort, meditation, and the development of wisdom. There are also eight Hindrances, or problems, that make for difficulty in treading the Path. These include such things as hatred, greed, and envy. I wonder if by now many of you are beginning to develop a distinct feeling of how exactly the content of the teaching reflects the kinds of ways we think, and phenomena we encounter, in psychoanalysis?

Buddhism is taught in an unbroken oral tradition, carried by the monastic orders, which goes back to the historical Buddha. The Buddha died aged eighty and is not a supernatural being. It is his memory and his life and teaching that are revered. He was an excellent psychologist, and knew a great deal about the unconscious mind.

The Buddha taught the Truths and the Path and the methods of meditation, which are the essential cornerstone of the whole spiritual practice. They are not esoteric either; they are *samatha* (which is one-pointed focus on one's natural breathing rhythm) and *vipassana* (learning the skill of splitting the mind into an experiencing and an observing part, exactly as we do in the practice of psychoanalysis, and then concentratedly focusing, for a given time each day, on the stream of thoughts and feelings—"free associations"—arising in the mind). One is not required to judge these thoughts and feelings or make moral decisions about them; one is required only to accept them all as of equal weight, and as a conditioned part of being human. The overall aim is to come to understand so thoroughly the multiple, subtle ways in which we are *attached* to our conditioned states and objects, even unpleasant ones, that we may move through the various attachments to the spiritually more advanced position of *Letting Go*.

Meditation is a powerful technique, and it is a misfortune, even dangerous, to be taught to do it without the religious context that supports it and gives it meaning. I will quote one passage from a book of essays called *Awakening the Heart* (Welwood, 1985). John Welwood's own essay contains these words:

> The psychologising of Eastern contemplative disciplines can rob these disciplines of their spiritual substance. It can pervert them into a Western mental health gimmick, and thereby prevent them from introducing the sharply *alternative* vision of life they are capable of bringing us. [original italics]

Welwood's brief study aims to clarify the understanding that Buddhism is a religion, particularly because of its transcendental possibilities; yet there are elements in it that are directly comparable with the practice of psychoanalysis. But our original problem remains. How does it come about that there are people who treat psychoanalysis itself as if it were a religion? For one thing, they may be more conditioned by the background Christian culture in which they have been raised than they are aware of being. To deepen our understanding of other possible explanations we can do no better than consult a book by Christopher Bollas, *The Shadow of the Object* (1987).

The first chapter of this book is called "The transformational object", and now light begins to dawn on our problem. The mother is the baby's first transformational object, in the pre-Oedipal phase, before language develops. The relationship of mother and child is a symbiotic harmony, an existential experience through which the mother effects continual metamorphoses in the baby, who is not, as yet, a "separate" object. The genetic core of the personality is still a potential, and is facilitated by the devoted attentions of the mother towards its realization. For the baby, the mother is an "environment", not a discrete person.

In adult life, there are some people who bring to certain aesthetic or religious experiences a readiness to encounter a displaced transformational object (from the longed-for primary mother). Theistic religion particularly lends itself to this regressive need through its authoritative promise to provide answers to the three questions I referred to earlier. An object, or system, which does meet this need becomes invested with a special intensity; it calls forth devotion, gratitude, and Faith. There may be a sense of the uncanny, so strong is the illusion of deep rapport between seeker and object. "It seems to promise the beseeching subject an experience where self-fragmentation will be integrated through a processing form" (Bollas, 1987, p. 33). The intense, sustained illusion of being selected by a "person" for a deeply reverential holding experience sponsors a psychosomatic memory of the containing environment; this is a non-representational recollection of a rapport that was the essence of life before words existed. Schizoid patients, particularly, require an adaptive technique which allows extremely regressed transference to develop "without the impingement of premature use of analytic interpretation. From this experiencing (in the counter-transference) of the early infant's environment, the analyst (can) interpret the past as it is re-created in the transference" (p. 41). I am quoting from Bollas's description of D. W. Winnicott at work.

It now becomes easier to understand that for some people, with certain configurations of need, psychoanalysis can represent (indeed *is* for a while) the transformational object. We can appreciate that they are having an experience identical to that of the convert in religion; the language and the indisputable sense of awe are the same. This experience is always, at first, unique and positive; but it does not always remain so, even in memory. I have referred to the state of *illusion* that reigns when this particular object-seeking regression occurs. For successful maturing through the analysis, the patient with a religious experience of the process must be slowly and skilfully *disillusioned* as the transference evolves towards its resolution. If the disillusioning happens clumsily or too fast, a negative prejudice of an anti-analytic kind, still carrying the unresolved intensity of investment, is created. At best, a prejudiced stasis (Jeffrey Masson comes to mind) and, at worst, psychotic breakdown can occur. A gradual, adaptive disillusioning by skilful analytic technique can parallel the best kind of early development, and the hitherto schizoid or false-self patient may have a new existential experience of coming to know, and be, the "unthought known", which is probably what Winnicott meant by the true self. But few resolutions are perfect, and there are a number of people, patients, ex-patients, frustrated religion-seekers, even a few psychoanalysts, whose religion, whether expressed by uncritical reverence or fierce critiques of the illusory object, is clearly psychoanalysis.

The title of my own short paper still remains mysterious. It relates to one of the ways in which psychoanalysis is *not* compatible with Buddhist teaching. The Buddha taught that there are what he called the Three Signs of Being, common to all human life. These are, first, that all beings suffer—in some ways, whether crudely or subtly, whether on a small or a grand scale; second, that all human experiences, affects, etc., are transient, impermanent; so far we probably have little difficulty in agreeing. It is the third Sign that is the stumbling-block. In Pali, the language of Buddhism, it is called *Anatta;* translated, this means there is no Self, or Ego. What, no self? Impossible, says the psychoanalyst, who spends his working life trying to repair the Self. Very briefly, the teaching is that the self, or ego, consists of purely conditioned, impermanent qualities; it is not an entity. We live with the *illusion* of entity, since that makes for consistency and ease in everyday situations. We may even say that we live with the excellent, apparent paradox that the Self is both an illusion *and*, in a temporal and pragmatic sense, "real".

The Western mind, philosophically attuned to the Christian stress on individual value, does not easily absorb this doctrine. It is as well not to twist oneself into knots trying to grasp it intellectually; slow realization of its liberating truth is the only way, within the context of the whole practice. It took me twelve years, and then suddenly it became fundamental to my understanding. Rather like those optical illusion pictures, which can only be seen one way until suddenly another way becomes obvious.

Does this discovery make one feel dispirited? No. Does it make one's life-work—striving to not only repair, but strengthen the ego—seem pointless? No. I work in the Western tradition; but my philosophy of life comes from Eastern teaching. To tell you the truth, I find it a wonderful paradoxical joke.

References

Bollas, C. (1987). *The Shadow of the Object: Psychoanalysis of the Unthought Known*. London: Free Association Books.
Boyd, W. (1990). *Brazzaville Beach*. London: Heinemann.
Welwood, J. (Ed.) (1985). *Awakening the Heart: East/West Approaches to Psychotherapy and the Healing Relationship*. Boston: Shambhala.

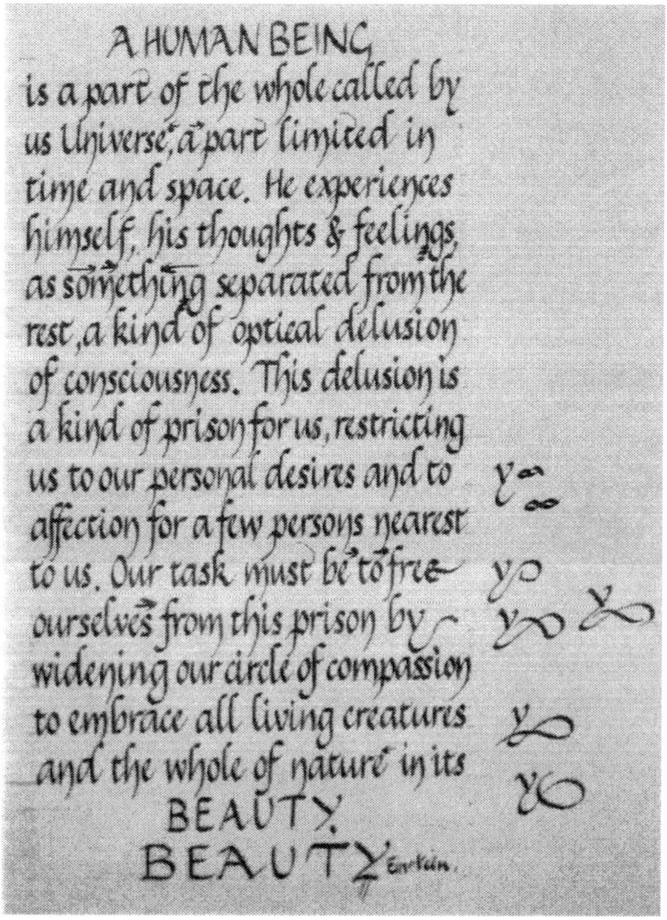

Figure 3. "A Human Being": calligraphy by Nina Coltart; a practice piece.

CHAPTER THIRTY-EIGHT

Self-regarding*

I t is only when one tries to reflect seriously on the notion of the self that one begins to get the sense that it refuses to be pinned down. We believe that we know ourselves, yet there are shadowy areas that evoke doubts in our minds. "Self" is one of those concepts of which one starts confidently: "Yes, of course I know what it is. It's ... er, well—" Immediately we start to try to locate, to categorize, even to describe, we find that we begin to stumble after one or two attributes of which we do feel sure. Yet, most of these can be speedily shown to be open to question, if not to complete refutation.

Take memory, for example. Somebody will say, "I know myself through my memory; I have memories which stretch back continuously, to before the age of two, and running through all those memories there is somebody who I experience and recognize as me". This is a common belief. Yet, only recently, memory has been

---

* Published on 13 November 1994 in *The Sunday Times* as an introduction to Nina Coltart's "Lunchtime Lecture", "The self: what is it?", given on 29 November 1994.

proved to be a shaky property. A rather fashionable subject of the moment, linking psychology and the law, is false memory. People who are prepared to swear on oath to a number of concrete facts—where they were at a specific time, with whom and what they said—can be irrefutably proved to be wrong in one or several particulars. These people are not lying in a usual, voluntary, conscious sense; but under the influence of fear, excitement, wanting to please, a wish for revenge, suggestion, the individual's memory is far more acquiescent in change, and malleable, than he would easily believe. The clinical state that illustrates my point is serious, even tragic. After severe brain injury, as from a road accident, a person may show a marked and consistent character change. Indeed, this example touches not only on what can happen to memory, but on the whole vexed question of what is the self? Post brain injury, a change, usually for the worse, can take place in the whole self. Some years ago, I was asked to see a woman who was depressed. Her husband, following a terrible car crash and being in a coma for three weeks, had become a morose, bad-tempered man who was utterly different from the man she had lived with for twenty-five years. One of the most tragic features of the change is that the patient appears not to remember what he was like before, though he can recall events and people in his own history. He cannot, therefore, struggle to reclaim "himself".

The self is such a piece of ready currency in the twentieth century that it is hard to believe that the whole concept of the self, approached from many different angles as it is (by anthropologists, social scientists, psychoanalysts, behavioural psychologists, theologians, and philosophers), only began to appear and preoccupy such thinkers around the early part of the eighteenth century. Before that, people had souls rather than selves, and very different they were. Souls were more or less alike, they did not make endless individual distinctions; souls were God-given and in the hands of God, to whom they would return after death to live through some sort of eternity. A question such as "Who are you?" would be answered in terms of generalities—one was a Catholic or a Protestant, a farmer or a trader. But introspection did not exist; descriptions of people, if they appeared at all in chronicles or history, were similarly formulaic, and usually employed to point up a moral lesson. Then, quite suddenly, individuals—selves—began to appear in literature. There are various pressuring reasons for this, but two that appeal to me particularly are: first, the spread of printing through Britain and Europe meant that never again would the literate be as isolated and non-communicating as had hitherto been the case; and second, the sudden popularity of Venetian mirrors meant that people could see themselves, not just each other. Authentic self-portraits began to be painted. And as Freud said, two centuries later: "The Ego is first and foremost a Body Ego". This became more real. The body might be the temple of the soul, but seeing it meant that one reckoned more positively with body as the vehicle of the self.

Philosophers, as if released from a theological straitjacket, began to speculate on the nature, even the existence, of the soul, and then the notion of the self began to take over, as less restricted by conditioned thinking. Hume is said to have "invented the self, and then dismissed it". It wasn't so much that he dismissed it as that he couldn't find it: he said, "When I enter most intimately into what I call myself, I always stumble on some particular perception or other—heat, cold, light, shade, love, hatred, pain, pleasure. I never can catch myself at any time without a perception, and never can observe anything but the perception ... a collection of perceptions which are in perpetual flux and movement". Rather suddenly, again, introspective autobiographical literature became a popular pursuit; Montaigne, an early entrant, had already produced his *Essays*; Boswell detailed his fascination with the personalities of others and also with himself and his moods; and Jean-Jacques Rousseau, in his *Confessions*, exploded into a narcissistic outpouring that has rarely been surpassed.

This introspective study of the self was a strong cultural influence by the time of Freud. The unconscious, and its systematic investigation, is one of Sigmund Freud's chief contributions to psychology. Freud's model of the mind allows for the mighty tensions he saw being held back, displaced, or sublimated; the clashes and conflicts that continually occur, as the deep, primitive drives of the lawless self press for expression, and the Ego, the more conscious "I" (but not wholly so) tries to modify them, hold them back, or bring them under the moral influence exerted by the Superego, itself a powerful and often violent agency.

I believe that one mistake that Freud made was that he started his great exploration of the mind of the human self by going down the path of one-person psychology, with all the raw materials and potential for becoming an adult individual already present in the brain. That is, he concentrated too exclusively on nature and did not attach sufficient weight to the continual influence of nurture, and relationships. After classical Freudian orthodoxy, psychoanalysis became eventually interested in object-relations: the use of the transference during therapy became more alive and intimate, and gradually the language of psychoanalysis and interpretation became more "experience-near" and convincing. Variations in technique developed alongside the newer theories of, for example, pre-verbal experience, of constant projection and introjection, and of the radically influential power of key relationships for the formation of the self.

Those of us who, though we had classical analysis, soon opened our personal style and technique to the object-relations developments, found that both lay and analytic literature contributed to our thinking and the tools of our trade. Although he offended many older psychoanalysts by his radical views, R. D. Laing was a far greater influence during the 1960s, and since, than analysts can usually hope to be, and I remember reading his two seminal works, *The Divided Self* and *The Self and Others*, with the sorts of feelings Cortez must have had as he gazed on the Pacific. Particularly, they shed light on the very difficult sorts of borderline patients who were increasingly coming into psychoanalysis.

One of the extraordinary features of the trend among the philosophers, which became steadily more dismissive of the self as the years went by, was how clearly they began to approximate to the psychologically astute and informed tenets of some Eastern religions. As I became a Buddhist about twenty-five years ago, and have practised ever since then, I am especially interested to compare and contrast some of the ideas on the self as they have developed in the West with those that I know from the inside in Buddhism. I hope to explore this further in my lecture.

CHAPTER THIRTY-NINE

Ingredient X*

During my last few years in full-time practice, which came to an end in December 1994, I began to have the feeling that the everyday psychotherapy was getting out of step with me. This sounds a bit narcissistic, on the lines of: "Everyone's out of step except my Billy". Perhaps that's the truth of it. We are all the centre of the universe for ourselves but it was because I was a particular sort of therapist—a psychoanalyst—that I began to develop this impression. In order to do the sort of work I did, which is all about trying to read the unconscious minds of other people and play back what we find in recognizable form, I had to have absorbed a lot of theory of a particular kind, and used it to develop a particular technique or style. However wide-ranging the adventures in which we accompany our patients, and however much each of these differs from the next, we tend to think and work and live within certain well-defined boundaries, by reason of our theory, our training, and our aims. The language that we use

---

* Unpublished typescript. Presented on 16 March 1996 as a Winnicott Centenary Lecture at the Squiggle Foundation.

to express all this is quite precise, and in spite of sophisticated evolution, is recognizable to people working within the same boundaries—which is, after all, one of the primary functions of language.

During my professional life, I did not use the media extensively, largely because of pressures on time. I would read some of *The Times*, and occasionally listen to the radio or watch television. Retirement offers, among many other riches, a sudden expansion in time, so that in a way it becomes more like space. I began to be able to follow up the vague impression I had had that the immediate world was changing in some odd way. More detailed acquaintance with the media helped. I am not talking about the world of technology, which increasingly leaves me gasping with incomprehension; the world I am talking about seemed mysteriously to be very close to our own; indeed, it seemed at times to be using, in a baffling way, some of the concepts I had always used myself, and yet at the same time it appeared largely unrecognizable. I am referring to what has happened within the broad field of what still seems to be called psychology.

In the 1950s and 1960s, psychology, *per se*, was a hard-nosed subject which was often a source of grave disappointment to enthusiastic young students at university, who had been under the misapprehension that it would deepen their knowledge of human nature and of themselves. The same sort of disillusionment, for much the same reasons, often awaited those who elected to read philosophy. Psychology students discovered that much of their studies consisted of impersonal tests and surveys, investigations into the behaviour of rats, and statistical conclusions to be drawn from these observations. Those of us who went in for psychiatry, or abnormal psychology as it was subtitled—though we had to get through a long medical training first, most of it irrelevant to our aspirations—did fare somewhat better, though many of you would now hardly believe the dehumanized way in which it was taught. Some few psychologists opted for clinical psychology, which at least brought them nearer to our world, and some again converged by undertaking further trainings in psychoanalysis and psychotherapy. Roughly speaking, on the road to taking mental illness seriously and trying to treat it, we did also learn quite a lot about human nature and about ourselves.

However, following upon the massive cultural upheavals of the 1960s, something happened: psychology and analytical therapy were hijacked. By then, analytical psychology and therapy had quite a long and respectable history; it is not exaggerating to say it had its own tradition. Its well-defined disciplines, thought, theory, language, and technique did not in themselves change, except in a natural evolutionary way; but all round the edges of this quite precise traditional field, great changes began to appear, burgeoned rapidly, and became what I think I must call "infected" by an increasingly sentimental, politicized, and irrationally optimistic *Zeitgeist*. Tradition itself became suspect, and often an object of contempt. Part of our tradition had shown that human nature is extremely complex, strongly influenced by the unconscious, and slow to change. By the end of his life, as we can see in his last great paper, "Analysis terminable and interminable", Freud was quite pessimistic about the effects of analysis, which is the most attentively detailed of any treatment that suffering humanity can undergo; this pessimism was largely due to what he saw as the strength and power of unconscious aggressive drives in people, which would ultimately resist treatment against all the conscious desires of the patient.

In the new psychologies, and pseudopsychological solutions that increasingly came on the market, all this hard-won traditional knowledge seems to have gone to the wall. There are several keynotes that sound through them, and, some years ago, Clifford Yorke, a psychoanalyst at the Hampstead Clinic, put his finger on one of them when he spoke of the devastating effect on children that the widespread notion of Instant Gratification was having. And not only on children, but on many of the infinitely curtailed treatments which are on offer to the public as solutions to any ills that can be named. There seem to be two major things that have happened in the speeded-up search for happiness that has occurred in the last 25–30 years. One is the great publicity given to certain idealistic, but very ill-thought-out, notions that are then presented to the public as if they are (a) pretty easy to achieve, and, more important in my view, (b) *Rights*. And the other thing that has come about is the wholesale ignoring of the Unconscious, virtually to the point of elimination. The new psychology, with its numerous burgeoning therapies, focuses entirely upon the conscious experience of individuals. Stress is continually laid on the ideas that not only has everyone a *right* to happiness, security, and good relationships, but everyone has the *capacity* for them: to determine one's actions, take full control of one's life, destiny, and behaviour, exert freedom of choice, and change rapidly in any direction which seems to offer the most gratification. All these Utopian aims are said to be achievable by a combination of some brief therapies, of various types, or by following prescriptions in some of the literally hundreds of magazines which devote themselves to this stuff, and by what is called some "work on" oneself. I first began to notice this phrase creeping into consultations, of which, for many years, I did four or five a week, about fifteen years ago; a certain sort of person would tell me, "I've been doing some work on myself"—sort of conspiratorially, as if sure of finding an understanding ally in me, which was certainly not the case. It did begin to give substance to the idea that something was occurring on the fringes of my world that I had not quite got a grip on. Rather especially when some of these characters would then tell me what was involved.

I always felt that I had to be clear with them that if they were referred to anyone by me for therapy or analysis, it would be a very different experience. The Freudian view of the ego buffeted by the instincts and impulses of the id, and by the harshness of the superego, and the analytical techniques of interpretation of the unconscious, had no place in the sunlit scenarios which seemed to be widely painted as the rightful habitations of the hopeful individual. It increasingly struck me that, in spite of the widespread emphasis I heard on complete honesty and openness in communications between people, the whole Human Potential Movement, as I have seen it called, was deeply contaminated by a sort of dishonesty. What we seem to hear less about is that the mindless advocacy of idealized states of being as *rights* can only bring about anxiety, guilt, and shame in people who do *not* achieve much, if anything, in the way of improvement in themselves or their state of mind. The hugely raised expectations can lead only to disillusionment, maybe after a brief period of euphoria, and this, in turn, in our culture of victimization, to an increase in blame of parents and early life. And as we know from years at the coalface, these are attitudes which in themselves are static, resistant, and depressive. It is always important in an analytical therapy, whose overall aim, or one of them, is that the patient shall finally take full responsibility for himself, to undo as soon as possible a state of mind in which parents or the early environment are felt to be at fault for the worst of the patient's suffering. They may be, but sticking in that groove is hopelessly anti-therapeutic. It is quite contrary to the dynamics of the here and now.

I was struck, in this prevailing atmosphere, by the enormous increase in a class of people called counsellors. It is now a cliché of our time that whenever something happens that might be deemed unpleasant or stressful, *teams* of counsellors appear on the scene within hours. Where from? Who are all these people? Let me say here that I am *not* referring to a necessarily small number of counsellors who receive a carefully organized and demanding two- or three-year training, such as is described by Ellen Noonan in her paper, "Tradition in training"—a significant title—in the very good collection of papers, edited by Laurence Spurling, called *From the Words of My Mouth* (1993). But, having said that, we realize that there are hundreds more of these people, all over the country, who have only the skimpiest of trainings, and the most superficial acquaintance with any traditional analytic theory, and by that I *simply* mean: "that which includes the dynamic unconscious". Brief courses of as little as three weekends are deemed sufficient; I recently met someone who was doing what was called "training to be a counsellor" by means of a short correspondence course! At no point in the course did she clap eyes on a living patient, or client, as they now seem to be called—a term I dislike, as I have said before, because it represents to me the purchasing partner in a purely commercial transaction. I do realize that these people buy our services, and I am not trying to disguise the financial element, but I prefer their suffering to be honoured by the old word, "patient". *The Times* carried a serious article the other day stating that in a culture of steadily rising unemployment, the only jobs on the increase were those of counsellors. The terms "counsellor" and "psychotherapist" are not protected, and anyone can set up in practice, self-styled by these titles. Therapy itself is frequently referred to as "pro-active", by which I take it that the goals—happiness and control of one's life as rights—are instated by the therapist, who then prescriptively and actively organizes the patient along such lines as he or she sees fit, according to his or her particular gimmick.

You may well be wondering by now where the mysterious Ingredient X comes in to all this, and indeed, you may well wonder. Ingredient X is a name for the combination of factors that go to make up that almost indefinable entity, a good therapist. I will give some thought to them in a moment. But, of course, I am speaking of a therapist in the tradition we know, the tradition in which Winnicott is such a key and towering figure. I cannot imagine how on earth one would define the properties of a therapist in the shallow, over-idealized, frequently politicized, and fragmented fields I have been talking about. A love of, and a quest for, truth is so deeply taken for granted in our tradition that I only now realize I did not even include it in my list of components of Ingredient X. Yet, I cannot help feeling that this quality must, at the very least, be vitiated in many of the less well-trained counsellors and therapists of today; I think many are probably not deliberately dishonest, but that their shallow optimism and their naïve hopes and beliefs produce in them, and in their clients, a self-deceiving state of mind in which sustained thought and learning and logic do not have a part to play. Feelings are what matter, not thought. Even simple observations seem to have no place, especially if they get in the way of some of the desperate pursuits of the new ideals. As an example, I might take the new-age view that men and women are basically the same, and equal in their rights, capacities, and needs, and if only they would learn to "communicate" more openly, most of the conflicts between them would be solved. This, of course, arises partly from the wholesale jettisoning of all that biology, physiology, genetics, and, I would add, history, have to tell us, as well as simple but attentive observation. Men and women are not the same; they are different in practically every way one cares to mention. Their drives are different, their aims and interests are different, the way they think and talk is different. However, the sorts of qualities that make up Ingredient X are human qualities that are shared by both, and these we think about and look for in ourselves, and when we are selecting people to train within the "old traditions", as they must now be called.

I start them with something that may be seen as invidious, almost certainly would be by the new-age psychologies, because, although, in fact, I do not believe it to be integral, there is a core concept in Ingredient X, which is giftedness. It can be seen as invidious because it is constitutional—nature, not social or political nurture. It is a concept that is recognized among therapists speaking to or of each other, and definition is not demanded. I suggest we leave it at that; that I leave you to reflect on it, and continue on with the other qualities that I believe we see in certain combinations, and which all, if giftedness is present at the heart of the matter, interact with it. I must first add two things: one is that I think giftedness is always part of vocation, if that is present—and it is not always, by any means; I will come back to it in a moment. The other is about Winnicott. I do not think there is any doubt, especially among those of us who actually saw him in action, that—however we might define it—Winnicott was extremely gifted. What has interested me recently is that, in my capacity as one of the publisher's readers for a publishing firm, Free Association Books, I read a typescript of a biography of Harry Guntrip, a lay analyst who was originally a clergyman, who died some years ago. It was by Jeremy Hazell (1996), and you will soon have an opportunity of reading it. Hazell had the most extraordinarily rich material at his disposal, because Guntrip had kept a detailed diary for nearly forty years, not only of his dreams, but of his two analyses, the first with Fairbairn, the second with Winnicott. He also had one or two other not very successful analytical therapies. The analysis with Fairbairn was, by some years, longer than that with Winnicott. Every single session with both was faithfully recorded. Whatever your opinion of the need to do this, it does give the most amazing window on two well-known analysts actually at work—the one place which is usually sacrosanct to analyst and patient, which is what makes it almost impossible, when all is said and done, to be sure in one's judgement as to whether anyone is a good analyst or not. What became clear to me as I read these fascinating accounts is that Fairbairn was a good, sound, decent, reliable analyst—but that Winnicott was gifted. More than that I can hardly embark on here without excessively prolonging this paper.

Back to vocation: there is no doubt in my mind that one can experience a vocation to psychotherapy. I am sure of it because I did myself. In fact, I think far more people have it today than towards the religious life, where the term originated—perhaps due to the widespread influence of the sort of stuff I was talking about at the beginning. Not only has God lost the compelling quality he used to have, but, if self-improvement and happiness are within everybody's reach as a result of some sensitivity groups and a bit of jogging, why sacrifice your life and libido to live in the cloister? There are five factors to a vocation in our field: giftedness, belief in the power of the unconscious, curiosity, strength of purpose, and reparativeness. If we do not limit its definition in this way, it becomes broader and sloppier and in no time we are simply talking about people who have the good fortune to like what they do and are reasonably good at it. The features I have just listed, by the way, distinguish a vocation to therapy from a religious vocation. Apart from the fact that the latter is felt to be a call from God, the professional religious is not usually interested in the unconscious, and is not notable for his or her curiosity; nor is such a person particularly reparative, certainly not in the sense we mean it. Last, the sense of mystery of one with a religious calling is located in God, whereas I find it far more satisfying and interesting to realize that it is human beings with their unconscious minds who are infinitely mysterious.

Long ago, in one of my *very* early papers (1967), I made a passing reference to psychosomatic illness, in order to point out how mysterious it is. And in spite of some analytic progress, and, on another front, advances in pharmacological therapeutics, it still is. If you are treating someone with a psychosomatic symptom, you may find that, by skill or intuition or sheer good luck, or a combination of all three, you stumble across an intervention which seems to reach and relieve the symptom. You can never be sure that it is going to work again; and you certainly cannot say, "Now I understand it, the mysterious leap from the mind to the body". Even less can you trace it back from the body to the mind. We have to remember that the patient lives inside that body, experiences the symptom as a purely physical event, and that he chose unconsciously to create it in the first place, and presumably has some considerable investment in keeping it that way. And, by definition, he created it without access to symbol formation, a capacity that true psychosomatic patients have not developed, due to some indescribable early frustration. The physical event is not the same thing as a hysterical conversion symptom, which always carries a symbolic message.

This brief excursion into one of the most mysterious events that human beings are capable of, and one of the most baffling and hard to treat, leads me to two components of Ingredient X which are important for a particular reason, and that is that they can be cultivated and strengthened in the self, while some of the others cannot. It is essential, by the way, to know which can and which cannot. One of this pair of components is tenacity of purpose, which I include in vocation; the other you might say is the same thing, but I do not think it is; that is patience. A person may well have overall strength of purpose, that sustains him in a life of commitment, yet he may be an impatient character in his everyday dealings, perhaps especially with other people. This simply will not do in a psychotherapist. I would go so far as to say that nurturing our capacity for patience and tolerance is vital from the beginning, and if you are lucky enough to have a fairly high natural boredom threshold, so much the better. Endlessly curious we may be, about the vagaries of human nature, but the fact remains that some passages in most analyses can be quite boring. Of course, I am not talking about the sort of simply excruciating boredom, which, if induced in you, should make you think very hard indeed about the patient's psychopathology. In fact, Winnicott said once, quoted in a paper by Nina Farhi called "Winnicott and a personal tradition" (1993), in Spurling's collection, that if a patient sustains your interest he is treatable, but if he truly does not, he is very ill, and you should not try to treat him. I am sure, however, that this is the comment of a *gifted* therapist, and not everyone would have that confidence.

Connected with patience, tolerance, and strength of purpose is the whole somewhat vexed question of the morality of a psychotherapist. I do not propose to go into this at length, as I have written about it elsewhere, only to say that it is false idealism to expect to become non-judgemental in our inmost selves. One of the many paradoxes of our profession comes into operation here. Of course, we make judgements of various kinds all the time while we are working. But we do not act out our moral judgements in our therapeutic behaviour with the patient; we explore what he has done and said instead, trusting in our faith that there is a powerful drive to the healthy and the good in the very fact of the patient wanting to know and understand himself. Here we are helped by steadiness of purpose and by patience. One of the last supervisions I did before I retired was of a young woman who was an absolute beginner, but had quickly built up quite a large practice through her connections with the Catholic church; she had been a nun for fifteen years before a brief training as a counsellor. She came to me with the idea that she should not make any moral judgements at all while engaged in therapy, and of course, with her highly tuned moral system, she found herself making them all the time, and was distressed and in conflict about this. It was a great relief to her to learn that she had a reliable and sensitive instrument built into her system, and that it was just a question of how to handle it.

Strength of purpose and patience stand us in good stead in the early years, when anxiety is often present. It takes many years to become entirely confident in our technique, self-reliant without self-consciousness, and free of all anxiety. We may realize that the anxiety is pointless, but we may not—and either way it is painful. We are anxious at the start about not knowing enough, and not having developed any technique of our own, and about feeling frightened of our patients, and of the harm that we believe our ignorance can do them. There is another paradox here, because this early anxiety is actually rooted in a sort of omnipotence so that we unconsciously fear that whatever we say or do has great power to damage the patient; the omnipotence is so far from our conscious sense of helplessness that it takes some insight to grasp it, but I have noticed that it can be a great relief to new supervisees to get hold of the idea firmly. We do have great power, of course, in some ways, and patients are both dependent on and attentive to us, but it is surprising how often a patient is not affected at all, simply does not notice, if a well-disposed, well-trained, potentially very good therapist makes a mistake, or is going through a patch of great ignorance, stupidity, or failure to catch on. We all have times of darkness in some treatments, when we simply do not know what is going on, or what to do.

This links with why it is important to see clearly the constituents of Ingredient X that can be nurtured and developed in the self. You cannot do anything about having a vocation; whatever it is, you either have it or you do not. Nor can you do anything about being gifted; you either are or you are not. Nor, I believe, can you do much about human curiosity: if you have none at all, you probably are not trying to be a therapist anyway; but you do not have to be almost insatiably curious, in fact, this could be experienced as thoroughly intrusive by some patients; a sustained and reasonably benevolent interest will do. You cannot do a great deal about being reparative, although again you are unlikely to be there at all if you have none of it, but it is a complex state, and structurally different from all the foregoing characteristics. And it needs attention during one's personal therapy, and will undoubtedly get it, since it is often rooted in unhappy or traumatic events in one's own life.

In fact, I am not sure that it is natural, that is to say inborn, to want actively to try to heal other people's psychic wounds and unhappiness. Wanting to relate closely to people, and to love and be loved, and to enjoy intimacy and interdependence is a different matter, and our understanding, and the theory, of all that we largely owe to Winnicott. But although empathy and intuition are both natural to some people, and, of course, are vital elements of Ingredient X, I do not believe they necessarily lead in the direction of true reparativeness; there probably has to have been trauma—and subsequently well-analysed trauma, at that—which I suppose is why a certain amount has been written about what has been called the "wounded healer".

Intuition and empathy are probably, by reason of being natural, part of giftedness; looking at them from a particular angle rather confirms that, because I think you would have to agree that they cannot be *taught*. They are not the same thing, but they are in the same category, and they do have that in common. Bion came to rely on them more and more, and saw them as the only means of reaching what he called O, the ineffable direct apperception of the truth of another person. The container for them, and for everything else we use and do in an analytic session, he saw as faith. He came to believe that faith and love, which he called L, were far more important than K, which stood for knowledge in his rather esoteric system of symbols. An analyst called Michael Eigen, who was strongly influenced by Bion, writes about Bion and faith particularly in a marvellous book called *The Electrified Tightrope* (1993), which I would recommend to you.

Finally, in our investigation of Ingredient X, there is the trio that has long pre-existed psychoanalysis, therapy, and counselling—all vital, and all serving to show us that we have no monopoly of anything much, except perhaps some rather sophisticated ways of thinking about the mind. These are faith, hope, and charity. I have written so often about faith myself that I am reluctant to repeat it here, except to remind you that I mean faith with a small f, in ourselves and in what we do, and to say that it, too, is something that can certainly be deepened and strengthened as we go along. Our faith in ourselves gets stronger as we develop our technique, and it exactly parallels the fading away of our early anxieties. The roots of it are built into place during our training, which is one of the reasons I am suspicious of the sketchy training courses that are offered to people today. It was St Paul who first spoke of this trio *as* a trio, and, in so doing, demonstrated an acute psychological insight; hope and faith initially potentiate each other, and out of them grows charity. At times, hope and faith are almost indistinguishable, especially during long, dark passages in the treatment of a severely depressed patient.

Charity is a word that has suffered over time; it is certainly not a word that has featured in our technical language. In fact, it has developed a sense that is more pejorative than not; the phrase "as cold as charity" lends it a glacial distinction. Yet we know that St Paul meant "love" and that he deemed it the greatest of the three. It is quite the hardest component of Ingredient X to speak about effectively, though I have written about it also, and will only remind you that it, or rather the development of the capacity to love, though basically a thing-in-itself, is also a skill, and a desirable one to cultivate as we go along. It has a backbone quality to it, it is robust and muscular, and, though the experience of it differs somewhat with every patient as it deepens and grows, it carries us through much therapeutic adversity, linked with its two partners in the trio.

Finally, though I would never insist that it has to be a constituent of Ingredient X, and it cannot, I believe, be developed if some rudimentary form of it is not present to begin with, a sense of humour is a great help. It, too, has to be pretty robust, and it should preferably include a large helping of irony. As I said in a paper called "Why am I here?" (1993), I know there is nothing particularly funny about the work we do, except in rather subtle ways. But they are important. *We* are not; and combined with an inner detachment which is also well worth cultivating, a sense of humour enables us to keep ourselves in a healthy perspective. I know that during the course of a therapy, we become immensely important to our patients. But this is very largely due to the power of the shifting shades of transference, and to such capacities for attachment, gratitude, and love that the patient brings with him or her into the treatment. We should never confuse the importance ascribed to us by each and all of our patients with anything intrinsic to ourselves. It is a function of the therapeutic object relationship, and it does not become us to react with complacency as if it were our rightful due. Detachment, which I found evolved for me from the practice of Buddhism, tends to make people shy away rather if talked about. They protest that it is contradictory to my views on the capacity to love. On the contrary, I see them as part and parcel of each other; it is essential that loving of the sort I mean is disinterested. Love can be so exploitative, both consciously and unconsciously—dependent, demanding, and narcissistic. This is absolutely not what is needed, and detachment and irony and humour keep it strong and uncontaminated. There is a difficulty about a sense of humour, especially when talking to a British audience, and that is that nobody ever thinks they haven't got one. I have noticed that it is not at such a premium with most Europeans and with Scandinavians. We may readily admit that we are not very patient, or that we do not have a sense of vocation; we may, somewhat less readily, confess to not being particularly curious, or even not very interested in being reparative. Freud admitted this last quite openly. But you do not catch anyone saying: "I have no sense of humour". Fortunately, it has never been a problem for me!

References

Coltart, N. (1967). The man with two mothers. In: *The Baby and the Bathwater* (pp. 1–22). London: Karnac, 1996.
Coltart, N. (1993). Why am I here? In: *The Baby and the Bathwater* (pp. 23–39). London: Karnac, 1996.
Eigen, M. (1993). *The Electrified Tightrope*, A. Phillips (Ed.). Northfield, NJ: Jason Aronson.
Farhi, N. (1993). Winnicott and a personal tradition. In: L. Spurling (Ed.), *From the Words of My Mouth: Tradition in Psychotherapy* (pp. 78–105). London: Tavistock.
Hazell, J. (1996). *H. J. S. Guntrip: A Psychoanalytical Biography*. London: Free Association Books.

Noonan, E. (1993). Tradition in training. In: L. Spurling (Ed.), *From the Words of My Mouth: Tradition in Psychotherapy* (pp. 18–39). London: Tavistock.

Spurling, L. (Ed.) (1993). *From the Words of my Mouth: Tradition in Psychotherapy*. London: Tavistock.

(C) REVIEWS

CHAPTER FORTY

*Reason and Violence**, by R. D. Laing and D. G. Cooper

In this book, Laing and Cooper present expositions of Sartre's three major works of the past decade. There is a lucid introduction, which for most profit should be re-read immediately once one has finished the book: it illuminates the difficult terminology, and particularly discusses the concept of "ambiguity" in Sartre's work and language for which the reader should prepare himself if he is to attempt understanding. Part One—"Question of Method"—repays careful and attentive reading, as the use of such concepts as praxis, totalization, depassment thereby become more intelligible: if some awareness of them is assimilated, then Part Three—"Critique of dialectical reason" is best taken at a run, without too much vertiginous dwelling on individual statements. The ideas it is expressing are vastly comprehensive and complex, and can best be appreciated in this way. Part One speaks more directly to the practising psychoanalyst, making one reflect on possible extensions of technique, and on increase in flexibility.

---

* London: Tavistock, 1964. 184 pp. Review published in 1965 in the *International Journal of Psychoanalysis*, 46 (1965): 394–395.

While the section on Genet presents a fascinating existential study in terms which are reasonably accessible to a clinician, the Questions of Method offer stimulating lines of thought on the extent to which psychoanalysis compares unconflictingly with Sartre's thought, and yet how far also Sartre "depasses" it.

Part Two—"Sartre on Genet"—is a masterly summary of Sartre's lengthy work, *Saint Genet*; the evaluation of the development of Genet's character from the viewpoint of "what one does to what is done to one", and particularly of the function of masturbation for Genet is of value to all analysts. The description is elaborated of how Genet's submissive homosexuality repeated for him the crisis which made him a thief: the day when, at the age of ten, an amiable, good, adopted child, he was surprised from behind by the adults with his hand in a drawer, and was raped by their pronouncement of what he then "chose to be"—i.e. "You are a thief". In his passive homosexuality, Genet becomes object for the other, reflecting back the other to himself, but then incorporating the self-reflected loved one in order to be him, and at the same time, in utter passivity, exercising total power: "I exist only through those who do not exist but for the being they receive from me". In this process of projective identification combined then with re-introjective identification, "the enjoyment received coincides with the enjoyment given". To achieve his "impossible dream" of being loved, Genet projects his made-and-chosen self into others, and is then penetrated by, "loved by", himself. The existential treatment of the "taking in" of the Other is already familiar to us from Laing's earlier book, *The Self and Others*.

In general, one of the most beneficial effects of *Reason and Violence* is to increase our awareness of the need to avoid crystallized thinking in our work, or what Laing calls "being stultified with fetishised pseudo-irreducibles".

CHAPTER FORTY-ONE

*The Technique at Issue: Controversies in Psychoanalysis from Freud and Ferenczi to Michael Balint**, by André Haynal

How pleasant to meet Dr Haynal, who picks up a subject potentially heavy to the mind, and makes of it a stylish, lively story, that can be read with profitable pleasure in an evening. Spiced with anecdotes from the lives of his three main protagonists, this study of the river of controversy flowing through psychoanalysis since early days gives one a sparkling overview of the often turbulent waters, and follows the mainstream through to the present.

In the beginning was Freud, and, for a decade or so, the Word was Freud. But then came a challenger from the East—Hungary: Ferenczi, at one and the same time Freud's most ardent, loyal supporter (and analysand), and yet, of all the first-generation followers, the one who pushed the boundaries irretrievably onwards and outwards, and pioneered new ground to the end of his days. Where Freud concentrated on theory, Ferenczi's great love was expansion of technique; Freud saw the patient as an object of rational study, yielding new insights for his model of the mind, whereas

---

* London: Karnac, 1988. 202 pp. Unpublished manuscript.

Ferenczi saw him as a suffering person interacting with, and affecting, the analyst. Freud, with genius, constructed a "one-person psychology"; Ferenczi, with intuition, opened up the whole field of "two-person psychology". Freud knew about transference and countertransference, but was rather afraid of them; Ferenczi embraced both as the best instruments for our purpose. Freud would have argued: "Developing theory will further technique", and he used the "classical" method of cognitive, didactic insights and reconstruction of memory. Ferenczi's view could be summarized as: "Developing technique will produce theory", and he evolved the "object-related" method with high levels of transference and countertransference work, interactive empathy, and the use of regression. Balint took up where Ferenczi left off, and the spotlight moved again on to the analyst himself as a whole person, and not only on his use of countertransference. Level-headed in furious controversy, Balint deepened and refined the study of regression as a valuable analytic experience.

But, with all the vigorous arguments down the years, often advanced with quasi-religious fervour, the British Society, enriched by the immigration of analysts of all shades of opinion, has held to one view dear to Freud's heart: that it is better for the health of psychoanalysis that its practitioners hang together, containing pluralism and controversy, rather than fragment; and this we do, knowing that the coherent strength of psychoanalysis lives in its aim and its topic (mental health and the abysses of the mind) and that this is not weakened by a multiplicity of personalities, styles, theories, or techniques.

CHAPTER FORTY-TWO

Mother, Madonna, Whore: The Idealization and Denigration of Motherhood*, by Estela V. Welldon

I n this readable book Estela Welldon holds our attention by her clinical experience, deployed skilfully to demonstrate the creative views which she has developed from it. She shows her respect for the Freudian and Kleinian traditions, and her divergences from them, derived from her long treatments of perversions presenting in women. "Women can't have perversions because they haven't got a penis" is one of the shibboleths she accurately dismantles, and along with it, some of its lesser, but still Sacred, Cows. Welldon satisfactorily demythologizes several Sacred Cows; in fact the intention to do so is implicit in the book's arresting title.

For too long, certain concepts were handed on from one generation to the next in our field, enshrined as *idées reçues*. Only men have perversions; perversions arise in a (failed) Oedipal stage of development; the baby is a woman's "second-best" achievement, a substitute for the penis; child sexual abuse is the province of men, where it occasionally exists; many female patients' accounts of

---

* London: Free Association Books, 1988. 158 pp. Review published in the *British Journal of Psychotherapy*, 6 (1989): 116–117.

sexual seduction in childhood are fantasies (the subject of one of the latest passionate debates, especially as to its origins); the Breast is always symbolic of the whole mother—many workers in our whole field of dynamic psychology will have no difficulty in recognizing this herd of Sacred Cows. Welldon persists reflectively in articulating her own structure of thought beyond these developmental stages in the history of psychoanalysis, without excessive provocation and without wasting energy on too much confrontational argument. This is not to say that all her ideas are original nor that she claims originality where there is already in existence parallel or convergent work from others; she acknowledges and uses this fully as she proceeds, and it is the richness of her clinical experience which brings her own authenticity to the form and content of her book.

She extends the boundaries of the study of the psychology of the Self beyond the limitations of both Freudian and Kleinian theory. Freudian theory is phallocentric, and both men and women are viewed as on the same developmental spectrum towards genitality, and woman is seen primarily as the being-without-a-Penis. Kleinian theory re-focuses on the Mother, herself constricted to repetitive representation by the Breast—goodness and badness emanate from the infant and fill the Breast; the fundamental *idée reçue* being that, other things being equal, the Breast is good-in-itself. In both traditions, it can be argued that scant importance is attached to the environment, since in both various innate driven characteristics in the infant predominate, and there is little true context for the almost infinite complexity of the interactions between two radically different sexes. Welldon is more conditioned by Kleinian views but they do not rule her thinking, and she clearly emphasizes early in the book that while Freudian theory is about male sex, Kleinian is about feeding, or what is, in passing, referred to as "the mammalian ecological function"; both views carry severe inherent limitations, which too often have not been questioned. Welldon is concerned with the profound differences between the psychic structures, and the self-representations, of the sexes, with her particular focus reserved for the power and influence, especially for ill, of the (more secret) self of the mother. She shows what it is like to have different types of mother, especially as a girl-child, what it is like to become, and be, a mother, with the effects of that childhood built into the system, where the conscious and unconscious of the mother are internalized, themselves moulded by the same process . . . and so *ad infinitum*.

In men, perversion is hostility expressed and tension released through one organ only, or its derivatives; in women (in whom the existence of perversion at all is still a controversial subject), it is expressed through the whole body. Both contain sadistic revenge. Both are sequential upon the early, pre-Oedipal relation to the perverse individual's own mother; but the man has an external, Other object which in some ways correlates with his own anatomical perverse fixation on the penis; in the woman, perversion is often self-directed—slashing, anorexia, bulimia, suicidal gestures—and this is also true of her abuse of her child, itself identified unconsciously either and most often with her own to-be-punished mother, and/or with the male who abused her in the past. The man's "aim", using the word in its rather specialized analytical sense, is different from the woman's, since he does not have to make the switch from his first love-object, while in the woman the mother is internalized (and often never truly abandoned), and then, in split, symbolic or whole form, projected into her own body or her child. For both sexes, Welldon clarifies, the greatest threat in infancy and childhood is not castration anxiety but the loss of the mother, and in both, abuse, neglect, or separation are to be avenged and punished.

The key chapter on Motherhood as a perversion, an idea rarely comprehensively acknowledged hitherto, will no doubt still evoke some of the resistances which met, for example, the studies by Rosen and Rascovsky on filicide. The will to survive in babies and children leads to extensive adaptations to a mother's perverse aggression, and the distorted introjects arising therefrom may mean either that the adult is unable to separate from the mother, or that he/she acts out the same behaviour with their own children. Here, Welldon returns to the central analytic myth, and asks why sufficient attention has never been paid to the more secret, more malignant, and, importantly, more conscious part played by Jocasta; it was, after all, she who was the "recognizer"—it must have been—of her own child. Therefore, she is more morally and emotionally responsible for the choice in which it is the role of Oedipus that has been stressed. And why has it been? To preserve the purity of the idealized concept of immaculate motherhood.

For many years, incest was one of the most powerful social taboos. Welldon says this is only partly dismantled—the facts of incest, and abuse generally, by the mother still have more difficulty in being accepted, and her contention is that the new taboo is secrecy. Here she goes on to a particular argument based on a premise that I myself cannot accept, if I have understood it correctly. She says that the secrecy enjoined upon an abused child by its aggressor is "intended to keep the family together"; and, in another passage, asks, "Is prostitution a symbolic manoeuvre to keep the family together?" Certainly, children who are subjected to paternal sexual abuse, about which more is now known, are often enjoined by the father to keep quiet, "or it will split the family". Certainly, fathers may turn to daughters sexually if the wife is pregnant, depressed, or not coping, and this may sometimes succeed in preserving the family "unity" if the girl suffers in silence, as she often does even without being told to; but I think there is a false argument here. Result seems to be confused with intention. But—and this is where I think I may not have clearly understood Welldon's argument, because naïve she is not—to look at such secrecy and see it as teleologically motivated by the wish for keeping the family going as a unit, seems to me to show a certain naïveté. For one thing, there is a lot of sociological evidence to suggest that this unity is not given the same high priority as it used to be, and for another, influential and less sophisticated factors such as fear —of exposure, retribution, punishment and shame ("castration-anxiety", in fact)—predominate in the maintenance of secrecy.

It is a hard task not to extend this review to the point of counter-productiveness, that is, the point at which potential readers would think they need not now bother actually to read the book. That would be a loss. Quite apart from its intrinsic interest, it is of real value to the clinician, in any part of our field, whether therapeutic, educational, or theoretical. Welldon says in her Epilogue that we still do not fully understand female sexuality. No, we do not—but, thanks to her book, we are a lot further on than we were.

CHAPTER FORTY-THREE

Forces of Destiny: Psychoanalysis and Human Idiom*, by Christopher Bollas

One of the most satisfying elements in Bollas's stunning new book is his gift for showing us himself at work. Not only is he an original thinker with a seemingly bottomless reservoir of ideas, but he can also write. He maps, with great precision, the geography of his ideas, and gives us detailed views of himself in that landscape, and makes it both inviting and possible for us to explore it too, and come to know it and use it. He tackles subjects which are new in concept (and some unfashionable, or taboo), and brings them into the forefront of one's imagination; he exposes countertransference innovations, difficulties, and use, with courage and sensitivity; he criticizes without personalizing and without rancour where criticism has often been stifled for reasons of politics or fear, and he articulates his personal idiom, revealing the inhabiting of his own destiny which is to make use of his experience to develop his views in good, clear language, free of jargon, and unencumbered by the venerable shibboleths of useful

---

* London: Free Association Books, 1989. 224 pp. Review published in *Free Associations*, 2(1) (1991), 128–132.

307

(and long-petrified) *idées reçues* which function so often as barriers to creativity in our work.

Within the confines of a review, I can only highlight a few ideas that hold particular appeal to me. The cornerstone of the book is the study of the Destiny drive, the subtle modes of being of the True Self. The False Self, often an ill-thought-out concept, is studied afresh from the viewpoint of Fate, which hardens the neurotic or schizoid carapace of the personal idiom, and impedes movement forward "on the right track". To free the personality from Fatedness, and facilitate the Destiny drive, is the true task of psychoanalysis, and the instrument is the skilful use of the whole personal idiom of the analyst, informed by knowledge and thought: disciplined within the analytic frame, spontaneous but not random, confident, yet not imposing or controlling. Bollas develops his view of how a person with a sense of destiny moves towards the living possibility of a Future, using "objects"—people and pursuits—as his Personal Effects on his journey. The Fated individual is deprived of Future, doomed to a damaged here-and-now; a doom which may only be darkened by repeated interpretations of the immediate transference in the here and now, and which also serve to deprive him of his Past, in analyst-centred ignoring of history. The uses of the analyst by the patient, explored in Bollas's first book, *The Shadow of the Object*, are here reviewed in greater depth, and subject relations theory developed. This is a view of the analyst's relation to himself while working, and his use of the countertransference; the analyst relates to his own True Self with inner appraisal, and it is the integrity of this relation which is the source of the confident use of associative intercommunication with the patient and of delicate, appropriate self-revelation. This is an example of Bollas's boldness—he is not referring to intrusive disclosures which would have a self-orientated need as their drive; he explores, and exemplifies in some detail, the enriching potential of this process if the analyst employs it with integrity, free-associating from within his self to the patient's self.

I particularly enjoyed the stress, explicit and implicit throughout, on the mildly heretical ideas that not only is the analysis enjoyable, but that positive, loving feelings in the patient are not always to be dismantled or translated by transference interpretation, but may be acknowledged and even celebrated. At the best, there are times of intense mutual pleasure as both parties, interacting subtly from the deepest springs of their own true selves, communicate the hitherto unthought known. That we are fulfilling our own destiny drives in our work, and that this is quite simply pleasurable, has been a subject of almost complete taboo in the profession. This is partly accounted for by an unsorted confusion between the notion of "gratifying the patient", and the psychic fact that for a patient to know that his analyst can love, hate, survive, and enjoy him is one of the most powerful ingredients in the process of self-articulation. That we cannot precisely label this ingredient touches on an idea which I was exploring when writing about faith in "Slouching towards Bethlehem", and which Bollas speaks of in greater detail. This is that for most of the time, and certainly at our most intensely creative moments, we do not know what psychoanalysis is. I should like to quote a passage here, from the chapter entitled "Off the wall", to illuminate the idea, and to give a feeling for Bollas's style:

> In the analysis of severely disturbed patients I think all analysts who are free of reassuring constraints of a particular dogma of practice . . . have a recurring experience of no longer knowing what psychoanalysis is. To some extent, we speak to the analysand to work through the unprocessed situation . . . to hear the voice of reason amidst confusion; we work upon or within our self, aiming to transform our inner state, to place ourselves in a position to make an interpretation. Much of the therapeutic work of a psychoanalysis takes place entirely within the analyst as he processes his own inner turmoil or useless ignorance, or in ineffective remove, in order to address the patient. . . . *This Not Knowing is an accomplishment.* It has taken me years of experience as an analyst to value this frame of mind and to know it for what it is—a necessary condition for the creation of a potential inner space, an inner analytic screen that we sustain, and which registers the patient's idiom. Interpretation does not emerge from the patient or myself. As Freud said, it is a dialect(ic) of two unconscious systems. . . . I believe, however, that those analysands who have truly changed very deeply are the ones who have "grasped" the analytic sensibility, who have found that freedom that emerges with a particular kind of not knowing that is essential to progressive registrations of the self and incremental intimacy with the other. *It amounts to a kind of pleasure . . .* [My italics, as I regard the two italicized passages almost as a credo statement, and invaluable, especially to younger, anxious analysts]

I think Sandor Ferenczi would have enjoyed this book, and felt heard and understood across half a century. His recently published *Clinical Diary* for 1932, only a year before his early death, contains ideas which sometimes feel as if they are the seeds of some of the ideas here. Bollas is more solidly held by his understanding of the necessity of the analytic frame, and he has the advantage by now that he is deeply rooted in a more substantial tradition of work which, nevertheless, can be traced back through the writings of Khan, Winnicott, Bion, Balint to Ferenczi himself, and thence to Abraham and Freud. Bollas also has a much stronger, surer intellectual grip on his own ideas than had Ferenczi, but both share the engaging quality of showing themselves at work in sessions with great honesty. Bollas marshals his Personal Effects for our benefit, and with a generosity which is the more useful to us for being sustained by thought, and lays the tools and nuts and bolts out before us.

For this is a handbook; there is no doubt about that. This is not a book for reading and consigning to the shelf. This is a "How To . . ." book, though the skill of the writing does not suggest a didactic or dogmatic approach: take it or leave it, he seems to imply, but it would be a loss for practitioners of our craft to leave it. In demonstrating how he applies himself to the everyday peculiar business of being an analyst, he stimulates us to expand our own technique. This book will help many analytical workers not only to be less afraid of what may be done, but also less afraid to talk about it. Courage and a desire to use the ideas may be drawn from them, the imagination kindled, and the sheer pleasure given by reading generates permitted enthusiasm for our own enjoyment and celebration of our work. He has rigorously anticipated most of the objections that are likely to be evoked, and met them seriously. This is no maverick with an eccentric message from Off the Wall but the sustained thought of an experienced independent analyst, steeped in the Independent tradition of the British School. The glossary is excellent, and the bibliography the well-tested library of Bollas's inner world, a treasured Personal Effect. His second book is a strong companion to its distinguished predecessor, *The Shadow of the Object*. I look forward with enthusiasm to the next, as Bollas is obviously "on the right track" for him and for us.

CHAPTER FORTY-FOUR

*Ignatius of Loyola: The Psychology of a Saint**, by W. W. Meissner

Here is a book of paradox, and, to many readers, the author himself represents a paradox. Dr Meissner serves two professional masters, two of the most powerful cultural figures of the last 400 years, St Ignatius and Sigmund Freud; he is a Jesuit priest, and he is a Professor of Psychoanalysis at Boston College. I imagine he is unique. Without his profound immersion in both his disciplines, he would never have brought off the achievement which this book is; with it he has produced a vivid, detailed and scholarly study of an extraordinary character, Ignatius of Loyola, who in his own life and character manifested many paradoxes. As I got deeper into the book, I was increasingly gripped by it, so alive is the portrait of a remarkable and charismatic man. I even felt by the end that he was, after all, rather lovable; through most of the book I had felt impatient, amazed, admiring, aggravated, and moved by turns, but rarely stirred to affection. I cannot help wondering if Dr Meissner heaved a sigh of relief as he laid

---

* New Haven and London: Yale University Press, 1992. 480 pp. Review published in 1993 in the *International Journal of Psychoanalysis*, 74, 1281–1283.

down his pen: there are massive sources for the Life, he had set himself a formidable task, and because of the intellectual and emotional requirements of both his professions, he must have been conscious of balancing on a tightrope throughout most of his journey.

I find I still cannot be sure where his primary audience was felt to be; I imagine a number of workers in our own field will read it partly on the basis of respect for Meissner's already-existing writings, but it will present them with a rare challenge, although it is very absorbing. Catholics, and indeed the religiously sophisticated, will read it, but if they have not already acquired more than a smattering of psychoanalytic methods, they will find it heavy going. In fact, I have to confess that at times I found it laborious, largely due to Meissner's psychoanalytic training and technique, which are strictly classical Freudian. It was not so much that it was difficult, as that I experienced a recurrent sense of deprivation, missing the fluent interpersonal subtleties of object-relations theory (especially in the short, sparse handling of Ignatius's very early life), and having to learn as I went along to make vital use of the rather ponderous concepts of early one-person psychology. But in the long run, there is an elegant coherence about the emerging picture, and, provided one has abandoned one's earlier longing for the mobility of internal object-relations in the psychic structure, one begins to realize that, for the evolving personality of the rigid, fanatical saint-to-be, there is a singular appropriateness about the rather formal conceptualizations of the classical era.

The scholarship of the book lies in Meissner's use of the amazing number of sources. From Ignatius alone, there are still extant an autobiography, a Spiritual Diary, the Spiritual Exercises, the Constitutions of the then-newly-formed Society of Jesus, and over 7,000 letters. Alongside are at least two biographies begun in his lifetime, and any number of studies and biographical attempts, most of them, as one reviewer said recently, "cloyingly hagiographic". This Dr Meissner is not. He is remarkably free of bias in either of his directions. On occasion, I did wonder whether he was not leaning over slightly too far in the direction of enlarging upon the psychoanalytic theories he has selected. Even at the very end of the book, in Sections 5 and 6, the psychoanalytic solidity of the work predominates, and in the very last chapter (called "The spiritual ascent"), when I had rather hoped for a spiritual overview, psychoanalysis holds sway. Nevertheless, very detailed attention is also paid to Ignatius's spiritual evolution.

Incidentally, do not be tempted to skip the last section (three chapters), thinking that you have had as much as you need; they are excellent. The Spiritual Ascent is one of the best things in the book, a masterly and lucid summary which draws many threads together.

Ignatius, or Iñigo, as he was called for the first thirty years of his life (he became Ignatius at the University of Paris, and presumably stuck to it to signal his change of identity), was born in 1491 into a noble Basque family in Central Spain, inheriting the culturally distinct tradition of the *hidalgos*, courtly, rich, and ready to fight for their king. His mother died at, or soon after, his birth and he was fostered with the family of the local blacksmith. "At the magic age of 7", he returned home, when his father remarried: the father died when Iñigo was sixteen, and soon afterwards the young man set out to seek adventures and fight where possible. He was badly injured at the Battle of Pamplona, and his leg was smashed up. He convalesced at home in the care of his stepmother, Magdalena, and during this time his long process of conversion began. He determined to change radically and become a beggar and a pilgrim, and a fighter for Christ. With fanatical fervour, he began to "work on himself", as would be said today, and soon set out on the first stage of his pilgrimage to Jerusalem. He stopped for about a year in Manresa, where the basic structure of his transformation was built up through hours of prayer, fasting, apostolic teaching, and living in a cave. It was here, at the peak of his fierce devotions and the first dramatic manifestations of his mystical ecstasies, that he wrote the Spiritual Exercises, still used by retreatants, and, incidentally, very self-revealing.

One of the extraordinary and characteristic features of this man, which I have seen nowhere specially noted, was his *walking*. Apart from leaving home on a mule, and very occasionally thereafter using a horse, Iñigo walked everywhere—and it must be remembered that his injured leg had healed badly and was painful and shorter than the other. These days, it is newsworthy if someone walks more than 100 miles or so; Iñigo and his ever-growing "band of brothers" walked thousands of miles in his lifetime: from

Manresa to Barcelona and Salamanca, to Genoa, across the Holy Land, back through Italy and France to Paris, then to Rome—taking it all, and influencing us to do the same, as a matter of course. Once in Rome, he more or less settled down, and slowly put into realization his long-held wish to found a new religious order, the Society of Jesus, of which he was then the head (or, significantly, "General") almost until his death.

His death occurred in peculiarly ironic circumstances. All his adult life, he had been ill more often than not, with a variety of probably psychosomatic, or self-inflicted (as a result of his long fasts and self-scourgings), symptoms. He had also been extremely controlling and authoritarian (which led him to be fanatically strict about blind obedience at all times to the superior, and ultimately the Pope, therefore Christ, when he founded his order). Sensing that he was near death, he told Polanco, an SJ member and his biographer, to fetch his confessor, and to obtain the Pope's blessing for him. Polanco did not obey at once, but postponed these tasks till the next day, thinking that Ignatius was no more ill than usual; but he was, and he died in the night, without being shriven or blessed. The irony was that Polanco had behaved much as Ignatius himself had often done, thinking that he knew best.

Meissner discusses at some length not only the question of whether Ignatius was mad, as some have thought, but, having decided that he is not (with which I, on the available evidence, agree), he then deploys all his clinical skill in teasing out the main psychological threads, and their interweaving, in this complex personality. More than once he warns us against reductionism, a tendency to which some psychoanalysts are unfortunately prone. For example:

> There is no question that many of the phenomena Ignatius experienced border on the pathological. The ultimate question for the psychoanalyst is whether these experiences can be located within some intelligible framework that allows us to find psychological meaning or purpose in them.

And again: "We do not want to run the risk of reducing a life of spiritual struggle to a pathological case history".

Separating out in Ignatius's personality the thinkable psychological elements, many of which support a diagnosis of neurosis rather than psychosis, we come, perhaps first and foremost, upon narcissism. Iñigo was a thoroughly narcissistic young man, with the strong ego ideal (including his paternal identifications) of the knight-warrior. During his conversion he slowly sought to change his aims and ideals, but the essential character of his narcissism remained virtually fixed. From being a warrior for lords temporal, he altered his aim, and embarked upon the ever-more-demanding service of Christ the King—the ideals of bravery, endurance, military obedience were more or less untouched, but pride, triumph, and omnipotence he sought to change into humility, self-denial, and obedience only to what he perceived as the will of God, in the imitation of Christ. This brings us to his masochism; without doubt, Ignatius was deeply masochistic, and the corresponding violence and sadism of his nature poured into his superego, and attacked him mercilessly, his sense of guilt and sin being apparently boundless. He wore a hair shirt and a spiked metal chain for much of his life. "To suffer (not to end suffering) is the highest virtue" (p. 237)—because Christ suffered on the Cross.

Linked with the conflictual superego–ego tension was his obsessionality. Iñigo suffered terribly from scruples, and was forever going over the same minutely-detailed pieces of ground in his perseverations, until his confessor told him he was not to confess "past history" any more, when the scruples seemed to abate. Unless he had a grandiose counterplan, Iñigo reacted well to being taken in hand and controlled by someone who was truly in authority over him.

Meissner elaborates in interesting detail the psychic revolution in Iñigo during the slow course of his conversion. He calls what occurred "transvaluation", and by this he intends to convey that Iñigo did not just substitute one set of ideals and values for another by an effort of will. This would, anyway, have been impossible, not to say shaky and superficial. "Values", Meissner says, "are action- and goal-oriented aspects of the self. . . . The value system . . . can be regarded as significant in the integration of narcissistic libido, and ego and superego activity, in a coherent and well-functioning self-structure" (p. 392). Iñigo gradually realized he could not reconcile his newly-sought spiritual value system with the older and more conventionally self-glorifying one. The new Christian values were slowly internalized and personalized, primarily by the synthetic function of the ego, but only so long as there was full accord from the superego. Iñigo's core identification from then on was with Christ, which acted as a central organizing conductor to his whole more or less pathological orchestra. Meissner devotes most of the last chapter of his book to these concepts, and describes them with energy and clarity.

There are so many aspects of this fascinating book, particularly the details of his mystical life, with its almost constant visions, tears, voices (interior or exterior), insights, and power, that it would take too long to describe them. It is these, presumably, which led one reviewer (a Roman Catholic) to label Ignatius flatly as a psychotic. But he wasn't. His ego slowly strengthened, his personality expanded, his capacity to love, teach, organize, and administer all matured steadily, none of which would have happened had he been psychotic. Dr Meissner has unravelled for us that Ignatius may have experienced some of the extremes of which the human mind, in its infinite complexity, is capable, and his conclusion is that he was very far indeed from becoming a deteriorated, paranoid, thought-disordered madman. Ignatius of Loyola set out to be a Saint, and, by God, he succeeded.

CHAPTER FORTY-FIVE

Body, Blood and Sexuality: A Psychoanalytic Study of St. Francis's Stigmata and Their Historical Context*, by Nitza Yarom

An attractive feature of this unusual short book is that it takes hysteria seriously. It is generally assumed in psychiatry today that the prevalence of hysteria, which gave Freud so much of his material for creating the foundations of psychoanalysis, has greatly reduced during the twentieth century; the understanding of character disorder, with special reference to narcissism, has taken the dominant place in the literature. But whether hysteria has really declined is open to doubt; it is hysterical manifestations that have changed, owing to several major sociological trends, such as improvement in the roles and opportunities available to women. Hysteria has also suffered by entering the vernacular as a pejorative term, but its loss as a rich and informative diagnosis has left psychiatry the poorer. Psychoanalysis, so often attacked from many angles today, can be said to have held the corner for hysteria, in spite of the reduction in its dramatic psychophysical symptoms, such as conversion. This book, which

---

* New York: Peter Lang, 1992. 148 pp. Review published in 1995 in the *International Journal of Psychoanalysis*, 76: 862—863.

skilfully weaves together a scholarly approach to mediaeval religious history with fluent handling of psychoanalytic theory, does much to redress the balance.

St Francis of Assisi, who developed the stigmata in 1224, two years before his death, is the first authentically recorded case. Since then, there have been about 300, predominantly Catholic women. Sixty-one have been made saints, though none since the late eighteenth century. During the nineteenth century, the status of stigmatics tended to change from saint to patient, dependent, nevertheless, on the Catholic strength of the social context. Writers who have made a special study of the condition, either historically or medically, are about evenly divided between those inclining to a psychophysical explanation and those who lean more towards fraud or conscious self-induction. The author of this book remains throughout commendably free of the several biases open to her, and indicates early on that her detailed investigations convince her that in the case of St Francis, we are dealing with authentic hysteria, that is, the unconscious production of a true conversion symptom. My own conviction would depend also on the fact, which she does not discuss, that, within a certain character structure, the whole religious and philosophical meaning of the lives of many who produce stigmata would militate morally and ethically against the use of fraud; fantasy certainly contributes to the phenomenon, but the superego and the relationship to Christ would not permit fraudulent imitation of the wounds of the Passion.

St Francis became famous in his own lifetime, not only on account of the stigmata, but also because his extreme and charismatic personality enabled him to found, successfully, his Order, and to catch the benevolent attention of the Popes of his time, who granted his Order favours; this, therefore, meant that as well as his own writings, biographies were begun while he was still alive. A fair amount of contemporary history is thus available to us, useful once disentangled from the hagiographical style of tradition. Yarom presents his history as the first section of her book. In the second section, she develops a detailed picture of the hysterical character of St Francis, in the context of his personal history; this she shows to be the *fons et origo* of the stigmata, thus seen to have its own logic in terms of his character development. Yarom has obviously been trained in the classical Freudian style, and while this is appropriate to her classical Oedipal study of "neurotic" hysteria, I would have welcomed a wider reference to post-Freudian developments. This could only have enhanced the work—McDougall, for example, makes full allowance for what she calls "archaic hysteria", and does not feel constrained by the earlier view of conversion hysteria being necessarily dependent on verbal development.

A substantial section of Part Two is given over to the Wolf-Man, with whom the author compares and contrasts St Francis. Her main reason for this is what she sees as the powerful effect of the father–son relationship on each; but whereas the Wolf-Man produced a classical obsessional neurosis at the age of 4½, Francis developed more or less normally until he was held up in moving on from an extrovert, boisterous adolescence into manhood. Yarom traces this to his unconscious conflicts over bisexuality, together with a real, external conflict with his dominating father. The Wolf-Man, as we know, can hardly be said to have resolved his problems by embarking on his lengthy analysis with Freud at the age of twenty-four, and forming a strong father-transference; whereas Francis, through his religious conversion at the same age, and a judicious balance of splitting, repression, and capitalizing on his masochism and feminine characteristics, achieved a pretty successful solution to his difficulties. He abandoned his family of origin and set out on his career as a mendicant monk, with a small band of followers. Yarom's lines of argument are skilfully presented, but the Wolf-Man and St Francis are in so many ways so different that I was aware of considerable mental effort in accepting this comparison as effectively more than padding for the book.

The section on "The hysterical personality of St. Francis", on the contrary, is excellent, and intrinsically valuable in its detailed reminders of the structure and functions of such a personality. "The historical context", which clarifies the title of the book, can be guaranteed to be of interest to all readers, whatever their primary discipline. Those with an educated cultural interest in the sociological and developmental aspects of religion will find much that is striking and memorable here on such subjects as the history of marriage, the development of the idea of Self, the evolution of transubstantiation in the Eucharist, celibacy, and the development of Mariolatry; interwoven with many of these is the enormous influence, still felt today, of the Fourth Lateran Council. This absorbing section provides a substantial and satisfying conclusion to a readable short book on a fascinating subject.

CHAPTER FORTY-SIX

*The Electrified Tightrope**, by Michael Eigen

For those who enjoy reading papers in the context of a background of information about the author, there is much to be said for reading the Afterword of this book first. It is a short piece of autobiography, which throws a special light on the author of these often extraordinary essays. It speaks to queries and theories that grow in one's mind as one reads them. For example, although I might have guessed at it, I was delighted that Eigen actually says,

> How can one call the therapist's exasperation impatience when it may take years to reach the blow-out-burn-out point? Therapist outbursts *can* be helpful. It is inhuman for the therapist always to be on good behaviour ... it is hard to imagine real work without [outbursts].

My pleasure related to the fact that to this day, thirteen years after I first gave the paper "Slouching towards Bethlehem", people who

---

* Edited by Adam Phillips. Northvale, NJ: Jason Aronson, 1993. 289 pp. Review published in 1995 in *Winnicott Studies: The Journal of the Squiggle Foundation*, 10 (Spring): 55–58.

have heard or read it still evince a sort of horrified shock at my description of "an outburst".

The Afterword, and its references to the varied interests of this unusual man, provides us with a historical sketch of how these subjects have fed into his destiny, that is, his chosen life work of analysis and therapy. He reveals that he has, at one time or another, "gone into" a wide spread of therapies—Gestalt, existential, those that work with the body. The analysts who have been his strongest influences are Searles, Klein, Winnicott, British Independents generally, Kohut, Laing, Lacan, and Bion. He has always pursued a more than passing interest in religion, and later in his life he studied Kabbalah and Jewish mysticism with two elderly Chassidic rabbis in New York. Religion, prayer, faith, mystical experience—all appear, woven into the texture of his analytic writing; to those who will have some idea of what he means, he speaks of "a sense of holiness" which can visit him while he works, when "it uplifts me as an analytic person and ignites sessions". His long apprenticeship included work with autistic and psychotic children, and with adults of very mixed pathologies. He gives us an overview of the sorts of subjects which interest him and which he likes to work with; this does not particularly focus on anything called "cure", but includes "ideal experiencing", psychosexual identity, interactions and countertransference, the clinical (rather than theoretical) "dramas of the Self", issues of pure-self feeling and self–other feeling, distinction and union, the body, the face. Both in the Afterword, and scattered through the essays, are views of what our work is, gleaned from experience: therapy is most helpful in "coming through"—coming through catastrophe, addiction, rigidity, psychopathy; it provides new experiences of old patterns, and new partnerships with unconscious processes; it soothes pain, assists growth, is full of contrasts and polarities, and constantly "brings one near the Unknowable". Invaluable aphorisms on technique crop up frequently: "do not prematurely interpret the negative transference" (which is often a name, he adds, for the analyst's frustration); "paradoxical injunctions are useful", especially with the acting-out, psychopathic sort of patient for whom he seems to have a flair; "let them luxuriate in their hatred"; use cross-talk, aggressive playing, use the comic if the patient arouses it in you; "do not force intimacy on those who cannot bear it . . . it is as undesirable to deluge the patient with therapeutic openness as it is to starve him with too great austerity". This last piece of advice is extremely necessary and rarely given. If only I could believe this book would reach the therapists who are proliferating round the edges of the older-established analytical fields, whose training is often scanty, and who often seem to rely on a sort of familiar over-friendliness as if it were therapeutic in itself—which, as Eigen emphasizes, it may well not be.

Adam Phillips's Introduction lays the foundations for a picture of Eigen which is so well supplemented by his own Afterword. Phillips draws our attention to the point that Eigen speaks in the tradition of Ferenczi and Rank, analysts who were inspired by, and steeped in, *the romance* of psychoanalysis—a concept Phillips uses technically as well as descriptively to link us, through Eigen's language and ideas, to the true Romantic tradition of the nineteenth century. Eigen, he says, brings a "new voice" to psychoanalysis; what at first seems to be "a thicket of metapsychological jargon" is soon recognized as Eigen's distinctive voice and language, exploring themes of Romanticism—but in psychoanalysis—such as "genius, inspiration, evil, the Devil, joy, ecstasy". Particularly in this respect, we should study the papers that make up the first third of the book: clinical stories, in which Eigen demonstrates what Phillips calls "unembarrassedly generous identifications with his patients".

Turning to these first four essays, we begin at once to catch Eigen's stress on the importance of our experiences, especially of our pleasure in the work, and in our identifications, however fleeting, with our patients' emotions, so that our mutuality becomes a great resource in the work. (Exactly what Kohut meant by empathy, defined as our main tool.) If we expand this resource by treasuring our experiences, we can increasingly trust our own thoughts and intuitions. What Eigen shows to be his main interest is, as I said above, not so much the idea of "cure", or even reasonably beneficial outcomes, so much as the capacity to stay with our patients resonantly through thick and thin, through every moment of their experience of therapy, and to study how they can use us, what they can do with their therapy—*if we can let them*. This last condition is the fascinating one, for Eigen; he points out how often analysts impose shapes, barriers, restrictive meaning on the material thrown up by the patients' self-explorations. We must listen for, and follow, the "instructions" from our patients, and give them space to do their best—or worst. The roads we are obliged to follow, if we are true to what the patient shows us of his needs, may be tortuously slow, long, dark, empty, and, which is worse, studded with gross pieces of acting-out. We have to respect the patient's absolute Otherness and *his* direction of search.

The first four chapters, and particularly "Psychopathy and individuation" and "Working with 'unwanted' patients", demonstrate how we need to develop "a huge confidence" in our assessments, that is, in our diagnoses of the patient's true needs, and work on deepening our strength of mind—not to be fearful, not to be too soothing, which can operate as a restraint, to maintain an optimum distance from them while staying minutely in touch with them. He does not underestimate the difficulty of the tasks, indeed says at one point, "Young and nervous therapists can't do it". But he gives such vivid illustrations of himself at work in clinical situations that we are learning as we read. On these "electrified tightropes", as he calls them in the fourth chapter, we have to allow for the patient's deepest, darkest needs, "his psychopathic acting-out of the grandiose self" (which may also be a lying, cheating, dishonest self) so that he may at last encounter "that sliver of ego" at the heart of the true self; then the return journey may be enjoyed by therapist and patient, when radical change towards tolerance of others, honesty, empathy, and humour are growing in the now clear and empty ground. Out of both these journeys and his faith, Eigen writes, "When goodness comes it will be the richer, the goodness of experience". If there is a phrase which sums up his treatment technique and philosophy, it is "Uncensoring awareness, which is the cognitive essence of compassion, is a critical condition for the profound unfolding of the patients' experience".

Eigen states that his attitudes do not mean that he condones psychopathy, but I think this must be an opinion that will provoke disagreement and criticism. He *does* say that it is all easier if you can like the patient, and many of us have the repeated experience that a difficult, dislikeable patient becomes even quite lovable if you can soldier on together into the darker depths. It seems to me that negative emotions and moral reservations of one's own must just be "held" through the great latitudes permitted by the therapeutic stance he describes; the patient has to feel that you are with him on the journey, whether this spells "condoning" to him or not. Too much weight allowed to the analyst's moralistic side would restrict the necessary freedom on the path to regeneration. And Eigen is the man to teach us; he clearly *has* found the narrow gate through which one must pass, and, trusting his diagnoses, has traversed the Electrified Tightrope with many patients.

I have chosen to devote most of this short essay to Eigen's clinical chapters, because of their packed value to a working therapist, but many of his other chapters deal with themes dear to my heart, and it is with great reluctance that I cut out much discussion of them. A first-class example is his detailed interest in faith: Chapter Eleven, "The area of faith in Winnicott, Lacan and Bion", and Chapter Seventeen, "Between catastrophe and faith", are the ones I shall turn to next when re-reading the book. Eigen feels to me as if he has thoroughly grasped the mysterious intricacies of Bion's thought as well as anyone ever has; he met him years ago and talked with him several times, and it is clear from the way Bion talked that he recognized a rare congenial listener. Eigen not only shares Bion's view of faith, but practises it constantly in his work; he has taken a lot from Winnicott and Lacan, but I don't think they spoke to him quite as Bion did. Bion came to rely less and less on knowledge (K) as the path towards Truth, and groped for a way to reach and express a more fundamental vision. His dictum about abstaining from memory and desire leaves nothing to hold on to except faith, as Eigen points out. In fact, "faith becomes the essential quality of the psychoanalytic attitude, at once a method and a saving moment". "Faith is the medium of access to psychoanalytic data", and especially to experience O, which is the unsayable, ultimately unknowable, emotional truth of a session. The analyst in faith goes out to meet O, with "guesses and convictions" about what is truly happening: he can never know it, with K, but he can know *about* it, and can feel and live it. Eigen is extremely interesting in this context, about another of Bion's well-known concepts—the Container: he criticizes some of the effects if the analyst is too aware of himself as the Container. He can "seek to influence the movement of O in ego-desirable directions", try to make it thinkable, manipulate it. This is not faith—it works *against* O, or allowing O to evolve. Faith alone will do, and deepen one's At-Onement with the Other and oneself. This then logically leads into prolonged discussion of False and True Selves, and back to Lacan and Winnicott.

This review must stop, without mention of The Face, or of Breathing, or of Omniscience, or of Soft and Hard Qualities—subjects which each have an essay to themselves. I only hope this unusual man, unorthodox analyst, gifted therapist, Romantic, has spoken enough through me to make you want to search until you find his book.

CHAPTER FORTY-SEVEN

Cultivating Intuition: An Introduction to Psychotherapy*, by Peter Lomas

Peter Lomas's new book, *Cultivating Intuition*, carries on in a tradition he has already established for himself in his previous writings, such as *True and False Experience* (1973) and *The Case for a Personal Psychotherapy* (1981). The subtitle of the volume under review is significant: Lomas gives the impression that there is, in the mildest possible way, something polemical about his works, as if he is *always* introducing psychotherapy, to audiences who need convincing that there is something in it, and that that something does not include some unattainable mystique. "Demystifying" is one of the words that come to mind to describe his work. Without being obvious about it, he produces "how to" books; his method is to give us pictures of himself at work, with particular attention paid to minutiae of style, especially in the language used. Nooks and crannies of a day in the consulting-room are explored in his idiosyncratic way, and without didacticism; he conveys details of his technique and his ways of thinking about what he is doing,

---

New York and London: Jason Aronson, 1993. 223 pp. Review published in 1995 in the *International Journal of Psychoanalysis*, 76, 426–428.

or about to do, as well as vignettes of him doing it and the patient responding. This gives us opportunity to compare and contrast ourselves at work and to react to his signposts.

Although it does not say so in the brief biographical blurb—and I think it should—Lomas is no longer a member of the British Psychoanalytical Society and has not been for many years. With an organization as hard to get into as this one, it is more interesting to know why people choose to leave than that they were admitted in the first place, which would have been to be trained as psychoanalysts. We may make some informed guesses when we have built up his self-portrait: perhaps an independence of spirit which reacted against the authoritarian teaching of some senior analysts, but also a liking for solitude, or at the most one-to-one encounters, and an inability to make positive use of the group structures in the Society, especially as this structure tends to engender tensions, paranoia, and subdued sorts of internecine warfare.

Lomas has a way of regarding a psychotherapy session that is appealing, as is much of what he lets us see of his technique, though he might object to this formal label attached to his ways of being with different patients. He says, "At every moment, in every session, we have to improvise, living on our wits, hoping for the best, often lost and uncertain". It takes considerable self-confidence, of an unostentatious sort, to be able to describe one's working day thus. This sort of style long ago offered me the model I sought when developing as a psychotherapist myself. Lomas says in a contingent passage, "There are certain forms of behaviour, spontaneity, encouragement, fun, tact, openness, humility and so on—that most of us subscribe to as essential aspects of fruitful relationships but that can easily be eroded by a technical approach based on a specific theory" (p. 9). He adds here that part of *the purpose of this book* is to indicate ways in which these things can be elicited, and, by inference, we gather, we can steer clear of the erosion process, enjoying the qualities he has just spoken of without exaggerated self-discipline, or too much solemnity, or rigid adherence to rules laid down. Too much theorizing "can have diminishing returns and impoverish our understanding, particularly in . . . relationships" (p. 98).

Following his title, the recurring stress in the book is on the use of intuition, on which he relies extensively but, he hopes, without idealization. He defines it thus in one place: "the gut feeling that is a distillation of all we know ..." One is walking on a tightrope in making extensive use of intuition, and, of course, Lomas knows this, but I feel that sometimes he forgets it; one of the main dangers of going out on a tightrope on one's own is that one does not experience the salutary correctiveness of inner analytic observers (Freud and others) and of theory that one has fully digested, and which can bring a certain necessary austerity to one's work where there is danger of sentimentality, a countertransference urge to confess, or what I call "over-personalization".

Lomas does not always evade these dangers. For example, there is a report of a conversation between the therapist and a patient called Glenys, in which I feel that his injunction, elsewhere in the book, not to reassure patients, goes completely by the board. Glenys is saying she's horrible, can't get on with people and ought to be on a desert island. Lomas responds,

> This isn't all of you. You love as well. I think I know how you feel. Sometimes at 3 a.m. I become aware of what a narcissistic, ambitious, egotistical person I am, and I despair of myself. But I know it's not all of me. You're forgetting the loving part of yourself. I don't think you're a horrible person. Quite the reverse.

Glenys says, "I believe you. I know you wouldn't lie to me" (p. 44). Lomas describes what he had done as "ordinary commonsense" and later again refers to her "need for reassurance and the usefulness, at that point, of giving it". I consider that Lomas compounds several technical errors at once. He is reassuring; without giving the patient any time to deal with what she is saying herself, he leaps straight in with the reassurance; he then gives what seems to me an extraordinary piece of self-revelation, embarrassing and gratuitous; I cannot help feeling that if my analyst had talked like that to me, I would have told him to keep his personal problems to himself. Lomas may respond that this simply shows that I am not Glenys — true enough, but self-revelation of this sort I would draw a line through as *never* being suitable for any patient under any circumstances. This is not the only example in the book, by any means, of the author transcribing bits of self-exposure often in an attempt to reassure, or make the patient feel specially understood. A section on "Abstinence" follows the above, with Lomas arguing against some of the more austere recommendations of Freud, and actually referring to their clarity and self-discipline as "lamentable" at one point. I feel mistrustful of his equating intuition—as he does in unremarked elision—with "ordinary commonsense". They are not the same thing. Intuition is not only the distillation of silted-down years of experience, but it carries the process forward and often contains, or points to, a piece of new insight. Ordinary commonsense we can get from friends or ourselves, and do not need therapists for.

While on this subject, I question the use of a portrait on the front cover of a book of this nature. After a while, when I was reading and annotating carefully, I began to be aggravated by it, and to ask myself what it was *for*? It belongs to the genre of "wise old eyes, kindly but enigmatic smile", and I infer that it is saying that if you are lucky enough to get a therapist who looks like this and not like a disastrous accident, then wisdom is guaranteed and you can lie back and relax. What *else* could it be for? Yet this is tacky and unsuitable.

Because the book is called *An Introduction*, it is chopped almost into sound bites, yet I hope the psychotherapists of tomorrow are sufficiently educated not to need this spoon-feeding way of imparting information. It becomes rather irritating, and one wishes Lomas would go more deeply into some of his subject matter. I could have done with a more intensive, more fully illustrated chapter on "Seduction", for example, since it is a subject only recently coming out of the closet. "The therapist", as the author says, "is in a position of formidable power" (p. 134), yet goes on, a few lines later, to "The patient is primed for seduction and the temptation for the therapist is great". Apart from his not dealing at all with the question of male patients and female therapists (a commoner combination than its opposite), I simply do not think what Lomas says here is *true* and therefore conclusions drawn may be invalid. Yet, on the whole, the chapter makes some sound points.

Where Lomas is excellent, and ideally should be read by young therapists, and those starting on the path, is in his study of language and its subtleties. This runs through the book, in his warnings against the dangers of labelling (p. 89 *et seq.*) and in his illustrations of severe limitations to concepts which can come about by various means (p. 96) so that we are lulled into taking certain ideas and phrases for granted, without re-examining our frequent use of them. He is respectful of the power of interpretation as our main tool (p. 132) and has some illuminating ideas on how to keep it fresh and likely to make an impact on patients. And—one of his favourite subjects—he is valuable on his conviction that the psychotherapeutic relationship is unique and *real*, not an as-if relationship; from this stem various sequelae, especially the need to try to reach the True Self of a patient behind the many ways in which False Selves are used as defences.

Certainly the book could be a useful introduction, but what I would like to emphasize is that psychotherapists of thirty years' experience can read it quickly and easily with themselves at work in mind, and receive really valuable reminders of how they may have got into language ruts, backwaters of thinking, ossification of their favourite concepts, and be helped to give all these daily tools of their trade a refreshing overhaul.

References

Lomas, P. (1973). *True and False Experience: The Human Element in Psychotherapy*. London: Allen Lane.

Lomas, P. (1981). *The Case for a Personal Psychotherapy*. New York: Oxford University Press.

CHAPTER FORTY-EIGHT

Some comments on "The silent cry", by Mona Serenius*

This is an unusual paper to find in a psychoanalytic journal, and some might judge it to be inappropriate. The author is a lay person, working in publishing, who has, as her paper indicates, had psychoanalysis herself. The main content of the paper is subjective and historical; of course there is no supporting theoretical structure, and it does not, except very indirectly, present any unitive viewpoint. Nevertheless, since psychoanalysts, too, are first and foremost human beings, whose life-experiences may have some major common features, and who may be impelled to their work by certain shared, if unrevealed, ego ideals arising from these experiences, the occasional paper which, personally and courageously, presents psychic damage and its origins deserves a receptive audience. This is likely to be particularly true for those who still have memories of the Second World War.

A British reader of my generation (mid sixties) inevitably compares and contrasts similar events as they happened here. I

---

* "The silent cry: a Finnish child during World War II and fifty years later" (1995), *International Forum of Psychoanalysis*, 4: 35–47. Commentary published in 1995 in the *International Forum of Psychoanalysis*, 4: 48–49.

came to the conclusion, after reading this paper, that the parallel scene in Britain to that presented as the background to Serenius's experience, the evacuation of children to the provinces, compared to the similarly-motivated migrations from Finland to Sweden, was not nearly so traumatic. I thought this for three main reasons.

First, the whole undertaking in England was better planned over a longer period; it may well be that the much-criticized Munich pact of Neville Chamberlain and Adolf Hitler in 1938 at least had the advantage that it provided a year in which to prepare for war on several fronts, military and social. The Finnish evacuations sound hasty, confused, and distressing from the start. One of the most shocking features is how often children were lied to; this almost seems to have been official policy, similar to the taboo on expression which came into force there at the war's end. Some Finnish mothers travelled with their children (though most did not) with, as it appears, everyone under the impression they would be billeted together at their destination; in fact, they rarely were; siblings also were split. Most evacuees from London (of which I had direct experience and of whom there were thousands) were organized into small groups within larger ones, and were conducted by a responsible adult—say, a member of the WRVS (Women's Royal Voluntary Service)—who was, nevertheless, not known to the children, and therefore able fairly freely to return rapidly to London.

Second, the journeys were not so uncomfortable and frightening; it was so arranged that all children had food, and access to lavatories, and that hundreds of special trains ran. Furthermore, because of the geography of the British Isles, no journey could take longer than a maximum of about twenty hours, and most were not nearly that. For the Finnish children, often alone or in charge of tiny siblings, trauma began with the very long and complex journeys.

But, third, and of dominating importance, for English children there was *no change of language involved*. Wherever they landed up— and it was unlikely to be more than 300–400 miles away—English would always be spoken.

It was certainly the war which brought most of the beginnings of development in psychology, especially that of children. It is pretty obvious from Serenius's account that lamentable ignorance reigned in Scandinavia in 1940 (as, on the whole, it did here), but it is much worse that the only investigations she reports from the post-war period there seem to have been undertaken by biased, even corrupt, politicized "scientists". Here, it was also in the 1940s that pioneering work began at what became the Hampstead Clinic, under the auspices of Anna Freud and Dorothy Burlingham; an example of the way it continued post war is the Robertsons' films on the effects of the separation on very young children. It is painful to read of how much of what was later studied was already present in Serenius's experience.

Her references to the behaviour of the children show classically how severe pathological defences were widespread: splitting, repression, denial, amnesia, blunting of affects, displacements of object. Presenting us with her own history, and vignettes from those of survivors in the Finnish and Swedish War-Children's Societies, she shows how damaged were the adults that these children became, how severely impoverished their lives in some cases. Serenius herself eventually found her way into analysis and seems to have been fortunate in the wisdom and skill of her analyst; but she presents a picture of a badly-traumatized person, nevertheless.

Serenius gives us the opportunity to link her self-revelation with more directly analytic ways of reflecting on it. She presents a rather "classical" survey of separation-symptology and, in spite of her being a lay writer, the paper is cast in terms which imply an awareness of object relations theory. Consideration by the reader of Winnicott's views on True and False Self is appropriate because that phenomenon is so clearly what Serenius is describing. The psychoanalytic reader can also make reflective reference to Kohut's self psychology, with special attention to the damaged narcissistic behaviours of traumatized children at quite specific stages, and later of the adults. And although Serenius still demonstrates a very common trait in people who were psychically hurt as children, a tendency to express herself as if what she suffered was humble and insignificant compared to the anguish of others, she nevertheless manages to convince us that what went on inside the children was, or became, literally unthinkable. Here it is enlightening to recall Bollas's *Shadow of the Object: Psychoanalysis of the Unthought Known*.

I would like to single out for special mention the immense value to Serenius and many others of the Finnish and Swedish War-Children's Societies. There was something uniquely precious and healing to them to meet and *recognize* people who had shared their early experiences, and many of the damaged and suffering states that had ensued, but had rarely been discussed or communicated. Her account of these meetings made me aware yet again of our task as psychoanalysts—to learn to recognize lost and suffering "children", Silent Cries, and to communicate that recognition.

(D) OBITUARIES

CHAPTER FORTY-NINE

Dr Maurice Friedman*

The untimely death of Maurice Friedman on 1 November 1989 left a marked void in the North London analytic scene. I had known him well since 1969, when he and I were both on the Clinic Directorate. I recall that the immediate impression he gave was one of warmth and good humour, and he seemed an attractive, unusual person. I lost touch with him for some years, when he was both more occupied outside the Society, primarily with Kingsbury Child Guidance Clinic, which he helped to found and build, and also not well some of the time. Then I began to widen my consultation practice, and from the mid 1970s onwards, I often saw and spoke to him, as he became one of the most valuable people on my private list of analysts and therapists to whom to make referrals.

Maurice did not have a high profile in the Society, which was the Society's loss. He was not a self-publicizer, being a man of exceptional natural modesty, nor did he write papers, nor participate in

---

* Published in 1990 in *The British Psycho-Analytical Society Bulletin*, 26(1): 16–17.

the bureaucracy of psychoanalysis. He had decided, early on, that his energies would be devoted to smaller, "lesser" causes, with the result that various struggling organizations in the more public sector benefited from his benign and cheerful presence. It was extraordinary and moving to talk, shortly after his death, with people who had worked alongside him in those places, and the tributes to him which poured over the telephone were spontaneous and loving; there was nothing forced about them, no sense that someone who had been caught on the hop was digging around in a store of social clichés for something to dredge up. On the contrary: "He was an absolute brick—there's no one I'd rather have worked with"; "He was tremendous, he worked all hours for us, and he could turn his hand to anything—diagnosis and assessment, supervision, groups, individual work, he'd just buckle down and get on with it"; and, over and over again, "He was an outstanding clinician". Kingsbury Child Guidance Clinic was probably his lasting love and legacy. An older, now retired, ex-consultant from there said, unselfconsciously and with great feeling, "Oh, when Maurice was there, and was the main builder of it—those were the Golden Days".

My contacts with him, apart from friendship with him and his wife, Etta, were concerned with placing private patients for anything from once to four times weekly analysis or therapy. If Maurice had a space, he would take a patient. There was no messing about. He didn't baulk at impossibly difficult pathology, from violent acting-out characters to schizoid, near psychotic, disturbance. We would have a longish chat over the telephone, he would see the patients, settle them in, and then write to me. This recurring pattern means that I now have a priceless collection of lovely discursive, clinical sketches in my possession; they were always vivid, humorous, and compassionate. Saying this reminds me that a word that cropped up frequently in talking about Maurice, both to colleagues and to patients, was "compassionate".

And here I think it important to mention also another of his strong and constant characteristics. He was a thorough-going analyst: he never wandered away from the disciplined use of the analytic frame, nor abandoned the strong underpinning of dynamic theoretical principles. But within that frame, he deployed his Self, with all the energizing skills of a richly wise and intuitive character. It has been another extraordinary experience to contact, talk with, and see many of the patients who were in treatment with him at the time of his death. His three children and I compiled a list of his patients (with some difficulty, I should add—Maurice was not noted for his organizational tidiness!), and between us, some of his colleague-friends and I broke the sad news to them, and saw many of those who wanted to come and express their grief, their appreciation and gratitude, their ambivalences, and their anger at this sudden bereavement.

Another word cropped up with striking frequency—"tenderness"—four or five times a patient used it about Maurice's availing of himself in the therapeutic setting. I thought this said more than they knew, since it is not a word usually associated with the impossible profession we try to practise. It was from the patients that I truly learnt a lot about "the analyst at work"—or rather, I should say, "this analyst"; because the unique blend of toughness, skill, and love in his work became increasingly apparent, through a window that we are rarely granted a chance to look through at this essentially private event. Also, I myself had the unusual opportunity to see patients whom I had seen for assessment in the past— and made extensive notes on at that point—and was able to scan in some depth the changes which had taken place. And I must say they were remarkable. I knew from long experience that "Maurice could handle anything"; indeed, I relied on it, and often prayed for him to have some space when I was trying to place someone difficult. I knew that he never lost a patient, but I had not previously had this opportunity to reassess them after anything from a few months to several years—and it was a rich experience, moving and impressive. Many of his grieving patients were able to attend his funeral service at Golders Green; the chapel was packed, although my own impression was that, apart from an almost solid showing of the Contemporary Freudians, the analysts, in accordance with Maurice's low profile already indicated, were thin on the ground. The thought flashed across my mind as I surveyed the big room crammed with his children, friends, relations from South Africa, colleagues, and patients—"*Si monumentum requiris, circumspice*". In his heart, Maurice would not have wished for more—*there* was the tribute to a wise and compassionate friend.

CHAPTER FIFTY

Jafar Kareem*

My good friend, Jafar Kareem, died suddenly and unexpectedly last year—and too soon: it is too bad there is no one to blame for deaths which we consider clumsily handled and badly mistimed. Jafar had the energy and ideas to pour into his life and work for another twenty years: why on earth snatch away him, of all people, when there are unhappy, ill old people longing for the Great Reaper to come and scythe them down? Of course, the big mistake Jafar made was to choose to be born with certain genes which were going to dictate the particular shape he ended up with—a typically merry, endomorphic, pyknic individual: if he had been a bus, he would have had "Coronary" written up on his front notice board. And that was what happened. His gallant frame succumbed—mercifully quickly—to a massive coronary thrombosis and, instead of a hateful life condemned to cardiac invalidism, Jafar was with us no more. And what an enormous gap he left, this short, stocky, jokey man, a great crater which covers a huge area of North London—to say the very least. For all

---

* Published in 1993 in *British Journal of Psychotherapy*, 10: 270–273.

I know, there are equivalent craters in Pakistan, Israel, Austria—all places where the indefatigable Jafar made his mark, won friends and influenced people.

When I first heard his life story—he told it to me himself, sitting in my living room one day soon after we had met—I was simply spellbound. I felt like those two boys sitting on the ground in the Pre-Raphaelite picture, *The Boyhood of Raleigh*, in which the boys are rapt in the presence of a storyteller (Raleigh himself?). It was difficult to absorb Jafar's life story all at once; one could hardly credit that he had fitted so much in. He was born in Calcutta, and was the youngest of a large family. His earliest life was clearly happy and stable—he could never have achieved all he did without solidly internalized good figures. He should, by his father's wish, have gone quietly on from school to university, turning himself into a respectable lawyer. However, it never did do to leave Jafar's own views out of any decision-making process such as this. The boy was a natural political animal and was, before puberty set in, already deep into the anti-Raj, anti-colonial disturbances, riots, and struggles that finally led to partition in India. Throughout his adolescence, he was a notable political activist, and an early sadness, which nevertheless strengthened his already growing philosophy of life, was that the political "success" of partition led to Jafar losing his own home in India. From thenceforth, he was a Pakistani. He was twice imprisoned before he was eighteen, when most of us were worrying about A-levels and our figures. A great friend of his, another student, was killed in a demonstration before his eyes—his philosophy of the need for healing and reconciliation took in another reinforcement and not, as one might perhaps have predicted, a streak of bitterness.

He did manage to fit in a psychology degree in Calcutta before leaving India for Britain to do postgraduate work. I find it striking, in view of all the places he subsequently lived in and where he ended up, that his first (and last) choice was Britain, and we should count ourselves lucky that no Raj legacy had destroyed his idealistic hopes about the UK. This was all very well for a while, but too quiet and tame for Jafar, who had what my grandmother called "a round bottom"—it was always pushing him up and off to another creative adventure, politically motivated for the most part. He worked with refugees in Austria in the 1950s, and with all sorts of displaced persons in camps in Europe. Not surprisingly, while he was visiting Vienna, a nascent interest in psychoanalysis, recalled from his student days, blossomed and he started his own analysis. When he had got a lot out of that, he moved to Israel, and there he did extraordinary mixed work—teaching psychology and psychotherapy; group therapy; individual therapy; assessment and diagnosis of both children and adults. By now, this gifted, versatile man could speak at least six languages well enough to communicate psychotherapeutically in them, a complex enough task in our mother tongue. Jafar spoke at least three dialects of his homeland: Hindu, Urdu, and Gujerati. He could speak English by the time he came to England. He learnt German in order to work in Austria and have his analysis, and he needed Yiddish in the camps and so he learnt that, and then, of course, working in Israel for three years, he learned Hebrew. Perhaps I should just add that his French and Italian would also enable him to move freely in those countries. And this was all for practical use as he had no special interest in linguistics as such. He was a truly gifted polyglot.

In England, he decided he must add another arrow to his bow by actually training as a psychotherapist, as his gathering vision of what he wanted to do in the future gradually took shape in his mind. So he became an Associate Member of the British Association of Psychotherapists. All this sort of thing takes time, and a marked quality that Jafar showed in a rather unusual way was patience. It was not the patience of the serene, undisturbed character. He had a chronic, underlying patience, along with faith, which sustained him as he gathered experience and worked towards his long-term goal. But he could be quite quick-tempered, ratty, and he did not suffer pretentious affectation gladly. Fools were another matter: he was sympathetic to a true fool, perhaps suspecting a hidden Holy Fool.

With care and patience, he and Jo Klein started the Black & White Group in the 1970s, in which pains and personal problems over race and racism could be openly discussed in a therapeutic atmosphere; it was the root and stem of Nafsiyat. (A period of useful work with families and children in the NHS ran in parallel with this.)

I cannot remember the exact date, but it must have been in about 1983 that Nafsiyat Intercultural Therapy Centre came into being: a psychotherapy organization, in no way different from the many others that were springing up, except in so far as it was staffed by, and specifically for patients of, mixed race and colour; and it succeeded—rapidly, and beyond anyone's dreams. In no time at all, Jafar and Heloise, his dear and devoted wife, a social worker, had nurtured and turned into an evolving success a completely mixed-race psychotherapy centre based on psychoanalysis. It not only filled a long-felt gap on the London scene but was soon recruiting consultants whom some had predicted would be the least likely to come: white middle-class psychiatric consultants and psychoanalysts. For those who knew Jafar, it was no surprise when a Nafsiyat training course became an integral part of the teaching curriculum (for the public, as well as students) under the aegis of University College Hospital Medical School Psychiatric Department. Almost in the twinkling of an eye (though it might have been a year or two) a diploma in the special skills required for mixed-race psychotherapy was available as a non-obligatory crowning of this course. The course acquired a curious prestige which I am sure was a spin-off from Jafar's own charisma; psychoanalysts who would not be seen dead teaching at reputable organizations such as Arbours, "because of its unorthodox methods", were pleased to be asked to give a few lectures or a special seminar on Jafar's UCH course.

Nafsiyat's approach worked hard to develop a theory and a language to deal in depth with issues of race and culture; the clinical methods shrank from no challenge. There is a form of psychoanalysis that barely acknowledges any influences due to external reality: everything is swept back along inner tunnels to early "phantasy" and the constant conflictual clashing of projective and introjective identifications. But Jafar and his co-workers saw that this was of no value to people who had just undergone specifically racial attack or victimization. Similarly, a rather typically (white) English "turning of a blind eye" to the power of deep cultural differences was confronted, where found, and set aside. Clinical approaches had to take such things into account if they were going to speak truly to these patients. This was utterly characteristic of Jafar's constant search for truth and his constant revealing of how therapies and theories could fail with people of other races, if radical differences in people were ignored (partly because of the fear, among the white middle class, of not being able to address them, let alone understand them). The work came to be called Intercultural Therapy, about which Jafar fortunately found time to write a book, with Roland Littlewood (Kareem & Littlewood, 1992), before he died. The diploma, on which he worked in tandem also with Roland Littlewood, was the Diploma in Intercultural Therapy.

It needed someone of Jafar's drive, creativity, imagination, and sensitivity to confront, with his therapy organization and his course and his many speaking engagements, the complacent and snobbish denials of so many in the psychiatric establishment, who to this day tend to assume that there will always be a higher proportion of "other races" in mental institutions, and that because of their "alien" culture they cannot possibly understand or benefit from psychodynamic therapy. The opposite has been proved to be true. Constant and scrupulous research, with impeccable statistical accompaniment, is carried out by various members of Nafsiyat; the evidence was certainly not going to be merely anecdotal.

Jafar was a complex man: apart from his amazing gift of tongues and the creative energy he poured out at every turn, he was—I think—a profoundly religious man. He was closely acquainted, through his various sojourns, with all the great religions of the world, and studied and practised them all, taking from each the common factors, which built up in him to a deep, reliable, religious and philosophical attitude to life. From his earliest life, he lived out in turn the best of Islam, Hinduism, Christianity, Judaism, and, finally, Buddhism. What a heady and a holy mixture, if truly absorbed by a great soul who could make room for the best in all, rejecting none.

Jafar's funeral, arranged most exquisitely and movingly by Heloise and his two children, was crammed with poetry, music and song—and people. Yet, if we think of all the achievements I have mentioned, we could also say, in one of the few languages which perhaps he *didn't* get around to in this life: "*Si monumentum requiris, circumspice*". Jafar's work and spirit live on, and we must not let them die.

Reference

Kareem, J., & Littlewood, R. (Eds.) (1992). *Intercultural Therapy: Theory, Interpretations and Practice.* Oxford: Blackwell.

(E) CURRICULUM VITAE

CHAPTER FIFTY-ONE

Nina Elizabeth Cameron Coltart

1A, WELL ROAD, HAMPSTEAD, LONDON NW3 1LJ, U.K.
Date of Birth: November 21st, 1927
Nationality: British

Tertiary Education

1. 1947–50   Somerville College, Oxford.
             M.A. Hons. Modern Languages: Spanish, French, Latin Subsidiary.
2. 1951–57   St. Bartholomew's Hospital, London, EC4.
             (Senior State Scholarship. Hospital Entrance Scholarship in Arts subjects)

Postgraduate Education

1960–66   Training analysis at the British Institute of Psychoanalysis, 63 New Cavendish Street, London W1M 7RD

---

* This *curriculum vitae* is in the form of a typewritten manuscript and was evidently prepared in 1989 for internal use at the British Psycho-Analytical Society.

Training Analyst: Mrs. E. M. Rosenfeld
1st Supervisor: Dr. J. Armstrong-Harris
2nd Supervisor: Mr. Masud Khan
Post-Graduate Supervisor Dr. P. Heimann

1964 Associate Member of British Society
1969 Full Member
1971 Training Analyst and Supervisor

Posts in NHS

1957 House Surgeon: Thoracic & Cardiac Unit, St. Bartholomew's Hospital, London, E.C.4.
1958 House physician: Paediatrics: St. Bartholomew's Hospital
1959 Senior House Physician: General medicine: North Middlesex Hospital, Edmonton, London
1960 Admitting Psychiatrist: Observation Wards: North Middlesex Hospital
1961 Registrar: Claybury Psychiatric Hospital (3,000 beds), Woodford Green, Essex.

At this point (end 1961) I left the NHS and set up a private psychotherapy practice, and started the theoretical part of the analytic training. I have continued in full time private practice, mixed psychotherapy and psychoanalysis, to the present. I also initiated, gradually built up, and now run a part-time Consultation Service concentrating on diagnosis and assessment for analytical therapy or analysis, which includes referral of patients to an appropriate analyst/therapist. For the last ten years, I have seen on average 200 patients a year in the Consultation Service. I intend to derive some data from the approx. 3,000 patients seen over 20+ years—one day!

Honorary Posts in the British Psychoanalytical Society

1969–72 *Member* of the (1) Membership Committee (2) Clinical Directorate
1972–82 *Director* of the London Clinic of Psychoanalysis.

Also, for shorter periods, but concurrent, member of the Admissions Committee.

Throughout the full 10-year period of the Clinic Directorate, I was also a member of the Board & Council, and a member of the Education Committee.

1984–87 *Vice-President* of the British Society, and Chairman of Board and Council. This entailed ex officio membership of every sub-committee which reported directly to the Council (e.g. Finance, Publications, Scientific Life of the Society, Rules & Procedures, etc.)

From 1970 through to 1989, I have always taught every year (Diagnosis & Assessment, Clinic Procedures, clinical seminars, Freud reading seminars, Adult Neurosis seminars), and by now, only 10 seminars on Technique to the senior students each year.

I have carried out the training analyses of a total of a 'round dozen' students, and so far, have supervised 24 students on their first or second training cases for the British Society.

External Professional Activities

I was the psycho-analyst representative on the Training Committee of the Arbours Psychotherapy Association for ten years 1973–83.

I visited Stockholm, Sweden six weekends a year for six years, running one large group of analysts on Saturday, and another on Sunday, for supervision.

I have also done the training analyses of four psychotherapists for various organisations, largely without prior intention, but they applied and were accepted when already with me; and a certain amount of clinical teaching outside our own Society.

Lectures Etc.

I have been giving special lectures on request to various organisations, including our own, for about twelve years (e.g English-Speaking Conference of Analysts 1981 and 1988, Anniversarial lectures for 2 Psychotherapy Organisations at the Royal Society of Medicine, basic lecture on psycho-analysis to political and religious groups, etc.)

In 1986 I travelled to New York and New England for three weeks (one as resident Visiting Analyst at Austen Riggs Hospital, Stockbridge, Mass.) and lectured or held seminars in various centres.

In March–April 1989, I was Visiting Analyst for six weeks to all the Australian Societies, mainly lectures and individual and group supervisions, as well as four public lectures in Melbourne, Adelaide, Sydney and Brisbane.

Publications

(Very few! I like keeping my papers to teach from.)

The Treatment of a Transvestite: *APP Journal*: 1985.

Diagnosis & Assessment for Analytical Therapy: *Journal of Contemporary Psycho-Analysis*, N.Y. 1986.

Slouching towards Bethlehem . . . *The British School of Psycho-Analysis: The Independent Tradition.* Ed. G. Kohon. FAB 1986.

Diagnosis & Assessment for Analytical Therapy (revised version): *British Journal of Psychotherapy* 1987.

Figure 4. "And the sprawling Bear": calligraphy by Nina Coltart.

Afterword

Gillian Preston

On 17 November 2007, I was standing on Brockenhurst railway station (in the heart of the New Forest), awaiting the arrival from Florida, via London, of this unknown quantity with whom I had been corresponding since October 2006, he having been put in touch with me by Neville Symington in Australia.

The train drew in, the automatic door slid back, and out stepped Peter, exactly opposite me (he reminded me instantly of Peter Sellers as Inspector Clouseau . . .). No need for introductions. I knew then and there it was a good omen, and thus began this extraordinary journey, which has culminated in this impressive collection.

Nina loved all things American. How appropriate then, that, out of the blue, an American, someone who only knew her through her writings, had this vision . . . not too strong a word . . . and who was determined to follow it through. Who else might have come forward, as this was something that needed to be done? Peter, despite a punishing work schedule, got there first. We all, especially I and my family, cannot thank him enough, or convey our admiration and gratitude for a job done with such sensitivity and affection.

Was I apprehensive? Not at all. Did I hesitate? Not a bit. With that gut feeling that comes only on rare occasions, I knew this project was right and necessary.

Despite the sometimes bittersweet aspect, I have enjoyed this new chapter in my life; one of the pleasures has been renewing acquaintances, and making new contacts with the eclectic group who presented themselves so willingly, and who have made such varied, colourful, and loving contributions, and not least, of course, our new friends, Peter and Cheryl Rudnytsky!

As a footnote, there was always one bit of Nina that often stood back, and looked askance at various aspects of life, as it affected her, and others, with mild disbelief . . . the "this can't be happening" feeling, which frequently resulted in us both having the most terrible and uncontrollable giggles, often in rather inappropriate places.

"Afterwords" need acknowledgements . . . to my husband David, for support and patience, especially in the matter of late suppers, and frequent forgetfulness and vagueness over day to day living, and to our daughter Penelope, who, on my behalf, Luddite that I am, often e-mailed on an almost daily basis, if not twice daily basis, with humour and loving interest.

INDEX

abuse, 169, 303, 305–306
affect, 52–53, 180, 254, 256, 262–263, 276, 292, 302, 335
aggression, 103–106, 110, 285, 305–306, 322
Amadeus Centre, 59
Amaravarti Monastery, 33, 59
anger, 20, 92, 171, 174, 177–178, 180, 214, 242, 341
Antinucci, P., 192–193
anxiety, 4, 13, 15, 55–56, 63, 106, 169–170, 172, 174–178, 181–183, 256–258, 286, 292
  castration, 305–306
Arbours Association, 41, 44, 59, 145, 176, 346, 353
attachment, 4, 17, 23, 36, 80–81, 172, 274, 295
Austen Riggs Center, xxxi, 200–201, 204, 207, 209, 211, 213–215, 353

Baker, R., 250, 258
Balint, M., 158, 161, 302, 310
Bergmann, M., 158, 161
Bettelheim, B., 159, 161
Bion, W. R., 105, 154–157, 161, 167, 175, 177, 179, 181, 293, 310, 322, 325
Bodei, R., 191–192

Boffito, S., 167, 185
Bollas, C., xxxi, 23, 57–58, 99, 110, 114, 160, 198, 203–208, 211–216, 218, 274–275, 277, 307–310, 335
Borgogno, F., 180, 185
Boston Psychoanalytic Society, xxxi, 215
Bowlby, J., 172, 185
Boyd, W., 272, 277
Breuer, J., 252, 258
British Psychoanalytical Society, xxx, 8, 44, 77, 79, 86, 98, 117, 165, 176, 179, 328, 352
Brown, M. M., xxvi, xxxii
Buddhist Hospice Trust, 267
Burlingham, D., 335

Cleese, J., 102, 110
Coltart, N.
  citations of works by, xxxix–xxx, 14, 46–48, 50, 52–55, 57–58, 62, 68, 100, 103, 107, 111, 113–115, 151–163, 166–169, 173–177, 179–186, 188, 290, 294–295, 309, 321, 354
  death of parents, xxxiii, 63, 69, 91, 117, 123, 128, 140–141, 165–166, 168–175, 177–178, 182–183, 190–192

grandmother, 123, 170–174, 344
nanny, 165, 171–172, 178, 183, 185
suicide, xxxii, 165, 168, 178, 182–184, 187, 190, 192–193
containment, 14, 16, 19, 56, 159, 176–178, 257, 275, 293, 325
countertransference, 55, 159–160, 174, 275, 302, 307–308, 322, 329
see also: transference

Davies, G., xxvii, xxxi
depression, 20, 31, 33, 54, 92, 107–110, 135, 170–172, 174–176, 183, 256, 280, 286, 294, 306
Diatkine, R., 47, 251, 258

Earle, A., 127, 213
Eco, U., 57–58
ego, 23, 50–51, 66, 90, 156, 171, 181, 253, 263, 276–277, 281, 286, 315–316, 324–325, 333
  ideal, 315
  super, 16, 45, 51, 158, 281, 286, 315–316, 318
Eigen, M., 293, 295, 321, 323–325
euthanasia, 136, 267, 269

Fairbairn, W. R. D., 289
fantasy, 12, 17, 46, 84, 175, 250, 264, 318
Farhi, N., 193, 291, 295
Ferenczi, S., 164, 190, 301–302, 310, 323
Flegenheimer, F. A., 45, 58
Freud, A., 335
Freud, S., xxxi, 9, 17, 50, 54, 67, 78, 100, 158, 162–163, 173–174, 179, 183, 188, 190, 216, 252, 258, 271, 281, 285, 295, 301–302, 309–311, 317, 319, 329, 353
Freudian ideas and theory, 17, 67, 174–175, 216, 282, 286, 303–304, 312, 319, 341
Friedman, M., 339–341

Gerrard, J., 26
Glover, E., 54, 165, 255–256, 258
guilt, 13, 15–16, 18, 20, 127, 157, 174, 184, 190, 286, 315
Guntrip, H., 22, 289

Hampstead and Highgate, 184, 186
hate, 13, 16, 19, 93, 159, 180, 208, 273, 281, 309, 322, 343
Hazell, J., 22, 26, 289, 295
Hecht, J., 191, 193
Horney, K., 176
hysteria, 54, 255–256, 290, 317–319

Institute of Psychoanalysis, 4, 41, 59, 63, 145, 351
introjection, 7, 19, 21, 24, 170, 282, 300, 305, 346

Kareem, J., 343–347
Khan, M. M. R., 171, 186, 310, 352
Kingsbury Child Guidance Clinic, 339–340
Klauber, J., 4, 7, 9
Knapp, P. H., 54–55, 58, 256, 258
Kohon, G., 166, 186
Kuiper, P. R., 250, 259
Kundera, M., 100, 111

Lacoursiere, R. B., 183, 186
Laing, R. D., 176, 282, 299–300, 322
Levin, S., 55, 58, 256, 258
Limentani, A., 54, 56, 58, 257, 259, 264–265
Lind, C., 108, 111
Littlewood, R., 347
Lomas, P., 165, 327–331
London Clinic of Psycho-Analysis, 43–44, 49, 55, 79, 249, 252, 352

McCarter, R. H., 55, 58, 256, 258
Meissner, W. W., 311–312, 314–316
Molad, G., 190–191, 193

Molino, A., xxix, xxxii–xxxiii, 22, 61–63, 98, 101, 111, 153–155, 162, 165–175, 178–179, 181, 183–184, 186, 192–193
motherhood, 20, 305

Nafsiyat Intercultural Therapy Centre, 345–347
Namnum, A., 50, 58, 253, 259
National Health Service (NHS), 50, 64, 345, 352
Noonan, E., 287, 296

object
  love, 171, 178, 183, 305
  relations, 16, 19, 21, 23, 282, 295, 312, 335
Oedipal ideas, 16, 18, 275, 303, 305, 319

Preston, G., xxvii–xxviii, xxx, xxxii–xxxiii, 26–27, 36, 59, 69, 81, 85, 91, 108, 110, 125, 140, 143, 145, 165, 170–172, 176
projection, 15–16, 19, 256, 272, 282, 300, 305
projective identification, 300, 346

rage, 17, 19–20, 159, 184
religion, 25, 81, 84, 271–272, 274–276, 282, 319, 322, 347
  Buddhism, xxv, xxvii, xxxii, 32–33, 59, 68, 80–81, 107, 113, 133, 140, 153, 165, 167, 169, 171, 175, 179, 182, 188–189, 193, 211, 267–268, 272–274, 276, 282, 295, 347
  Christianity, 32, 133, 140, 165, 175, 182, 192, 267, 274, 276, 313–316, 318, 347
repression, 18, 52, 178, 193, 254, 319, 335
Rosenfeld, E., 173–175, 177–178, 352
Rossi Monti, M., 46, 58
Rudnytsky, P. L., 165, 186, 358
Rycroft, C., 165

Saint Francis of Assisi, 318–319
Saint Genet, 300
Saint Ignatius of Loyola (Iñigo), 311–316
Sartre, J. P., 299–300
schizoid
  borderline psychotics, 55, 256
  patient(s), 275–276
self, 83, 86, 276, 279, 304, 308, 319, 322, 331, 335, 340
  -confidence, 128, 328
  conscious(ness), 134
  disclosure, 22, 164
  -esteem, 264, 269
  knowledge, 53, 178, 255, 263
Serenius, M., xxvi, xxxi, 111, 334–335
sexuality, 16, 105–106, 110, 136, 300, 306, 319
Sherborne School, 123, 125, 172–173
Sinason, M., 41
Skynner, R., 102, 110
Somerville College, 80, 123, 127, 129, 146, 173, 351
splitting, 18–19, 52–53, 62, 156, 254, 272, 274, 305, 319, 335
Spurling, L., 287, 291, 296
Stensson, J., 95–96, 98
Stone, L., 250, 259
Symington, N., xxx–xxxii, 66, 357

Theravadan centre, 33
transference, 7, 12, 14–16, 19–20, 25, 40, 47–50, 53, 63, 164, 176 178, 184, 214, 250, 253, 254, 257, 275–276, 282, 295, 302, 308, 319, 322 *see also*: countertransference

Voluntary Euthanasia Society, 184, 267

War
  First World, 19, 170, 173
  Second World, 4, 165, 333
Welldon, E. V., 303–306
Welwood, J., 274, 277

Wermer, H., 55, 58, 256, 258
Williams, P., 189–190
Winnicott, D. W., xxviii, 4, 19–20, 51, 55, 58–59, 164, 171, 179, 186, 263, 265, 275–276, 283, 288–289, 291, 293, 310, 322, 325, 335
world *see also*: War
　analytic, 23, 151, 183
　external, 15, 21
　inner, 104, 184, 258, 310
　internal, 13, 15, 19–20, 23, 54, 56, 58
Wright, L., 191, 194

Yarom, N., 318–319
Yeats, W. B., xxxii, xxxv, 166, 179, 181, 183
Yorke, C., 261, 265, 285

Zetzel, E., 54–55, 58, 256, 258–259